A HERO'S JOURNEY

A HERO'S JOURNEY

MOSE M. KINSEY

Copyright © 2017 by Mose M. Kinsey.

Library of Congress Control Number:		2017902422
ISBN:	Hardcover	978-1-5245-8495-5
	Softcover	978-1-5245-8494-8
	eBook	978-1-5245-8493-1

All rights reserved. No part of this book may be reproduced or transmitted in any form or by any means, electronic or mechanical, including photocopying, recording, or by any information storage and retrieval system, without permission in writing from the copyright owner.

This is a work of fiction. Names, characters, places and incidents either are the product of the author's imagination or are used fictitiously, and any resemblance to any actual persons, living or dead, events, or locales is entirely coincidental.

Any people depicted in stock imagery provided by Thinkstock are models, and such images are being used for illustrative purposes only.
Certain stock imagery © Thinkstock.

Print information available on the last page.

Rev. date: 02/17/2017

To order additional copies of this book, contact:
Xlibris
1-888-795-4274
www.Xlibris.com
Orders@Xlibris.com
754586

Acknowledgment

I would like to credit my youngest daughter, Roanea Bluecloud Kinsey, for encouraging me to put my family history on paper. Christmas 2015, one of my gifts from her was a book that asks questions about my life. It was a hundred-or-so-page book that asked questions about a person's life and you simply fill in the blanks. I left the book on my kitchen table for about four months before picking it up again and taking a serious look at it. Roanea and Lincoln were born toward the end of my military career, and they didn't really experience that part of my life. She never knew her grandparents or her aunts and uncles on my side of the family. I would always talk about them and some of the experiences I had as a child. The older she got, the more interested she became in knowing where her dad came from and his history. She had become interested in the things I experienced as a child growing up in the segregated South. More importantly, why I chose to leave home and do something different from the rest of my family. What made me different? The book was so detailed in its questioning that I thought, why don't I write my autobiography. The book was essentially a mini-autobiography.

When I started writing the book, I didn't tell anyone what I was doing. I wanted to keep it a secret until it was completed. I didn't let Roanea know until I was about fifty pages into the book. She was ecstatic and couldn't believe that I was writing about my own life.

The other person instrumental in encouraging me to write the book is my human resources assistant manager, Jenyatta Moore. She said, "I hear you talking about the hard times you have had as a kid and the things you have accomplished during your life. You should write your autobiography and get it out to the people who know you but don't know how you have gotten where you are now."

I would like to thank the girls in my office (Ana Hernandez, Janie Perales, Olgalidia Garcia, and Vanessa Alvarado) for keeping the book a secret as well. Marlee was very helpful in helping me with details of the kids' high school years. When I told my other kids that I was writing the book, I was over 100 pages into it and they wanted to read what I had already written. Some of them read what I had written up to that point and I told them that this would be all they would see until the book was completed. They have been patiently waiting while simultaneously chomping at the bit for more.

Parenting Philosophy

There are two words that every parent must master and operate under when raising children. Those two words are standards and consequences. Parents must set standards for their children to live by. When those standards are broken, there must be consequences that are applied for the broken rule. If no consequences are applied, then the broken rule becomes the new standard.

You set the standards when the child is a toddler; you can't wait until they are in their teens. When a child is old enough to make the distinction that sugar tastes better than salt, this is the time to start setting standards for your child. Children are expected to break things or make poor choices; it's a part of them weaving their way through life. When this happens, parents are responsible for letting the child know how to prevent this from happening again in a positive way. My own kids rarely got the belt, but when they did, it motivated change.

My Children:

Cassandra Irene (Turner) Felton
Husband Richard
Housewife
Son – Demarcus Johnson
Daughter – Keyonna Johnson
Daughter – Traquel Johnson
Son – Jimmy Johnson

Danny Lamar Croft
United States Army (3 years)
Deputy Sheriff (22 years), Valdosta, Georgia
Fiancée – Nakiuma (Nikki) Wade
Daughter – Jordan Tyson
Daughter – Mia Brown
Daughter – Peyton Brown
Daughter - Danyelle Croft

Dedric McLoyd Kinsey
United States Air Force (10 years active, 7 years reserves and current reserve unit Albuquerque, New Mexico)
Department of Defense, El Paso, Texas
Fiancée – Maira Corral
Son – Kwantell Kinsey (United States Marine Corps, Camp Lejeune, North Carolina)

Orenthal Juan Kinsey
United States Army (Retired)
Hunter Airfield, Savannah, Georgia (computer programmer and repairer)
Wife – Dagmar Kinsey
Son – Christopher Schirmer
Son – Jeremy Carter

Dwayne McLoyd Kinsey
United States Army (10 years)
Department of Defense, Atlanta, Georgia (budget analyst)
Daughter – Monique Kinsey
Daughter – Kyana Kinsey
Daughter – Kayla Kinsey
Son – Isiah Kinsey
Son – Kobe Kinsey
Son – Jordan Kinsey

Falisha Michelle Kinsey
Radiology, Augusta, Georgia
Son – Travareas Moore

Roanea Bluecloud Kinsey
Senior – Georgia Southern University

Lincoln Meadows Kinsey
United States Marine Corp, Camp Lejeune, North Carolina

A Hero's Journey

July 29, 1953, was an unusually hot summer day. About 5:00 PM in the evening at the home of Lola Mae Kinsey and Thomas Elbert Kinsey, there were some exciting events going on: The birth of their sixth child and third son, Mose McLoyd Kinsey. I weighed 9 pounds 7 oz. The midwife, Mrs. Mattie Mae Bradford, delivered me and she was quite surprised that I was such a big baby. Mrs. Bradford was the midwife for most of the black families in Norman Park. She lived next door to us so it was very convenient for Mom. Mrs. Bradford was required to turn in the legal documents to our County Health Department so that a birth certificate could be made and recorded in my name. Somehow, Mose McLoyd Kinsey ended up Moose McLoyd Kinsey. This was discovered years later upon my signing up for the military. Turns out that Mrs. Bradford was very good at delivering babies but fell a little short on spelling.

Two Very Different Parents

My dad was short stocky man, about 5 feet 3 inches tall, having a dark complexion, and weighing about 145 pounds. He stood upright in a direct way. He was also a man of very few words. He spoke rarely, if at all. When he did speak, we listened closely because he would always say something that made a lot of sense or it seemed that it was the final piece of the puzzle that made things fit perfectly.

Dad grew up prior to and during the Great Depression of the early 1930s. He was born on March 1, 1908, in Thompson, Georgia. My dad had a hard life growing up in the segregated South. He was forced to drop out of school while in the sixth grade. He couldn't read or write so he felt being in school was a waste of his and the school's time. Dad thought he should be working to earn a living. He began his working career in the cotton and tobacco fields. That was all the work there was back then for poor uneducated black American males. He would often tell the story of a man making him so angry that he felt that he had no choice but to fight him and he beat the man very badly. Thus, he had to flee his home for fear that the man's relatives and friends would come after him with the intentions of killing him. Dad said he left town, and he would often pray that the man survived the fight. He would always say that he should have just left town instead of letting anger take control of him, and he regretted it ever since. Several years later, he found out that the man did survive the fight.

My dad would also use this experience as a learning point with us kids, that we shouldn't allow someone to make us as angry as he once was. He let us know that his anger almost put his family in danger as a young man. He wanted us to become tolerant of certain things, especially if someone called us names. He would often tell us that retaliation could be very costly if we let name-calling get to us or if we let our anger get the best of us. After that incident, Dad went to live with relatives in a town near Osier Field, Georgia. It was a small farming town near Pearson and Kirkland, Georgia. He began work there in the tobacco and cotton fields.

The farm next to the one that my father worked was sharecropped by a black farmer named Fleming Horne. Fleming and his wife Mosuri were raising five children and all of them worked in the fields. My mother was one of those five children.

Mom had an even more difficult start in life than my father. Her father died before she was born. Her mother died before her teen years, giving birth to her third child. Neither survived the delivery. This tragedy forced my mom and her sister Galley to live with her mother's brother (Fleming Horne) and his wife (Mosuri Horne) and their family. Mom was born on December 25, 1918, in a small town near Osier Field, Georgia. Her situation with her uncle and family was not a good one for her and her sister. The two of them were not treated like their cousins. They did most of the cleaning chores in and around the house. The two of them were the first kids to go to work in the cotton fields when it was time to start work. My mom was rarely allowed to go to school and eventually stopped going at age twelve. She too did not learn to read or write during her few years in school. Mom was so desperate to leave that situation with her uncle and aunt that she ran off and married my father at age fifteen. My oldest brother, Thomas Elbert Kinsey Jr. (deceased), was born in 1934; my mom was sixteen years old.

My father eventually got a job with the railroad as a brakeman. He settled with my mother along the railroad route in Norman Park, Georgia. The railroad began to wind down in this part of the South and Dad was laid off after twenty-three years. Dad always carried around a souvenir from that job; he had a scar on his chest about one and a half inches long and about one-sixth inch wide. He said one night that the train was making a very quick stop and a piece of steel came off the track and hit him in the chest. He was taken to the doctor and the doctor said that it was okay to leave the lead in place in his chest.

After settling in Norman Park, Dad worked as a logger. He and my brother-in-law worked together cutting down trees and taking them to the lumber yard. My dad barely made enough money to pay the bills and put food on the table in that profession. After several years of working in pulpwood, my dad began working as a janitor at Norman Junior College located in Norman Park, Georgia. Being a janitor was stable work where he could work five days a week and earn a little bit more money per week.

My dad was a very proud man. He would never consider asking anyone for anything. He was the head of our household and he tried to make sure that we had what we needed, not necessarily what we wanted. One of the most painful things in my young life was not being called names as a black kid growing up in the segregated South or being extremely poor. It was seeing my father work very hard all week long and not being able to sign his name to receive his pay. One of his kids had to sign his name where he marked an X on his paycheck. If one of his kids wasn't with him, then the cashier would sign his paycheck for him. I could tell by the expression on his face that he was very embarrassed by it.

Education was not a priority for poor blacks during his era. Dad said that their school was a one-room, one-story building. Kids of all grade levels would be in the same room. The higher-grade kids would sit in the back of the classroom. He would always say that he cut up in class and that's the reason he never learned to read or write.

When he turned thirteen years old, he knew that it was his turn to start earning a living and not waste his time in school any longer. Dad would say that he wished he had taken school more seriously and gotten his education. I don't think he ever understood that we were proud of him being able to take care of us and teach us to be good neighbors in our community. We were not a touchy-feely-type family.

My mother was quite different from my father. She was about 5 feet 5 inches tall, having a light complexion, weighing about 140 pounds and was very talkative in her home. She was my dad's total opposite. She, however, was the disciplinarian in the family. You didn't want to get a spanking from Mom because as she spanked you, she would carry a full-on conversation. Sometimes those conversations last for three or four minutes or more.

The Kinsey Family

One of my earliest childhood memories were my immediate family. I remember that my oldest sister (Mary Nell Kinsey) and her husband lived with us in our small house. I can recall riding in a pulpwood truck to the woods watching my dad and my brother-in-law cut down trees and drag them out of the woods. At the end of the day, we would head home and my mom and sister would be upset that bugs were in my hair and eyelashes. I would always go from the truck straight to the washtub for a good scrub down.

When I was a little boy my oldest brother had left Georgia for Indiana. My aunt Galley and her husband moved there and my older brother, Thomas Jr., decided to go with them to break the cycle of uneducated colored farm hands in the Deep South. While in Indiana, he decided to join the army. After serving a tour in the army, he settled down in Chicago, Illinois. He lived there for most of his adult life while working in a factory. I had never seen him until he returned home to visit at Christmas in 1967. He was thirty-three years old and had a family. He also had a very bad drinking problem. The entire time he was here, he either drank or talked about drinking. I didn't see him again until the early 1980s after he was divorced and returned to Moultrie to live. He succumbed to alcoholism in 1989 at age fifty-five.

The third oldest in our family is my sister Leatis. The fourth child in our family is my brother Leroy. The fifth kid in our family was my sister Dorothy. Dorothy developed diabetes in 1985 at the age of thirty-four. At that time, I was a drill sergeant in the U.S. Army stationed at Fort Benning, Georgia. I got a phone call from my sister Leatis saying Dorothy was in a coma and no one knew what happened to her. She called me back a few hours later saying that she had gone into a diabetic coma. She went on to say that her blood sugar was well about 500. Leatis explained that Dorothy had lost her eyesight, her kidneys stopped functioning, and her heart had been severely damaged. I immediately *came home to see her. We didn't quite know what type disease diabetes was at that time. The doctor explained it to us. The doctor said that it was a* very bad disease if a person doesn't take their medication, and in her case, her not knowing that she had developed the disease could have been fatal.

Dorothy immediately began dialysis treatments three times a week because her kidneys didn't work. She did regain some of her eyesight in her right eye. She went from eating doughnuts, candy bars, and very large plates of food to eating salads and small portions in her plate and taking her diabetic medication. She was very lucky; a kidney became available three months after she lost hers. She was rushed to Emory Hospital in Atlanta to undergo the transplant. I was being transferred from Fort Benny, Georgia, to California as an army recruiter. The week prior to leaving for my new assignment, I stayed in Atlanta with some friends so that I could be with her for the transplant.

In 1995, Dorothy's condition with diabetes was so bad the family had to place her in a nursing home. I left California to attend my youngest son Dwayne's graduation from basic training at Fort Jackson, South Carolina, and I also came home to see our family and to check on Dorothy. It was very heartbreaking to see my forty-four-year-old sister in a nursing home. She had gotten to the point that she couldn't be cared for at home and had to be under more professional care. She could receive that care in the nursing home. We talked about when we were kids growing up and our friends. She would laugh at our conversation. I told her the next time I come home, we would see if we could take her home for a visit. She simply said okay. At the end of our visit, she said, "I love Mose." I said, "I love too Dot."

My wife Marlee, son Orenthal, and daughter Roanea left early the next morning, traveling back to California. We arrived at home in Fresno and no sooner than I opened the door when the phone started ringing. I picked up the phone and it was my sister Leatis, and the first thing she said was, "We lost Dot." I couldn't believe it; I had just talked to her. She seemed so normal to me. As I reflect, I think God allowed her to stay alive until I came home so that the both of us could see each other for the last time. Marlee called her mom, Jo, and dad, Wade, in Utah and asked her mom if she could come and stay with Roanea and Orenthal while we fly to Georgia for the funeral. We did return home to Dorothy's funeral. For me, the funeral was very emotional because I had not been around Dot that much due to my military career. She was two years older than me, and we were a lot closer growing up than the rest of my siblings. Mom said it was God's will that she left us so young, and I just nodded my head in agreement.

I am the sixth child in our family. Timothy is the seventh and final child in our family. Mom was forty-two years old when Timothy was born. Tim was a surprise to everyone. Mom would often tell the story of her and my oldest sister Mary Nell being pregnant at the same time. Mom was pregnant with my brother Tim, and my sister was pregnant with my niece Mary Ann. They say that it was the talk of the neighborhood. Mother and daughter pregnant.

First Years of School

Memories of my early years of being in school have stayed with me for all my life. I didn't like riding the bus to school all the way to Doerun, Georgia. The ride lasted two hours because of the bus driver having to pick up kids along the route.

My first grade teacher stood out for several different reasons. First, her husband was the school's principal. Secondly, my parents couldn't afford twenty cents per day for our lunch in the school cafeteria. Mrs. Hooker would sell cookies for a penny each at lunch for the kids that could not afford to eat in the cafeteria every day. Thirdly, I was kind of her pet; I would carry her cookie box to the playground every day for lunch. She would always ask me to open the door when it was time for us to go outside. Mrs. Hooker was the reason I didn't mind taking that awful bus ride every day to school.

Mrs. Wise, on the other hand, was quite different. She was my fifth grade teacher and she prided herself in turning out kids that were good spellers. I was one of her prized students when it came to spelling. What people don't know is that there was a price to pay to be a good speller under Mrs. Wise. She would have five students sit on one side of a table and she would sit on the other side and she was armed with a 12-inch wooden ruler. If you misspelled a word, she would grab four fingers on one of your hands with the palm facing up. She would take the ruler and give you four or five lashes across the palm. It was very painful but very effective.

Mrs. Corben was my third grade English teacher. Mrs. Corben was probably in her early fifties. She dressed very conservatively and wore glasses. I was grateful that she didn't use Mrs. Wise's tactics. We were expected to complete a reading assignment and read from books that must have been issued to twenty previous students. There were torn, missing pages that were written on or had gum on some of the pages, and they had to be taped up to keep them together. I thought to myself, they must have retrieved them from the city dump. The first day I walked into her classroom, I thought that those books were for the janitor to take to the dumpster. The school itself was in very good shape.

Homemade Toys Were Fun

Toys were very rare in the Kinsey household. We had virtually no toys to play with. Well, maybe one exception would be *marbles*. Every kid in our neighborhood had marbles. They were cheap, easy to maintain, and everyone played with them. Another relatively cheap toy was a *used tire*. It was our individual car and we rolled it with style. We would name them after cars; mine was an impala. We kids would often race with our tires just like the race car drivers. Our imaginations would take over and it would seem like we were professional drivers at the Kinsey 500. We would make the sounds as if we were doing 200 miles per hour and some of us would have the occasional crash; the others would simulate pulling the driver out of the burning car and another would be the ambulance pulling up to transport the driver. We would have our own Kinsey 500 right there near Norman Park, Georgia, on the hood race track. We often made our own toys. A *roller packer* comes to mind as one of many toys we made. It was made of a syrup can. We would take a nail and put a hole in the center of the can on the bottom side. Then, we would take the lid and put a hole in the center of it. We would gather wire from a burned-out tire or field wire. Next, we would run the wire through the holes in the bottom of the can and the lid and have the wire long enough to reach your waist while in a loop. The final thing was to fill the can up with dirt and close the lid and off you go with your new roller packer. Another favorite toy we made were *camel walkers*. Most canned goods brought from a store came in 16 oz. cans.

We would take the cans, pull that nail out again, and put holes in it about an eighth inch from the top directly across from each other. Take some wire and run it through both holes and loop the wire high enough that it would reach about halfway up your thigh. When you step on them and begin to run with them on, they would kick up dirt as if you were on a horse. We made our own *bow and arrow*. We would cut a small limb off a China berry tree about a half to three-quarter inch in diameter and about thirty-six inches long. Cut a notch about a half-inch below both ends on the same side. Take a piece of wire and run it to both ends and tie them off while making sure that you leave the limb in a bow shape. Next, we took the straightest branches we could find to use as the arrow. We would then take a Royal Crown Soda top and place the end of the limb centered in the bottletop and take a hammer and hammer its closed end on the limb, making it into an arrow.

Early Life-Altering Experiences

We lived across from a wooded area. My buddies and I would often go into the woods to play in the trees and swing on the vines that hung on the trees. My brother, Leroy, and his friends went to swing on the vines as well. One day Leroy had jumped on a vine that had been ridden quite a few times, and it had become very flimsy and weak. He started to swing on the vine and it broke, and down came my brother. He landed on his back so hard that it knocked the air out of his lungs. He was gasping for air. We all ran over to help him. By the time we all reached him, he had started breathing again. It was very scary. None of us knew how to revive him had he continued not to breathe. We were just glad that he was okay and that we didn't have to try to start him breathing again.

Experiences Kids Encounter

Childhood tragedies do occur during school years and our elementary school was no exception. During the summer months while out of school, we couldn't afford to go to the recreation pool in Moultrie to swim. So, some of our friends would swim in a small creek near their home. One day in early July, I remember us coming home from the tobacco field for lunch and my mom came out to the truck and told us that James Huewitt McBride had drowned in the creek. We were about thirteen years old at the time, and we all were devastated at his death. I couldn't believe that someone could die that young. It was like a dream for me. I began thinking about just the week before, when we were all laughing and joking together in their front yard. I thought, once they get him to the hospital, he would wake up, but he never did.

The first time I felt that I was different as a human being was during my first grade year in school. I was with my mother at the store near Norman Park, and I asked my mother why white kids don't go to school. My mother said, "They do."

I said, "I don't see them at my school," and my mom laughed. Once she stopped laughing, she said to me, "They go to a different school than you."

I asked her, "Why?"

Mom said, "White folks don't go to school with black folks. We are a different color, that's why. That's why we live in different neighborhoods too. All our neighbors are black."

I hadn't realized it until she said it, but she was right. All our friends were black, and they were the only neighbors we had. The neighbors that lived next door to us. The neighbors that lived around the corner and the ones that lived past our church and down U.S. Highway 319 were all black families. These families represented a small community within our little town.

Equality in Education in the South

In 1954, the United States Supreme Court decision on *Brown vs. Board of Education of Topeka* ruled that segregation was unconstitutional. In 1955, Brown II called for "desegregation with all deliberate speed." In 1957, the president had to send U.S. troops to Central High School in Little Rock, Arkansas, to protect black students because Arkansas' governor had dispatched the National Guard of the State to deny nine black students enrollment.

Another example of strong resistance to change was in Prince Edward County, Virginia. They abandoned the entire public school system, leaving education to private interests that excluded black children from their schools. In the mid- to late 1960s, the United States Supreme Court had reached its limits on waiting for school systems to follow the law and integrate their schools. The Civil Rights Act had passed several years earlier, and many schools throughout the country had not followed the law. So the United States Supreme Court issued a warning to all school systems that were receiving federal funds that they would lose them if they did not follow the law.

In 1967, it was Norman Park School's turn to open its school doors to all its citizens. Mom talked to me and my sister Dorothy about going to school here at home the upcoming school year. She said, "Mose and Dot, you will be going to school right here in Norman Park next year." Mom went on to say, "You live here and we decided that you live here, and you will go to school here." Charlie A. Gray School was an all-black school, which went from first through eighth grade. Mom said that some of the black families had a meeting to talk about whether they are going to send their children to Norman Park or Moultrie schools. Mom said that most of the families agreed to send their kids to school right here in Norman Park. She also said that some parents said that they were just not willing to take the risk of sending their kids to school here and having them wind up getting hurt. Mom said that she and my dad explained to the other parents that the people in Norman Park were different from the people that they have seen on TV in Alabama and

Mississippi. Mom said that Reverend Leonard asked them how they feel about their boss. They said that their boss treated them fine and were not verbally abusive to them. He also asked them whether their kids were any different from their parents, and they said no. Mom said that she never knew that this many people in our community were afraid of their kids being hurt while trying to attend school. She said that people were truly scared, and it made her question whether she was doing the right thing. Reverend Leonard, Mom said, was sort of the mediator for the group.

A New Beginning

This was the longest summer of my life. Not knowing what was going to happen to us on the first day of school in Norman Park was a worry for everyone. We had seen the violence on TV from other places in Georgia and from other states and one couldn't stop thinking or talking about it the entire summer. My parents had told me and my sister that no matter what is said to you, you do not say anything back. If someone bothers you, you tell your teacher.

Some of my friends had received different advice. Some of my friends were saying if someone messes with them, they were told not to take it but to fight if a must. As we visited each other over the summer and began to talk about going to this school that we were not allowed to attend in the past, we realized that this was real and could be a huge challenge for us to be accepted by our new classmates, teachers, and staff.

One afternoon, a friend that lived next door and I was going to town, and on the way, we saw some high-school-age boys as we were approaching the store. One of the older boys said, "There's seventy-eight of them starting this fall." My friend and I didn't say anything; we just kept walking. They didn't call us names or try to stop or hit us. They let us pass to go into the store. I was thinking while I was in the store, what are these guys going to do when we come out of the store? My friend didn't say anything to me, and I didn't say a word to him. We were just surprised that these guys said that to us. When we finished buying what we came for, we walked outside of the store, and the guys were gone. As we walked back home, we were looking and walking very fast. I didn't tell Mom or Dad what happened to us because I felt that they would not let me go to school in Norman Park the next year. I wanted to go to school there, and I didn't want to ride the bus all the way to Moultrie for two hours like I did to Doerun. I was willing to endure just about anything rather than be on the bus for that amount of time.

The entire summer was all about desegregation of the country's school systems. The evening news would interview proponents and opponents of the law. The advocates for the law being followed were positive and sincere. The advocates opposing the law were mean and hateful about the law. By summer's end, some of the community's potential students had backed out of enrolling in our local school. They succumbed to fear in the press, which, in my opinion, was a planned event. What the blacks in our community didn't realize was that the people on TV were not from our hometown. They were from across the country and in some parts of this state, but none from here.

The week prior to the start of school was very intense. My friends and I were getting a little scared at the thought of walking into an angry mob at the school's entrance. As I would visit friends that final week leading up to the start of school, I would ask them whether they were still going to Norman Park School. Most of them were still coming, and that encouraged me because by now I was waffling back and forth. One of our neighbors came to the house to talk to Mom about the school situation. She asked my mom if she was still going to let me and Dorothy go to our local school.

My mom said, "Yes, they are going to school here, and nobody is going to stop them." She told the neighbor, "These kids have opportunities that we never had." I thought, well, that narrowed my options dramatically.

We had worked in the fields all summer long earning money for our school clothes. For the first time, Mom took me shopping at Lazarus Department Store. Lazarus had the popular clothes that teenage boys wore in those days. My older brother, Leroy, shopped there. I was excited to shop there. Mr. Lazarus was very friendly to everyone that came in his store. He treated you like the store was yours and that he was there to help you look your best. He would often comment on what you are trying on. He would give you a yes or he would say, "You might want to look at this one, young man." He always made you feel welcome in his store. I think the main reason I shopped at Lazarus that summer was that Mom wanted to make sure that I wore decent clothes when we did enter school.

Sunday night before the first day of school, I couldn't sleep. I was thinking of what was going to happen the next day at school. How would we be accepted in the school in our own hometown? Not knowing or realizing as a boy, everything I bought in the stores here, I paid taxes on, and some of the tax money that was collected from me and my parents went to the school that I couldn't attend. I would lie in bed with my eyes open, thinking, Would I be in class with one of my friends? Would my new classmates want to sit next to me? Are the teachers willing to teach us? All we knew was what we saw on TV from Mississippi and Alabama, and that wasn't the best example to encourage new black students in the South. If Alabama and Mississippi were the benchmark, then students, teachers, principals, and school superintendents did not want us taught in their schools. I managed to get about two hours' sleep that night.

The next morning Mom said, "Mose, it's time to get up and get ready for school."

I said, "Okay, I am getting up."

She said, "You wear those blue colored pants with that beige shirt."

I said, "Yes, ma'am, I see them."

After getting dressed, I just sat in a chair until Mom came out of her bedroom and said, "It's time for you to go." She also said, "Mose, if someone says something to you or call you something, you tell your teacher."

I said, "Okay, Mom."

I left home walking. It was probably the longest walk in my life at that point. As I walked, the deep sense of uncertainty grew increasingly. I would constantly look far ahead to see if some of the other black kids were walking so that I would have someone to walk with. I reached town and I saw no one. I walked through the Norman College campus, and I saw no other black students in sight. I am thinking now; did everyone back out except me? The Future Farmers of America building was at the beginning of our school campus, and there was a side road running beside it, and it was there where I saw the Browns' children walking toward school. I waited on them to catch up with me and I walked on to school with them. As we approached the school, there were no white adults waiting outside the school with signs; not even a crowd of students was present. Everyone was getting off their bus and going to their class.

I was so relieved to see no one in our town at our school protesting. I walked on to the office to get my class schedule so that I could see where I needed to go. The principal, Mr Smith, handed me my schedule and said, "Mose, you are in Mrs. McCrary's homeroom." He pointed and said, "Go down the hallway, make a right, and Mrs. McCrary's room is down there on the right." I followed Mr. Smith's instructions and when I reached Mrs. McCrary's room, I just went inside and sat in the very last row near no one. Other students piled in the class and as they walked past my desk, they would look over at me. Some of the kids would deliberately not look at me, but some couldn't help themselves. Like all kids or teenagers, they were as curious about me as I was about them. This was something new for everyone and in some people's eyes, it was a very big deal. I am sure that the students of this school didn't know what to expect of the new kids entering their school either. Kids and young adults only have what their parents tell them to rely on. If parents resented integration, then their kids would probably be told negative, and, in most cases, untrue things about the incoming students. Parents that accepted the fact that integration was going to happen are the parents that prepared their kids for the transition in a positive way. My personal experience with this school during the transition was highly successful. The first year, there were only a few complaints of name-calling, which I never witnessed. I don't know if it was my personality or me rarely speaking to anyone, but my classmates welcomed me very well.

No one ever called me names or tried to harm in any way that first year. Mrs. McCrary immediately noticed there was a lot of curiosity in the room so she said, "Good morning, class, my name is Mrs. McCrary and I am your homeroom teacher and some of you may have me for class later in the day." She said, "Let's begin by telling each other our name and where we live." When it was my turn to tell where I lived, I said, "My name is Mose Kinsey and I live on Mill Street in Norman Park." As I surveyed the room, I realized that I was the only black student in Mrs. McCrary's homeroom. No one in the room came up to me to welcome me to the school, but that was fine by me.

The bell rang and I rotated through all my classes that first day and I didn't have issues with anyone at school. I walked home and Mom met me at the door. She asked me, "How did it go at school?" I told her it was a lot different from what I expected. She said, "In what way?" I said there were no parents at the entrance protesting and none of the students called me names. She was in shock! She couldn't believe it. I think she too was convinced by the TV that all white people hated black people. That may not have been the total case with us, but at least nothing happened that first day of school.

Childhood friends

Childhood friends will sometimes get you in trouble without even trying. My friends and I loved playing marbles all the time.

One day I was headed up to the store to pick up something for Mom and a friend of mine asked me if he could go with me. I said yes. We made it as far as the turpentine shed and my friend said, "Mose, I have some cigarettes, do you want one?"

I said, "No, my dad told me not to smoke."

He said, "Okay, but can you look out for me while I smoke one?"

I said okay. After his smoke break, we went on to the store and from there we returned home. Mom said to me, "You haven't been smoking, have you?"

I said, "No, Mom, my friend wanted me to but I didn't." She said okay.

Mom must have smelled the smoke in my clothes or someone told her that we were at the turpentine mill smoking cigarettes. I didn't care that she had found out about the cigarettes; I was just happy that she believed me.

He and I decided to visit our friend that lives in the country. On the way to his house, my buddy pulled out a box of matches and started striking them and throwing them into the dry brush. The brush would catch on fire and I would put it out. The third time he did it, the flames were just too big and he finally tried to help but it was too late. The fire got away from us and burned several acres of land. The fire department had to come put it out. We never made it to our friend's house. We instead went to our friend's house on U.S. Highway 319. We remained there until dark and then we proceeded home, hoping no one would know that it was us that started the fire.

Of course, that tactic didn't work. When I got home, Mom said, "What were you doing with matches?"

I said, "Mamma, I tried to put the fire out, but my friend kept throwing lit matches on the grass and it got out of control."

She simply said, "You shouldn't have been with him." That was the worst and last whipping I received from my parents. I never got into trouble again.

Home sweet Home

The home that I grew up in lacked most modern amenities. We lived in a two-bedroom wood-frame home with no plumbing or insulation. Our house was not very big. One of the bedrooms was dedicated to my mom and dad. The other bedroom was for us kids; half of the room was for the boys and the other half was for the girls. Our living room was for my oldest sister Mary and her husband. Our living arrangements were very tight, but we managed to get along with each other. It had a wood-burning heater for heat in the winter. Mom cooked on a wood-burning stove to prepare our meals. We didn't have a bathroom. We used a washtub as our bath tub. It was about 3 to 4 feet in diameter and about 1 foot deep. The only modern plumbing we had in our house was running water. We used an outhouse as our restroom. Our kitchen was used to take baths in with the washtub because it was close to the running water.

Operating the heater and stove was not that hard once you learned. My older brother (Leroy) and I would take turns collecting firewood for the heater and the stove. The woods across from our house provided the firewood that we needed to heat and cook. During the wintertime our heater was utilized to its fullest. We would have a two-and-a-half-gallon kettle on top of it heating our bath water.

Inside the heater, we would often put sweet potatoes underneath the coals to cook as a meal. To maximize the space on the heater, there would be a smaller quart-size kettle filled with water for coffee. Despite the fact that we had only one heater in our home, it warmed the entire house very well.

Cooking for two families on a wood-burning stove in the summertime presented a challenge for Mom. Mom would cook once a day. She would start about 8 or 9 am while it was still cool. When Mom cooked, she would always have a small towel around her neck. By having the rag around her neck, she would have her sweat rag with her always. A typical meal prepared by my mom was a two-and-a-half-gallon pot of collard greens, two chickens cut up and fried, a big pot of rice, a big pot of corn, two large trays of corn bread. She cooked it all on this wood-burning stove and no one in the family imagined what an incredible challenge it was for her to do this until years later. One of my favorite meals that Mom cooked was piping hot biscuits, sugarcane syrup, pork, and beef sausage with ice tea. I would ask Mom for four or five biscuits to go with the syrup. I was thin as a rail. I guess the weight that I should have gained was passed on to the adults in the family. It's a wonder that I didn't weigh over 200 pounds as a kid.

Washing clothes was a major task for my mom as it was for many poor families in our community. Mom had a cast iron smudge pot that she used for our dirtiest clothes. She would set the pot between two blocks, put firewood under it, and build a fire under it. Mom would fill the pot up with water, add washing powder, and let it heat up until it came to a boil. She would place our clothes in the wash pot for washing. When the clothes in the smudge pot was ready to come out of the hot water, there would be two washtubs filled with cold water sitting beside the smudge pot to rinse the washing powder out of the clothes.

The tubs had scrub boards in each of them. They were used to agitate the dirt, grease, and grime out of the clothes and it was done by hand. Mom would use a broomstick as an agitator as she stirred the clothes in the smudge pot. She also used it to take the clothes out of the pot and put them in the tubs. My father had put up a clothesline made of wire in the backyard so that Mom could hang the clothes there for drying. We had several pecan trees in our backyard, so Dad ran metal wire between two of the trees to support the clothes on the line.

The line was over 30 feet long so Dad had to use a support pole about midway the line to assist in holding up the clothes. Years later my dad saved up enough money to get Mom a washing machine with a wringer on it. The wringer was attached to wring out excess water from the clothes prior to putting the clothes on the line. My younger brother Timothy was about four years old and he decided to help Mom with the clothes. Mom was attending the smudge pot and she heard my brother yelling. She dropped the pole that she used to stir the clothes in the smudge pot and immediately ran over and unplugged the machine and unlocked the wringer and freed my brother's arm.

The wringer was two 18-inch horizontal bars that are spring loaded and pressed together so that as the clothes go through the wringer, they will squeeze the water out of the clothes. My little brother's arm wasn't broken, but his eagerness to assist my mom in washing clothes was certainly broken.

Trying to sleep on those hot, humid nights in July and August in South Georgia was a challenge. We couldn't afford an air-conditioner in our house. You had to remain hot and muggy. My brother and I would sometimes open the window and pull the covers over our heads. We could hear the mosquitoes buzzing around our heads from underneath the sheets. The cool breeze coming through the window was worth taking a chance on getting bitten by the mosquitoes. If you made the mistake of falling asleep and the covers came off your head, the next morning you would see the evidence that the mosquitoes didn't go away. We couldn't afford a home telephone, but we did have a black-and-white television set. The television helped us cope as a large family living in one house. My dad and I would watch baseball on the weekends. My mom loved the soap operas such as *The Loretta Young Show* and *Patten Place*. I loved Westerns such as Roy Rogers, Gene Autry, Hop-along Cassidy, Raw Hide, *The Rifleman*, and *The Lone Ranger, Leave it to Beaver*, and the *Circus Boy*.

I remember the first time I saw a television with color. I was going to Mrs. Sheppard's house to see if she needed her grass cut. She would pay me $1.50 to cut her lawn with her push mower. That day I decided to take a shortcut and walk behind the church to get to her house. The preacher lived in the house next door to the church. As I passed the preacher's back porch, the door was open, and I looked through and saw the television set and it was showing color. Once I finished my grass-cutting job, I went home and told Mom that I had seen a television showing in color at the preacher's house. She said, "Boy, you had better stop walking around folks' houses. They will think you are looking to steal something from them."

I said, "Mom, I was just looking at the television," and she said, "You don't go that way again."

I thought, Wow, Mom was more concerned about people thinking that I wanted to steal from them rather than me seeing a color TV for the first time in my life.

Mom and Dad were like that though; they never wanted us to get into trouble or give Kinsey a bad name in our community.

Growing up poor had its share of challenges. Visiting the outhouse at night was always a frightening experience. The outhouse is normally placed at least a couple hundred feet from your house so that you wouldn't notice the smell. First, they were not equipped with a lighting system. Secondly, there were critters that either crawled or walked at night that you would rather not meet outside at night. Everyone would be conscious of ensuring that they used the outhouse prior to the hours of darkness. Well, as you would have it, about 11:00 pm one night, I was so full of water that my eyes were floating. I looked throughout the house to see if my brother, Leroy, was home, but he had not made it home. At this point, I was bending over with bladder pain. I told Mom that I was going to the outhouse, and Mom responded, "It's very dark out there. Can't you wait until tomorrow?"

I said, "No, Mamma, I must go now."

She said, "Get your dad's flashlight."

I yelled to her as I was going out the door, "I couldn't find it."

She yelled back, "Look out for snakes! They are crawling this time of the year."

After hearing her say that, I stopped and thought about it, and the pain started up again and I moved on toward the outhouse. I could barely see the image of the outhouse as I made my final approach to the building. After a successful trip to the outhouse without contacting any ground travelers, I opened the outhouse door and stepped inside. I immediately began to release water from the faucet. About five seconds into the downpour, I heard something move on the floor to my right. All in one motion, I jumped and turned my body toward the door, hitting the door with my head, knocking it open, and landing on my feet on the ground outside of the outhouse. It must have taken me only five seconds to reach our back door. I ran inside of our house, yelling to my mom there was something inside the outhouse. Mamma turned to me and said, "Boy, you must have fell into one of the washtubs out there because your pants are soaking wet."

I said, "No, Mom, I was using the outhouse and something moved in there."

My dad checked the outhouse the next morning and thought that an opossum had come in through the side of the outhouse. I asked my dad, "Do they bite?" He said that the opossum was probably more afraid of me than I was of him. I told dad I thought that I was more afraid because I left the outhouse and the critter didn't.

Money was very scarce in our house as well. Aside from cutting people's grass to earn money as a juvenile, I often would walk along the dirt road or the highway to pick up pop bottles that drivers would throw out of their cars on to the shoulder of the roadway. I could redeem the pop bottles at the store in Norman Park for 2 cents each. I would leave our house carrying a two-and-half-gallon plastic bucket for carrying my find. My goal was to collect at least ten bottles when I went on a search. Once my goal was met, I would head for the store to exchange my goods for either legal tender or goods at the store. Often it was for goods at the store. A 16 oz. Royal Crown Cola cost 6 cents, and a Baby Ruth Candy Bar only cost 5 cents. Sometimes I would get a cola and bag of peanuts. Peanuts were 5 cents a bag. I would drink some of the cola and take the bag of peanuts and pour them all into the bottle of pop. While walking home, I would take a drink of the pop by turning the bottle upside down and allow the peanuts to race to the neck of the bottle, then I could release a few in my mouth. I would return the bottle in my hand and begin to chew on the peanuts. It was a great treat. The Babe Ruth Candy Bar would be kept in a safe place at home for later. This was a very well-deserved treat for me after a very long and hard search for pop bottles.

Growing Up Black in the South

Norman Park was a small farming town of about 600 people during that time. It's located about 200 miles south of Atlanta, Georgia. Our county's (Colquitt) population was about 15,000 people and Moultrie is its county seat.

Many would say that our town is in the Deep South and I concur; however, as a young adult, I didn't see the extreme hatred and physical abuse of blacks that I witnessed on television coming out of Alabama and Mississippi and other parts of the country. I must admit, there were towns and cities in Georgia that were not like our small town, and they had issues much like Alabama and Mississippi. We were treated differently, but it was a subtle difference. I can't speak for everyone, but during my childhood, we did have separate drinking fountains in public places, restrooms, restaurants, and theaters, just among a few. The governor of our state at that time was no different from most Southern governors. To get elected, they must represent segregation. To see the governor of a state come out on television and condone and even take part in racist acts was a very disheartening era for our state and our country. As a young black kid in the South, you saw no hope that life would get better for you as for as having opportunities toward a better life. Especially when you have the governor of your state stand at the entrance of the university to deny minorities access to the registrar's office so they could not enroll. These are people that are supposed to represent every human being in their state. The government is charged with ensuring that people's basic human rights are protected under the laws of each state and the federal laws of this country. I saw the leader of our state acting like the mob in front of him. He was a total disgrace to this state, and he didn't realize it because he was so intoxicated with hate and an eagerness to impress his constituents who had that same hate.

Moultrie, Georgia, is located about 10 miles south of Norman Park. There my family could shop for clothes. Back then, if Mom could find clothes without holes in them and they looked clean, then she would buy them. The cost was minimal: a dime for a shirt and about 15 cents for a pair of pants. Mom continued to shop at Goodwill for me until I began working in the tobacco fields. We were in Goodwill one Saturday, and I asked Mom if I could go to the restroom and she said, "No, your dad must take you to the courthouse."

I said, "Mama, that man (Caucasian) went to the restroom in the back of the store."

Mom said, "I know, but we cannot use it. There are restrooms for us (Negros) at the courthouse."

I went to the car and told Dad that I had to use the restroom, and he said, "Okay, come go with me."

We walked across the street and to the east side of the courthouse, and there were stairs leading under the courthouse and right to a sign that said Colored Only. We went through the door, and there was the restroom. It was in decent shape because the county prisoners kept it clean.

After I finished using the restroom, my dad took me on the first floor of the courthouse to show me the restroom that I was not allowed to use. I asked Dad, "Why do they let the prisoner go in the restroom, and we cannot go in there?"

Dad said, "The prisoner cleans the restroom but cannot use it."

I told Dad that if I was cleaning the restroom and had to use it very bad, then I would go right there. Dad turned around and began to smile, and we left for the store where Mom was shopping.

We had a movie theater in Moultrie, and of course, it was segregated as well. It was called the Colquitt Theater.

We kids would work doing the summer cropping tobacco during the week. On the weekend, some of us would ask my dad to take us to the Colquitt Theater. We would go to the 7:00 PM movie. The white patrons would sit on the ground level of the building, and the black patrons would sit upstairs to watch the movie. We would buy our tickets, a box of popcorn, and a Coca-Cola then march upstairs and get a seat and watch the movie. Once the movie was over, we would walk about two blocks north of the theater to Starkey's Restaurant. All of us would sit at a table and order foot-long chili dogs, fries, and a large Coca-Cola. Dad would come to Starkey's about 10:00 PM to pick us up. On the way back home, my dad would listen to us talk about the movie all the way home. He would occasionally ask us questions about the movie, and I am convinced that it was to ensure that we continued to have a good time.

During the late 1950s and early 1960s, there were very sad times for blacks across America. The Deep South was the primary focal point. We may have a good day at school, but in the evening as we were sitting around the television set, things changed very quickly. There would be an air of sadness as we watched Chet Huntley and David Brinkley bring horror into our living room each night—the horror of blacks being hosed down by Alabama's firemen and others being beaten with batons by the town's police officers. Colored people were protesting for the right to vote as citizens of the United States of America. I remember one evening the news was on and the broadcaster, Chet Huntley, took off his glasses and wiped away some tears from his eyes. I think he must have thought that the cameras were off or they had cut away for a commercial. The emotions that Chet Huntley displayed that night showed the world that all white people didn't agree with this type of treatment of other human beings in our country.

Again, I saw the same emotion from another popular news reporter when President John F. Kennedy was assassinated in 1963. Walter Cronkite had to take his glasses off and fight back the tears right after he announced that the president was dead. People across the country loved him despite the narrow minds of a few in the Deep South and other areas of our great nation that practiced hate and bigotry in their homes. I often thought as a kid, Why did God make us different? Didn't he create us all? Are human beings the work of God? Why would someone hate the work of God? Will the people that hate God's work go to heaven? Will people that hate other people be allowed into heaven? Those are just a few things that I thought of as a young boy growing up in America at a very sad time in our country.

Some state patrol officers were not particularly nice to colored drivers back then. Our family was returning from Thomasville, Georgia (Thomasville is located about 30 miles south of Norman Park), and as we crossed into the Colquitt County line from Thomas County, my dad was pulled over. The patrolman walked up to our car and asked Dad, "Let me see your license, boy." Dad gave him his license. He looked at Dad and said, "Do you know why I stopped you, boy?" The patrolman looked like he couldn't have been a day over thirty-two years old, and Dad was about fifty-five years old at the time.

The patrolman said, "You were weaving across the road; have you been drinking, boy?"

Dad said, "No, Officer."

He told my dad, "Well, I am going to have to punch your license for crossing the center line." He reached into his coat pocket and came out with a hand punch, and he held Dad's license up and punched a small hole in it and gave Dad the license back.

In those days, a driver could lose their license if they had a certain number of punches on their license. My dad took the license and placed it back in his wallet, and he drove off.

Mom said, "Elbert, you were not weaving in the road."

My dad said, "I know, Lola Mae, but what can I do? Nobody's going to believe me over the state patrol." He looked at my mom and said, "We just should pray about it."

Despite this type of treatment from law enforcement officers because of his race, my dad would always render them respect when he encountered them.

Business Venture

I wanted to become a businessman at a young age. When I was about thirteen years old, one of the fundraisers for our school that year was candy that looked like a gold nugget and was filled with something that tastes like Reese's peanut butter in the middle. I figured that I could cut out the middleman (the school) and earn all the profit for myself. The plan was to knock on doors on weekends until all the candy was sold. Per the school, we sold a ton of candy that year. I thought, well, I can sell at least ten cases. That equates to about 120 cans of candy. I ordered the ten cases of candy and began to plan my route for each Saturday. Six weeks passed, and I was on edge waiting for the candy to arrive at the post office. I asked my mom if I had gotten any mail, and she would always tell me, "No, I haven't seen anything."

Two more weeks passed, and I arrived from school, and I walked in the house looking for Mom, and she wasn't there, but my sister Leatis was there. I asked her where was Mom, and she said Mom had gone to the store. I told her that I was waiting for my candy to come in. She turned and walked away with the loudest laugh that you could hear. I asked her why she was laughing. She turned to me and said, "Boy, Mama sent all that candy back.

"We were at the post office, and Mr. Weaver said, 'Lola Mae, a bunch of candy came in for Mose. Do you want to pick it up for him?' Mom said, 'No, send it back. What that boy ordered all that candy for?' She told me not to say anything to you about the candy."

When Mom came home, I asked her why she sent the candy back. She said if I didn't sell that candy, I would have to pay for it. She said that she wasn't willing to take that chance. I said, "Mom, it was in my name."

She said, "Then why did I have to sign for it? Mr. Weaver knew that you were not old enough to order that candy."

I was crushed. All my dreams of making a large profit selling that candy had gone right down the drain. In later years when I came home from the military for vacation, Mom would sometimes bring up the candy. We would have the longest laugh from that situation. That candy entrepreneurial venture didn't get off the ground, but the one at school did. My classmates continued ordering candy from me. As the school year progressed, a lot of the uneasiness slipped away, and a little of normalcy crept in. I began to feel comfortable with my new surroundings and its people.

After settling into the new school for a year or two, I was tempted to play sports for the school. The skills I had developed came from playing with the Underwood kids, Eugene and Emanuel. Their neighbors, Daniel and Linda Fay Purvis, also played with us. They had a basketball goal, and we often played basketball on weekends.

Sports Motivated Me to Stay in School

My eighth and ninth grade years in school, I would hang out at the Norman College Gym playing pickup games of basketball. I knew some of the college players. Jimmy and Bob Elliot were two of the school's star players, and they would play during off season in the gym. They were from Cambridge, Maryland. I would go to the gym on Saturday mornings because they had the key to the gym.

After playing with them for several months, they would choose me on their team all the time. Jimmy was about 6' 3", and Bobby was about 6' 5" and could jump out of the gym. My ninth grade year in school, all my friends encouraged me to go out for the school's basketball team. I didn't feel that I was good enough to make the team, so I didn't try out that year. Instead, I continued to play with the college guys at Norman College.

That summer after work and on weekends, I was in the gym every day playing basketball. The guy from college said to me, "Mose, you should play for your school team. You are good." Several of my friends were trying out for the team that year. Coach Eddie Owens was head coach of the team. When school started, I signed up for tryouts. I made the varsity team as a sophomore. The high school players were not as big as the players that I had been accustomed to playing against. The first year I played with the college players, I would get all banged up, so I learned to play a lot tougher to compete with them. Our first week of practice was mainly running and wind sprints. It was normal for me because of having to run with the college guys.

Our school was the smallest classification of schools in Georgia. We were a class C school. K-12 with a senior graduating class each year of about fifty-five students. Ronald Zorn stood at 6' 3" tall as our starting senior. Ed Norman, Doug Gointo, Danny Baker, Mickey Key, Ricky Himbree, Danny Singley, Ben Weaver, Earol Stephens, Leroy Little, and Robert Brown were on the team. Our team had been the doormat for every team in our region prior to this year. In those days, seniors were the starters for the game. I was a sophomore on the varsity team, and

I certainly was not expected to start the game. We were trailing in the second quarter and Coach Owens put me in the game. I finished the game with over 18 points and over 10 rebounds and 2 steals. In practice, Coach would always run me with the defense team. During the next practice, Coach started putting me on some of the offensive plays.

The next game was much the same; I would come off the bench and score 20-plus points, 15-plus rebounds with 2 to 3 steals a game. Our seventh game of the season, we went to Adel, Georgia, to play the Cook County Yellow Jackets (Class B School), and I scored 33 points coming off the bench, and we lost by 3 points.

The next day after our P.E. class, Coach Owens called me into his office and said, "Mose, I talked to Mr. Smith and you are starting the next game."

I simply said, "Yes, sir," and walked out of his office.

When I reached my friends, I told them that Coach said that I was starting the next game.

Our next game was at home and we won the game. I had not realized the impact of me starting the game as a sophomore and causing one of our senior players to sit during the start of a game. It's something that I had not asked for, nor did I think it would be important when Coach told me that I would be in the starting lineup. Even after telling me that he had consulted with our school's principal prior to allowing me to start the game, I didn't think about the senior that I would replace. The day following the game, I was on my way to P.E. class, and one of my friends stopped me and told me that one of the senior players' mother had just left Coach Owens' office after having words with him about why her son did not start the game the previous night. I went on to the gym and dressed out for class. We went on the gym floor and Coach eventually came out of his office after being on the phone. He didn't say anything but "Let's get started." I wanted to tell Coach that I didn't mind not starting, but that would have let him known that my friend was eavesdropping on his conversation with a parent.

Coach has never let on to me or anyone else that this happened. Of course, I am sure the other person on the phone with Coach when I walked in the gym was either Mr. Smith or his wife, Bonnie. The player was and still is a great guy. He never knew that I knew that this happened. He may not know that his mom came to Coach's office. I do know that Coach took a lot of heat for coaching us, and he has never talked to any of us about it. He is truly a great man and coach.

We made the region playoffs. We won our first game in the tournament, and that put us up against the Doerun Deers of Doerun, Georgia. Doerun was a second seed in our tournament. They were expected to beat us by at least 20 points. Well, we were up by 1 point by game's end. We beat them 46 to 45, and I scored 21 points. We were celebrating on the floor, and Ed Norman came up to me and said, "Mose, you just won us a trip to Macon."

I said, "Macon? What do you mean?"

He said we are going to the state playoffs.

We weren't quite good enough to get past Georgia Christian School out of Valdosta, Georgia. They had a guard. His last name was Crisp, and he could hit from anywhere on the court. Coach put me in charge of holding him under 30 points for the game. Coach knew that if Crisp would score over 30 points, then we would lose. I chased him all night long, and he still ended up with 20 points. Despite us holding Crisp under 30, they still won and went to Macon as a number 1 seed in the Class C State Tournament. We finished the year region runners-up but earned a trip to the state tournament. We were pitted against East Coweta County in the first round of the state tournament. We beat them, which made history for Norman Park High School. The next round had us playing Arlington out of Atlanta. Arlington beat us en route to a state championship title. The next year James Harris was our center. Standing at 6' 5", he helped dominate the rebounding statistics in our region. We won over fifteen games that year in route to a number 1 region seed.

We breezed through the tournament and then Georgia Christian School was the last school standing in our way of being region champions. When that game began, I needed 8 points to reach 500 points in a single season. We not only got me the 8 points, but we beat them handily to give Norman Park High School their first boys region championship. Our girls team were coming off a state championship run. They were awesome. They were led by Jill Middlebrooks, Kay McKellar, Judy Hart, Patsy Hall, Judy Hall, Wanda Smith, Jeanie Pierce, and Gail Barker. Our team, unfortunately, were put out again by Arlington of Atlanta.

I did play baseball, and I ran track while in school. In baseball, we were region champions. Track, I ran the 100-yard dash, 400-yard dash and threw the shot-put (4 lbs. steel ball). In region, I won gold in the 110 yard and the shot-put and bronze in the 440 yard. In state, I won bronze in the 440 yard. The same guy (Willie Frank Banks from Doerun, Georgia) that beat me in region beat me at the state meet.

One of the things that helped us prepare for the 1972 season was that some of us were sent to Georgia Southern College for a one-week basketball clinic. Coach Owens talked to the returning team and three of us wound up going to the camp. Ricky Himbree, Danny Singley, and I were the players going to the one-week camp. Ricky had a 1968 Mustang, and it looked good. I had no idea where we were going, but a map did help us out. We went on this road and don't know if it was a shortcut or we had to detour, but it wound up being an adventure for the three of us. We came up to a lakelike area and down at the lower part of it; it had a ferry boat that we drove the car on and we were ferried across. I had never done anything like that before. Once on the other side, we continued our journey on to Statesboro, Georgia. We talked about that ferry all the way to the university. We reached the camp location and were assigned rooms in a dormitory. There were athletes from all over Georgia. One of the athletes there was Wayne "Tree" Rollins, who went on to play in the NBA. Wayne's birthday was the second day of camp, and some of the guys were trying to lure him out of his room. Well, Wayne grabbed a fire extinguisher and began to spray all of us. As you would have it, one of the coaches intervened and made the crowd disperse and go to bed. That was the end of the celebration. The camp was designed to work on our basic basketball fundamentals such as dribbling, setting screens, pick and rolls, and how to defend your basket. I think the training improved our basketball skills a great deal. I would certainly recommend it for future ball players.

Dad's First Basketball Game

My dad was the janitor for Norman College until the school closed in 1971. He was transferred from there to our high school in Norman Park. Dad was a homebody-type person; he never goes anywhere but home. He had not seen me play basketball. So when he arrived at our school, all the teachers were telling him, "You must see Mose play basketball." About seven games into our schedule, we were playing Whigham High School at home and like normal at the end of the third quarter of our girls' game, we would get up and head to the dressing room to get ready for our game.

Toward the end of our girls' game, we came out of our dressing room and lined up at the door, waiting on the final seconds to tick off the clock. One of my buddies ran up to the door and said, "Mose, your dad is here to see you play." He pointed toward the door's entrance. As we exited the door to start our warm-up drills, I began looking to see if I could locate him so that I could wave to him. I looked toward the end of the gym's bleachers, and there he was, sitting there with my sister, Leatis. I waved at him and he waved back. I couldn't believe that he came to the game. I knew that he supported me playing basketball. It was just one of those unwritten rules that Dad supported you from home because that was his sanctuary. He doesn't like the spotlight. It was a very close game, but we managed to win it by the skin of our teeth. When I made it home, I asked him, "Did you like the game?" and he just simply said, "Yes, it was good." Of course, he didn't need to talk because my sister was doing all the talking. That's my dad, a man of very few words.

The way I could spend time with my dad other than watching baseball was going fishing. I knew that he loved to fish, so on some Saturday mornings, I would ask Dad if he wanted to go fishing. I would always say I will dig the bait. He would tell me okay. I would go outside and dig the bait, and when I finished, I would tell Dad that I had the bait, and he'd come to the car and we would leave for the pond. Norman College had a farm, and it had a huge pond on it, and that's where we would always fish. Once we reached the pond area, the first thing I would do is start gathering firewood for the stove and the heater. When I finished with the wood, I would join Dad fishing. I would ask Dad, "How many fish have you caught, Dad?" He would tell me, and I would tell him that I would catch him. He would catch a fish, and then I would catch one. I don't think I have ever outfished him.

When we were getting ready to leave the fishing creek, I would always go over to his fishing spot to see how many fish he had caught. I would say, "Dad, where's your fish?" He would point to where his fish were and I would walk over and lift them up, and as usual, I would say, "You got me again." He would just smile. One of the fun parts of our trip to the fishing pond was that Dad would let me drive the car to gather the firewood. He would also let me drive the car from the pond up to the hardball highway. That's how I learned to drive a three on the column transmission shifter. Our car was standard shift, but the shifter was attached to the steering column. Once you mastered the operations of the clutch, the shifting was very easy.

Smokey Joe

One of Dad's many vehicles that he drove was a 1960 Chevrolet Impala. We named it Smokey Joe. It was reliable and cranked-up on the first turn of the key, and it would take you anywhere. The problem was that it smoked very badly. We would be riding down the road, and it would leave a very visible smoke signature for miles. We often joked that the smoke trail that it left behind was thicker than the mosquito truck spraying for mosquitoes. People would pass by us, and they would look over at us, and if their looks could kill, we would all be dead. Most kids riding in their parents' car wanted to ride in the front seat; not us, we would run to the car to be the first one to make it to the back seat so that no one could recognize us.

Our neighbors loved it because we would keep the mosquito population down. My sister was extremely excited that I was going to take the test for my license so that I would be the one that gets the looks from other drivers as Smokey Joe sprayed the highway with smoke. Smokey Joe was our only transportation. Dad couldn't afford anything else. It was ride in Smokey Joe or stay at home.

A License to Drive

When I turned fifteen years old, I was more than ready to get my driver's license. I had been practicing with Dad for the past five or six years on dirt roads and at the fishpond. I got the study guide from the State Troopers Station at our courthouse in Moultrie. The troopers would be set up in our courthouse two days per week to administer the written and driving tests. I went one Tuesday morning to take the test. As I approached the counter where the officers were standing, one of the officers turned to me and said, "What can I do for you, sonny boy?"

I said, "I am here to take the test for my learner's license, sir?"

He said, "Have you studied for the test?"

I said, "Yes, sir."

He said, "Come go with me then."

He had me sit on one end of the table, and there was another gentleman on the other end of the table. The other gentleman had already begun his test. The officer said, "Come here, boy, take this test, and sit back over there, and when you finish, bring it back to me."

I said, "Yes, sir." I took the test and went back to my seat and sat down and began to answer the questions on the sheet. After writing in all the answers, I got up and took the answer sheet back to the officer.

The officer said, "You done already, boy?" He also said, "When people finish that quick, they normally don't pass." I just looked at him and didn't say anything. He then said, "Have a seat, and I will have the results in a minute."

When I returned to my seat, I noticed that the gentleman taking the test on the other end of the table was about half done with his test. He also seemed very nervous while taking his test. After about five or ten minutes, the officer reappeared at the counter, and he motioned for me to come up to the counter. When I arrived at the counter, he said, "Where do you go to school at, boy?"

I said, "Norman Park High School."

He said, "Norman Park! You don't go to Bryant High School?"

I said, "No, sir, I live in Norman Park."

After that exchange, the officer refocused on why I was there. He said, "Okay, boy, you did pretty good on the written test; you passed."

I said, "Thank you, sir."

He said, "Have you been practicing on your driving, boy?"

I said, "Yes, sir, on dirt roads, a lot."

The officer said, "Give me a few minutes, and I will have you come up and take your picture for your learner's license." After my picture was taken and the officer was about to give me the license, the officer said, "Be careful on these roads."

I said, "Yes, sir."

New Set of Wheels

Later that summer, Mom, Dad, and I were in Moultrie, and we were passing by Knight's Fish Market, and across from Knight's, there was a car lot. The lot had a 1961 Chevrolet Impala sitting outside the lot facing the road, and it was red.

On the windshield, it had $295.00. As we were passing by the car lot, I said to Mom, "There is a car on that lot for $295. Can we go back and see it?"

She said yes. Mom turned to Dad and said, "Elbert, turn around and let's go look at that car." So we went back to the lot to look at the car.

As we pulled, up the salesman saw us from inside the building, and he got up and came outside and greeted us. By this time, we were at the Chevy. He said, "Good afternoon, folks, you're interested in that Chevrolet?" The car was a 6-cylinder, three on the column, bench seats, four doors, and no hub caps. The salesman saw that I was asking all the questions, so he said to Mom, "Hey, ma'am, why don't you let your son drive the car, and he can tell you what he thinks about the car?"

I took it for a drive and it drove very well, and it had no smoke signature unlike Smokey Joe. I asked Mom if I had enough money saved up to get it, and she said, "I think you do." Mom kept money for me during the summer from working for Mr. Middlebrooks. Mom told the salesman that we wanted the car. The salesman said, "Okay, ma'am, who do you want to carry the note on the car?"

She said, "I think we have enough money to pay cash for the car."

The salesman said, "Okay, ma'am, when do you want to pick it up?"

Mom said, "We will be back on Monday."

We then left the car lot and headed back home. I was so excited about getting the car that I didn't get any sleep over the next two days. While I was working, Mom and Dad went that Monday and purchased the car and had it in the front yard when I got in from work that day. I immediately washed it and began to clean it up. I bought a can of spray silver paint to paint the rims since I didn't have hub caps. Several weeks later, I wanted to put a name on the car. That was a popular thing to do back then. As I was thinking of a name to put on the car, I was watching a Disney movie about a coyote. The movie was called *Chico the Misunderstood Coyote*. So, I decided to put Chico on the car. The names were often placed on the rear quarter panel on both sides of the vehicle nearest the taillight. The car was red, and I had the gentleman at a sign shop put Chico in dark yellow. Until this day, some people in Moultrie only know me by the name that I had on my car, Chico. Chico was supposed to be my car, but the family used it and I was all right with it, but at least we were finally able to retire Smokey Joe.

Local People Who Impacted My Life as a Kid

A Teacher's Concern

This year Mrs. Betty Stallings was my homeroom teacher, and I was in one of her English classes. My buddies and I were all concentrating this year on winning the region crown in basketball. It was going to be a very hard task because of Georgia Christian School. They would always find a way to win the region championship. We were practicing evenings and sometimes on Saturday mornings so that we would be prepared for the season. Once the season started, we poured everything into each game we played. I can remember being so tired after a game that I would sometimes sleep through my alarm clock. We played Echols County away, and I played in every minute of the game.

We had to travel back and be in school the next morning by 8:00 am. My buddy, Leroy Little, stopped by my house and knocked on the door to wake me up. I got ready and walked to school. I had to stop by Mrs. Stallings' room to report that I was in school. Mrs. Stallings said, "Mose, you are not a privileged character." I knew what she meant when she said it. This statement alone changed my life and my way of thinking from that day forward. Those words made me think of how people viewed me based on things that I do. It made me realize that people are watching how you conduct yourself or even how you react to success. It was something I needed to push myself to come to school no matter how tired I was. If everyone else on the team made it to school on time, I should have made it on time too. That statement has helped me keep things in perspective throughout my life. If I did something that warrants praise, I would never ask for it; I may act as though it was nothing. Since that day, I have always made it a priority to be on time and come to work every day. I was never late for school again after the conversation with Mrs. Stallings. I truly appreciated her honesty and her willingness to let me know how others viewed my character because of me coming to school late. This encounter was not a coincidence; God works in mysterious ways, and Mrs. Stallings was the vehicle He used to get His message to me that I wasn't anyone special and that gifts that He gave me He could have given to someone else.

Different Summer Job

The next summer Mrs. Stallings had talked to me about a summer job program for high school kids at C.E. Building Products (more recently known as Wells Aluminum) and asked me if I was interested. I said, "Yes, ma'am, I would."

She said, "You would be working for my husband, and his name is Roscoe."

I replied, "Yes, ma'am." Mrs. Stallings explained to me where to go to apply for the job. When we got out of school for the summer, I went the next Monday to apply. I reported to C.E. Building Products' front office for an interview. The lady that talked to me said, "Are you the Mose Kinsey that Roscoe's wife Betty teaches?"

I said, "Yes, ma'am."

She said, "You are already hired. We just need to fill out your paperwork."

I said, "Thank you, ma'am." I was very quiet around people back then, so I didn't say that much to anybody. The lady came back and said, "We are done with your paperwork. Are you ready to work today?"

I said, "Yes, ma'am."

She called someone on the radio and told them to pick me up at the plant entrance and take me to Roscoe's line. The lady directed me to the front gate, and there I waited on the person to come get me. By the time I arrived at the front gate, a guy walked up to me and asked, "Are you Mose?" I said yes. He said, "Come go with me."

I walked through the gate, and the guy took me to the plant and over to Roscoe's line. Roscoe met us there, and he said, "Hey, Mose, come over here, and let me introduce you to the fellows." After that, he said, "You will be working over here." My job was to keep the doors and windows going down the conveyor belt. Also, to help take them off the belt and help the guys if they got behind on their jobs. It was easy compared to cropping tobacco in the hot fields.

Roscoe treated his guys like they were buddies. We would always have a fun time while working on his line. He would tell jokes while we were working. Roscoe would have us motivated from the time we walked in the plant and until it was time to leave. Several times on the way home, there would be a guy outside the gate trying to get us to join the union. He would say, "Hey, kid, it's time for you to join." I told him that I wasn't sure if I wanted to join. He said that the union looks out for you, and it only costs a couple of dollars per week. I said to him, "I have a good boss, and he takes care of us guys." Finally, I told him that I had to buy school clothes with my money. He didn't ask me anymore after that encounter. I hated leaving that job because I liked working and earning my own money. In the end, school was a better choice for me because I loved playing basketball.

A Dairy Farmer's Kindness

Ben Weaver was one of my teammates on our basketball team. His father was a dairy farmer, and Ben's mom worked in our principal's office. We were runner-up winners in our region in basketball behind Georgia Christian School. I was getting ready for the trip to Macon, Georgia. I asked Mom if she had some money that I could take with me for food or snacks. Mom said, "I have $2.90; you can take it with you."

I said, "Okay, I probably don't need it all. What I don't use, I will bring it back."

She said, "Don't worry about it."

The day we were leaving, a lot of parents came to see their kids off to Macon. As we were boarding the bus, some of the parents were at the bus's door shaking the team member's hands and wishing us a good game. Just prior to me boarding the bus, Mr. Weaver reached his hand out to shake my hand, and he said, "Mose, good luck, and have a good game." There was something in his hand, and he released it in my hand. I immediately knew it was paper, and I thought, Wow!

I took whatever it was and put it in my pocket immediately, and at the same time I said, "Thank you, Mr. Weaver."

We boarded the bus, and when I got in my seat, I reached in my pocket and pulled the paper out, and it was a $10 bill. I was in shock and had no idea that Mr. Weaver was going to give me money. I was so grateful for the money. I did share the money with other teammates that were in similar situations like me. Mr. Weaver and other whites in my community are the people that helped shape my way of thinking. That all people don't hate. Mr. Weaver is one of the reasons that I give to people that are in need without hesitation. I have been convinced that the hand of God has always been with Mr. Weaver. His act of kindness and generosity has and always will be remembered.

Coach Grantham's Advice

One day I had to leave school early, and a kid that had attended Norman Park School previously was on the road walking past the school. As I was leaving the school's parking area, he flagged me down. He then asked me for a ride into town. I said, "Okay, get in." I took him to town and went on my way.

The next day at school, Coach Grantham called me into his office and said, "Mose, who was that riding in your car yesterday?" I told him the kid's name, and he said, "Yes, that's who I thought it was."

Coach Grantham said, "Mose, I don't think you need to be hanging around with that character. He will get you into deep trouble." He said this guy is known for doing some bad things out there in our community. I said he stopped me and asked me for a ride into town; I didn't think anything about it. Coach said, "You don't need to be giving him any rides in the future."

Coach Grantham's warning was a great help to me as well. People do judge you by the company that you associate yourself with. If you hang out with people that do bad things, then they assume that you do the same thing. I have used that advice throughout my life as well. Coach Grantham didn't have to warn me of this kid, but he did and I am grateful to him for the warning. He showed a great concern for me and what could happen to me if I would have accepted this kid as a regular friend. This is another lifelong lesson that I learned right there in the small town of Norman Park, Georgia.

Mr. Middlebrooks, My Summer Boss

I often tell people about my times as a teenager working in the tobacco fields. If I hadn't had a good boss, I probably wouldn't be talking about the good ole days working. Mr. Middlebrooks was much like my dad; he was a man of very few words, unless he was telling you what needed to be done for the day. I never heard him say anything bad about anyone. I remember him dropping me off at a cotton field to hoe the weed out of the rows of cotton. When he came back to pick me up, he looked down the rows, and all he said was, "It looks good, Mose." He would often drive the tractor that pulled the tobacco harvester while we cropped. At the end of the rows or when we would stop to take a break, everyone would be talking, but he would just sit back and listen to us. If he noticed someone cropping the tobacco too green to cook in the barn, he would simply say, "You are cropping too green, Mose." He wouldn't yell or scream. He treated all his workers with the utmost respect.

Our water cooler was a five-gallon wooden barrel. We would put a ten-pound block of ice in it and fill it up with water. There was only one dipper to drink from, and Mr. Middlebrooks would drink from the same dipper the rest of us would drink out of. His actions showed us that he was no better than us. Mr. Middlebrooks worked just as hard as we did.

One Sunday evening, he came by the house and asked if I could help irrigate one of the fields. I said, "Yes, sir." We went to the field and loaded up the irrigation pipe on the trailer and moved to another field and started dropping the pipe. Once the pipes were dropped, we immediately started connecting the links of the pipe to one another. Once all the pipes was connected, Mr. Middlebrooks or Billy Gene (his son) would go start the engine down at the pond. The engine would draw the water from the pond through the irrigation pipes and up through the sprinklers and out on the plants. It is now about 1:00 am and Mr. Middlebrooks is still working as hard as Billy Gene and me. He would not ask you to do anything he wouldn't do or hadn't already done himself.

If a piece of machinery broke down and we needed someone to go into town to get a part, he would want to continue to work while someone else gets the part. Mr. Middlebrooks was the hardest working boss ever. He would always tell the workers to be ready at 6:00 am to be picked up for work. Mr. Middlebrooks would come by about ten minutes to 6:00 am. I can't recall him ever being late to pick me up for work. My work week was Monday through Saturday at noon. My check would be $55.00. I would take it home to Mom to put in the bank the next week. Mr. Middlebrooks was very much like my dad that he never missed a day of work unless he was so sick that he just couldn't make it. I have been truly blessed to have had examples in my life like my dad and Mr. Middlebrooks.

My Little League Baseball Coaches

Mr. Murphy, Mr. Revere, and Mr. Dawson wanted to put together a Little League baseball team of black kids in Norman Park. Mr. Murphy stopped by our house and talked to my dad about me playing with the team. Dad asked me if I wanted to learn how to play baseball, and I said, "Yes, sir."

Dad and I watched baseball together all the time on television, but I never thought about playing. The coaches were all men of God and were deacons in our church (Morning Grove Baptist Church). The black kids in Norman Park didn't have anything to do on weekends. Mr. Murphy's two oldest sons (Earl and Eddie Dean) were a few years older than me, but I could play on the team as well. Mr. Revere's Jake was also a few years older than me. Curtis and other kids in the black community made up a good-size team.

The first day of practice was very confusing to me. We didn't know what to do at all. We all had to be taught the very basic of the sport. We had to be taught how to field a ball both on the ground and in the air, how to hit the ball, and the basic rules of play. We worked on learning the game for about two weeks because none of us had played baseball before. Our coaches were very patient with us, no screaming or shouting (other than to the outfield). If you made a mistake, you were not ridiculed or embarrassed in front of your peers. They always encouraged us to do our best.

I started off playing first base. Earl played Shortstop and he was about three or four years older than me, and he was the biggest kid on the team. He would field the ball and throw it to me as hard as he could. At first, I was afraid to catch the ball because Earl threw it so hard. Early on when the ball was hit, I would hope it didn't go to Earl. As luck would have it, every ball that was hit went to him, and I had to catch it. In the end, it made me a much better first baseman and my fielding skills improved a great deal. The lessons I learned from those coaches helped me more in life than the baseball skills. How to talk to someone when they have made a bad play. They would talk to you very calmly and would use that situation as a learning point. They were very understanding and not all chastising. The way they instructed us on how to play the game of baseball, it was with great compassion and enthusiasm. We were treated fairly and equally as individuals and as teammates. No one on the team had preferential treatment. We were, essentially, treated like one big family.

My Dad

My dad's personality is what sticks out to me. He was very quiet and hardly ever spoke to someone unless they asked him a question. During my school years, I would see him most on weekends. He never missed work, so he was never home until late in the afternoons. He would have a garden planted most years. In the evenings, you would see him standing up out in the garden a lot. I remember one incident where my dad had gone to Moultrie Loan Company with one of my sisters and co-signed for her on a $300.00 loan, and Mom found out about it. Mom was upset. She argued with Dad for over three hours. Dad finally left the house and went to our church, and he was there for about five or six hours. When he returned, Mom was back to normal. She didn't say anything else to him the rest of the day. She knew that he had left to go pray. When he was going through things like that with Mom or if anything was very heavy on his mind, he would go to the church to pray.

I recall a situation concerning one of my sisters and a former boyfriend. She told Mom and Dad that she had ended the relationship with the guy. Well, she lied and continued seeing the guy until he threatened her. Well, she was finally serious about not seeing him after this occurred. About two weeks had passed, and she had not seen him. He began to ride by our house. Dad came outside, and he stopped and asked Dad if he could speak to my sister, and Dad said, "No, you best be leaving from around here."

One of my dad's friends was visiting. The guy told my dad, "I will leave after I see her."

My dad said, "I don't want any trouble, but you need to leave from around here."

My dad's friend told the guy, "You heard what Tom said. You need to get your ass out of here right now."

The guy took off in his car and not two minutes later, he was back. He would ride past the house and look over at us. My dad's friend said, "Tom, I know how to stop this." He left walking, and the next time the guy passed by our house and turned to go up the street, there was a single rifle shot fired. The guy's front windshield just shattered. He speeded up and got out of the area, and we never saw him again that night.

My dad's friend came back to our house and said, "Tom, I don't think he will bother anybody down here again." He was right. The guy never came back in our neighborhood again.

My dad set the bar high for his kids to follow. He was a man of great integrity. He always stood for what was right, especially if you were one of his kids. He constantly drilled that into you. He would tell us about how he would turn in things that he had found on the job. Being the janitor, he would find that people forgot or misplaced things quite often. If he found it, he wanted the rightful owner to get it back. He would find money, wallets, purses, checkbooks, and valuable items such as watches and jewelry. These were examples that Dad would use when talking to us kids about doing the right thing. He had a big heart.

Mr. Joe Griffin's business was harvesting turpentine. He hired people to harvest turpentine during the year. Turpentine was harvested by skinning a small enough area on a pine tree so that it would drain its sap into an aluminum tray over time. One family came into town and the husband worked for Mr. Griffin. Well, for some reason they abruptly left Norman Park and wound up leaving their daughter behind. My mom asked my dad if it was okay to keep the girl until other family members could be reached.

Jonnie Mae was about fifteen years old, and she stayed with us until she was grown and moved out. A similar situation arose with the same seasonal work of turpentine, but this time it was two boys left behind. Our neighbors (the Sims) took one of the boys, and my mom and dad agreed to take the other boy. They also stayed with us until they could get jobs and move out on their own. They were okay with taking on the extra responsibility of raising other kids with their own. I have always said that my dad only had a sixth grade education, but he has a Ph.D. in humility and humanity.

My Older Brother, Leroy

Leroy had a work ethic that mirrored my dad's. I don't recall him ever missing a day of work. He never got sick. Leroy also got his start working in the fields right alongside us. He, like my dad, couldn't read or write; however, Leroy could sign his name. He married his high school sweetheart, Mary Lee Underwood.

Leroy worked for Norman College farm, which was located on the Doerun-Norman Park Road just past our high school. That's where Dad and I always fished. Some Saturdays during the school year, Leroy would get me to help him and his boss (Mr. Collins) castrate some of the pigs on the farm. The smaller pigs were very easy to work with. You simply placed the pig on his side and put your knee on its neck and open his hind legs, and Mr. Collins would start in with the razorblade. The larger pigs were much more work. We would corner one, and I would walk straddle the pig front head to hind quarter, reach down, and pick up his rear legs. As I stood up, I would back up in the corner with his head directly jammed in the corner. I had both my feet and legs in between his front legs. Then I would stand straight up and raise his hind legs up and spread them so that Mr. Collins could walk up and begin to use his razorblade. At the end of the castrations, we would head home with the meat. My dad could prepare the spoils very good.

My brother worked there for a few more years. After Norman College closed, Leroy started working for a concrete company based out of another county in Georgia. The team he worked with would build or restore bridges on highways. He learned his job so well that he could read the blueprints on how to build the bridge. After twenty-plus years on the job and his job foreman's health was deteriorating, the team relied heavily on Leroy to tell them how to build the bridges. Once his boss retired, the company wanted to promote him to foreman. Leroy thought, not being able to read or write was his main concern. He didn't want the responsibility, and a coworker was awarded the job. Although the coworker was awarded the job, Leroy continued to build the bridges while the coworker received the credit. Several years later, the coworker that was awarded the job passed away. The owner of the company told my brother that he knew who had been responsible for the team's bridges being built. He said he knew that it was him all along who was reading the blueprints and keeping the team together. The final thing he told Leroy was, "You are the foreman." My brother's daughters (Charlene and Mary Pat) taught him how to do his paperwork, and he was just fine.

Leroy was a great inspiration for me, personally. He and my dad were men who believed very strongly in taking care of their family, and they set the example for me and my younger brother to follow.

Coach Owens

Coach Owens was my head basketball coach. He believed in hard work. Wind sprints was his middle name. When I first started playing basketball, we wouldn't work with the basketball for the first week of practice. We would do endurance training, wind sprints, figure 8 without the ball, and walk through plays without the ball. When we finally got the ball, it was for figure 8 running drills and running dribbling drills. Our plays were designed as a series of picks and screens to free a player up for the ball. We could run those plays without the ball also. Coach was very intense during the game. Coach was always concerned about us staying academically eligible to play. He would constantly check on our grades to see if we were close to failing. We had to maintain a C average to play on the team. Coach didn't want you to fail a grade or he would threaten you with sitting on the bench. As hard as he worked us in practice, no one wanted to sit out a game. We figured that we had earned an opportunity to play the next week.

Coach was a strict disciplinarian. One afternoon my brother's car broke down, and he stopped by the school to get my car to go get another tire. They searched for me. I was supposed to be in P.E. class, but I left school a little early that day. The first time I had ever left school early. Coach was not happy, to say the least. Most people think that coaches take up for their players when they are wrong, but not Coach Owens. Our talk the next day was not good. He left me with this. Do you think you deserve to start the next game? I couldn't say anything but no. It was very hard, but it was something that I did, and I had to endure the consequences. It seemed like on eternity sitting the bench watching my teammates play without me. The fans were looking at the bench and pointing at me. All I could do was try not to acknowledge them and focus on looking at my teammates on the court.

About three minutes in the first quarter, a timeout was called. My teammates made their way to the bench, and I would stand up beside them and try to help encourage them to run the plays. As the first quarter was over, and the team came to the bench, by this time,

I was thinking, "Well, I guess I want get in the game during the first half." Coach turned to me and said, "Mose, get in and get their power forward." I was in shock but relieved. I went into the game, and we all played very well, but we lost the game by 4 points. I pinned that loss on myself for not doing the right thing, something my father spent his entire life teaching us. I let a lot of people down, my teammates, our fans, Coach Owens, and my dad. I appreciate coach today for holding me and the rest of my teammates to standards. Rules are put in place to be followed. When a person breaks those rules, then they earn the consequences that apply to those rules. No one should be exempt from the consequences once rules or laws are broken by an individual. I honestly don't know where I would be or what I would be doing right now if I hadn't had all these people in my life to guide me this far.

There are many others in my early years that certainly played a huge role in shaping my character, but these men and women stood out more so than anyone else.

Making a Career Change

My senior year in high school, I worked nights for a plant in Moultrie. I worked from 11:00 PM to 7:00 AM in the morning. My job was to take the large rolls of weaved twine off the weaving machine with a lift that moves on rails in the ceiling. I would remove the rolls and take them to a storage area off the main floor. I would do this all night. I guess I had been working there for almost eight months, and we got a guy in for me to teach him my job. He learned my job and was doing well. I came in one night, and I looked on the floor to observe the weaver to see if a roll needed to be taken off. I saw the guy that I trained to do my job, and he was running a machine. I went to the foreman and I asked him, "Why was he on the machine? I was next in line to go on the machine."

The foreman simply looked at me and said, "Mose, he married one of our supervisors' daughter, and they told me to train him on all the jobs in my department."

I said to the foreman, "That isn't right, man."

He said, "I just did what they told me to do."

I didn't know if I could talk to someone else, so I just complained to myself and just kept working. The next day, one of my close friends, Robert Davis, stopped by my house and asked me to go with him to the Army Recruiters Office. I told him that I would go with him. He said that he was interested to hear what they had to say.

He and I went to the federal building in Moultrie. The recruiters were waiting for him to arrive. One of the recruiters said, "Are you his friend?" I said yes. He said, "I can get the both of you in on the buddy plan."

I said, "What is that?"

He said, "You both sign up, and you will go through training together."

I said, "My mom don't want me to go in the military."

He said, "I can talk to your mom."

I said, "No, that's all right."

He said, "Well, all you must do right now is go to Albany and take the written test. If you pass the written test, then you can go take a physical and get a job."

I said, "I am not sure because I work the night shift at Moultrie Textiles, and I wouldn't do well on the test because I will be sleepy."

The recruiter said, "Just go take it anyway." I said okay.

Two days later, I got off work and met Robert and the recruiter at Bull's Restaurant. We had breakfast, and off we went for Albany. We arrived at the testing site about fifty minutes later. The recruiter put all of us in this room and gave us the test and turned us loose to take the test. I must have fallen asleep on the test ten or more times prior to me finishing that test.

The recruiter returned to the test site to pick us up. He picked us up and took us back home, and on the way, he asked me if I had made up my mind about going in. I said, "I don't know."

Two days later, the recruiter called Robert and me into the recruiting station. Robert stopped by the house and picked me up, and we went to the recruiter's office. When we arrived at the federal building, I started to waffle on whether to go in or not. We went on upstairs to meet the recruiter, and he greeted us with a big smile. He looked at us and said, "Do you guys want the good news, or do you want the better news?"

We said, "The good news first."

He said, "You both passed the ASVAB test."

I said, "What is the better news?"

He said, "Both of you qualified for a $2,500 bonus."

I said, "What, you are joking, right?"

He said, "No, you guys did very well. When do you all want to leave?"

I said, "I am not sure I want to go in."

Robert said, "Come on, Mose, we can go in together on the buddy plan."

I told them that I had to think about it. Robert and I left and went to my house. We were at my house talking, and suddenly I stood up and said, "You know, they did me wrong on the job, and I am not going back there." I told Robert that I was going into the army.

He said, "We need to let the recruiter know."

I said, "Let's go up there tomorrow when I get off work."

We went to the recruiter's office and told him that we were ready to go. He said, "What month?"

We said August.

He said, "Okay, I will get the paperwork ready for you to sign tomorrow. Bring your birth certificate, Social Security card, and driver's license, if you have it."

We got all the paperwork that he requested. We returned to the recruiter's office the next day and began to fill out paperwork. The recruiter said to me, "I thought you said your name was Mose?"

I said, "It is Mose."

He said, "Not per your birth certificate."

I said, "What does it say?"

He said, "It says Moose."

I said, "That can't be right."

He said, "Who did your birth certificate, the hospital?"

I said, "No, Mrs. Maddie Bradford; she was Mom's midwife."

He said, "Do you want to change it?"

I said, "No, let it ride the way it is."

Once we finished the paperwork, Robert and I left and went back home with the plan to leave in August. A couple of days passed by and Robert and I got to talking about going in, and we finally decided that we would just leave as soon as possible. The recruiter called Robert with the new date, and it is just days away. We would leave for Atlanta MEPS Station on July 30. The recruiter put us on a bus from Moultrie to Atlanta. We arrived in Atlanta in the evening time. We checked into our hotel rooms. About 9:00 PM, we decided that we would see what Atlanta looks like after dark. There were clubs several blocks from where we were staying.

Well, I guess it was about 9 or 10 PM, and Robert called my room and said, "Hey, Mose, let's go see what's going around here."

I said, "Okay, I will meet you downstairs in five minutes."

We met and walked out on the walkway and looked in both directions. We saw people dressed casually, walking toward a glass-front building. I said, "Let's go check that out and see what's going on inside." We went in and as I looked around, it had boxing photos everywhere. Joe Lewis, Floyd Patterson, Rocky Marciano, and of course, Muhammad Ali. The place also had a television screen playing old fights. In the middle of the place, they had a bar, and behind the bar, there was a dancing stage, and there was this girl dancing in a bikini-like outfit. Guys were all around the bar watching the young lady dance. Robert and I had never seen anything like this. I said to Robert, "Hey, Rob, I think you have to be over twenty-one to be in a place like this?"

Robert said, "Yes, you're right, but let's stay a little longer."

I said, "I don't know, man. What if the police come in and we are in here, and we are not twenty-one? We could be arrested and not leave for the army tomorrow."

He finally said, "Yes, you're right, let's go." We left the bar and walked around a little more and went back to our hotel for the night. Our recruiter had already told us that the shuttle bus would be by to pick us up around 4:30 am.

The next morning as we were waiting on the shuttle to pick us up for the trip to the Military Entrance Processing Station (MEPS), we realized that we were not the only young men looking for a change in careers. Many other guys were waiting with us for the shuttle. The shuttle delivered us to the MEPS for our physical and induction into the military. There were guys and a few girls going into all the branches of military (army, air force, marines, and navy). As we talked to one another, we found that we all had our own separate personal reasons for choosing the branch of service that we signed up for.

One of the sergeants rounded us up, and he separated the males from the females and sent us separate ways to begin the physical. After our physical, we all wound up at the counseling office for our branch of service. The counselors were the military personnel that would assign us to our job and whatever guarantees our military branch promised. When it was my turn to go in and talk with the counselor, I went in and sat down, and the guy said, "Moose Kinsey is your name?"

I said, "Yes, Sergeant."

The sergeant said, "Well, Moose, you qualify for our $2,500 cash bonus because you did so well on your test." Then he said, "You must enlist for a minimum of four years, and you must go into the *combat arms* field as a part of this deal." Combat arms means that if we were in a war, your job puts you on the front lines with the enemy. I told the recruiter that I was all right with going into combat arms, but I didn't know if I wanted to stay in for four years.

He said, "Take a little while to think about it, and I will get with you later."

I came out and had a seat and thought to myself, What if I don't like the military? I would be stuck for one more year. I was now the last recruit in the room, and the sergeant said, "Hey, Moose, you made up your mind yet?"

I said, "Yes, Sergeant." I said, "I want only three years."

He said, "All right, what job do you have in mind?"

I said, "I like the big guns."

He said, "That would be field artillery."

I said, "Yes, I think I will like doing that."

The sergeant finished my paperwork and rushed me down the hallway with the other recruits that were just minutes away from swearing in. We reached the group, and the captain said, "Okay, everyone, it's time to become a part of the greatest organization in the world, the United States Armed Forces."

Recruits of all branches of the military swore in at the same time. We all went inside the room, and the captain read us the oath of allegiance to our country, which made us officially in the military.

Army Basic Combat Training

After swearing in, we had about thirty minutes to board the bus for Fort Jackson, South Carolina. The trip from MEPS in Atlanta to Fort Jackson, South Carolina, was about six hours. We arrived at Fort Jackson around midnight. A sergeant got us off the bus and took us to the supply room to get our linen for our bunks (beds). Once we were all off the bus, the sergeant introduced himself and welcomed us to Fort Jackson, South Carolina. It was now about 2:00 am in the morning. The group finally finished at the supply room, and we were off to our barracks (living quarters). We reached the barracks, and the sergeant took a headcount to ensure that all fifty of us were present, and he assigned each of us a bunk. As the sergeant called our names and bunk number, we took our linen and filed out on formation and into the barracks. We located our bunk and made up our bunks and went back outside into formation and waited for the sergeant to release us for the evening.

The sergeant walked through the barracks and came out and said, "I am very unhappy with what I see in this barrack." I knew he was referring to how we made our bunks. Some were made, and some were not made at all. He said, "We are going into the barracks and gather around bunk number 7, and I will show you how to make a bunk correctly." It was now about 3 am in the morning. We went inside and stood around bunk number 7. The sergeant came in and took the linen and made up the bunk. He took a quarter out of his pocket and threw it on the bunk and the quarter flips about twenty times. The sergeant turned around and looked at the group and said, "When you finish making yours, the quarter better flip thirty times in the air."

We looked at each other like, No sleep tonight. The sergeant said, "I am going to give you ten minutes to make up your bunks and the time starts now!" As everyone was scrabbling to get to their bunks, he said, "Oh, by the way, it's 3:25 am, and first call is 4:30 am." He walked out of the barracks and stood outside in the formation area. When I finished working on my bunk, I took a quarter and threw it on my bunk and it flipped one time. I went, Oh, boy, that's not going to cut it. I retightened it again, and it flipped twice. By now, time is running out, and I just waited on the sergeant to call us to the formation area.

Thirty seconds later, he yelled, "Get out here, you maggots!" It takes us about ten seconds to reach the sergeant and form in somewhat of a formation.

The sergeant says, "Who thinks they have the bunk that will pass inspection?"

One of the guys in the back of formation says, "I think mine will, Sergeant."

The sergeant tells the group to wait in formation because if his quarter doesn't flip thirty times, everyone must go back and redo their bunks. We hear the sergeant yell, "Hell no! Where did you learn this, Private?"

The private said, "Junior ROTC (Reserve Officer Training Corps), Sergeant."

He said to the recruit, "You better give these knuckleheads a crash course on how to tighten their bunk." The sergeant came back outside and said, "Private McAffrey will give you instructions on how to make your bunk in the morning." He looked at his watch and said, "You scumbags better go ahead and hit your bunks because 4:30 am is right around the corner."

We rushed inside the barracks and went to bed. It seemed like within the short time I laid my head down, it was time to get up. The lights came on, and there stood another sergeant yelling at us to get up. He said, "Get up and stand beside your bunk." He introduced himself and welcomed us to Fort Jackson as well. The sergeant said very loudly, "You dirt bags have thirty minutes to shit, shower, shave, get dressed, make up your bunk, and be in formation. Oh, the last one in formation owes me fifty push-ups."

While Kilgore was executing his fifty push-ups for being late, the rest of the platoon was learning how to march. Kilgore rejoined us prior to going to breakfast. The sergeant marched us to breakfast.

As we approached the mess hall (dining area), we had to form a single file line leading up to the door. Just inside the door, there was a desk there for a person taking headcount of all recruits eating breakfast. When you entered the door, you would have to give that person your last name and whether you were R. A. (Regular Army) or U.S. (United

States Draftee). As I entered the door, I would sound off loud and clear, "Kinsey R. A.," and walk to the serving line. I would pick up a drinking cup and a tray for my food.

The cooks would put food on your tray as the line moved slowly. We sat down at a table nut. We could not talk to one another or you would have to get up and leave the mess hall. The sergeants would always say, "If you are talking in my mess hall, you are done eating and must get up and leave." I was sitting there eating, and I heard the loudest "Get up! Get out of my mess hall!" The recruit had taken only one bite of his food before talking to his buddy next to him. I learned very quickly that you listened and follow instructions or you would pay dearly. As I finished my five-minute meal, I left the mess hall at a rapid rate of speed. After exiting the mess hall door, I saw the one bite recruit in the "front-leaning rest position" (push-up). The poor guy had been executing push-ups since he had been outside. What a learning curve for the rest of us. We went from there back to the barracks to use the latrine (restroom) and continued to tighten up our bunks. The sergeant came back to our barracks about 7:00 am and yelled, "Fall outside right now!"

We formed into a formation, and he guided us to the administration section for in-processing. It was there that we processed for pay, identification cards, and mail. We went from there to the barber shop for haircuts. I thought it was kind of comical that the barbers would ask each one of us what kind of haircut we wanted, knowing that he was going to cut our heads bald. This took about a half day to complete. That evening, we moved to the clothing section to pick up our everyday attire. We split up into groups to avoid long lines. I moved to the boot section first. The civilian worker put a foot measurer down beside my feet and said, "Step in this, recruit!" I stepped in the foot sizer and he yelled out to the privates retrieving boots for him, "Hey, size 12."

The private emerged with that size 12 boots and gave the boots to the gentleman and said, "Hey, recruit, put these on and let me know how they feel?"

I put the boots on and walked down the aisle and back, and I told the gentleman that they felt good. He then said, "Good, move to the point, recruit."

The next point for me was underwear. The gentleman there asked, "What size boxers do you wear, recruit?"

I said, "Sir, I have never worn boxers before."

He said, "Welcome to the army, recruit." He then said, "You look like a size 32."

I said, "Yes, sir, I am 32 in the waist." He then threw me a bundle of boxer shorts and said, "Move to the point, recruit."

I was at the T-shirt section next. The guy there said, "How many inches are you across the chest, recruit?"

I said, "I don't know, sir." He then took a tape measure and ran it around my chest and yelled to the recruit bringing out shirts, "42." The private brought the guy some bundles of T-shirts, and he took them, gave them to me, and said, "Move on to the next station, recruit."

I finally reached the fatigues or utility uniform (field pants and shirts) station. I knew my pants and shirt size when I reached that station.

Once we finished being issued our clothing items, it was time for us to head back to the barracks. The sergeant put us into formation, and we began marching back to our barracks. We reached our barracks, and the sergeant said, "There is a method to storing your clothes in the wall locker. I will demonstrate to you how to fold your socks, shirts, underwear, and the placement of your pants and shirts on hangers in your wall locker." The sergeant was very detailed in what he needed us to do. After his demonstration, he said, "Here's what I am going to do. I am going to inspect the wall locker of your choice in thirty minutes so you all should work together as a team."

There were a couple of the recruits that had been in Junior ROTC in high school, and the group relied heavily on them in getting us through this wall locker inspection. The sergeant gave us a diagram of our wall locker. The diagram showed where everything that we were issued should be placed in the wall locker. The recruit showed us how to roll our socks, fold our T-shirts, and how to place our fatigues. The sergeant shows up after and goes directly to PFC McAffrey's bunk. He opened the wall locker, and to me it was the ultimate wall locker display. The sergeant, however, disagreed and trashed it saying that nothing was right. We knew if McAffrey's wall locker didn't pass, then ours would stand a snowball's chance in hell. The sergeant finally got tired of inspecting us around 1:00 am. He said, "I won't be here tomorrow, but my counterpart will and if you all don't get it together, you will be, 2:00 am tomorrow morning, getting into your bunks."

Morning came very quickly. We began learning how to march this day. We learned to do individual movements such as left face, right face, about face, present arms, order arms, parade rest, and attention. The group also learned to march as a group or a unit such as forward march, right flank, left flank, rear march, column left, column right, mark time, and group halt. Marching was fun, and it came natural for some of the recruits. We also attended classes on military customs and traditions and how to wear the uniform. By the end of the day, we were all tired out but had that one task that none of us seemed to be able to master, the bunk. We got to bed around 2:00 am the next night. We finished that day and it was time to head over to the drill sergeants. These were people that I dreaded seeing. Stomachs dropped, eyes popped, and teeth chattered all at the thought of meeting our drill sergeant.

The drill sergeant was a necessary icon of both evil and sainthood standing in our way of success. We all knew that this day was coming. It was no secret; we knew that we had to go through the drill sergeants to make it through basic training. It was about 5:30 pm and the cattle trucks lined up along the company area, and we all knew what was about to happen. We came out of our barracks with bag and baggage, ready to face our nemesis, the drill sergeant. As we boarded the cattle trucks bound for the training battalions, we were both frightened and saddened—saddened that we were leaving such a peaceful environment, yet frightened that we were heading for a life of misery for the next several weeks. As the cattle trucks approached Delta Company Fifth Battalion First Infantry Division (D 5/1), we saw the drill sergeants lined up on the physical training field. The truck stopped and the door flew open and a drill sergeant jumped on the doorstep and yelled, "Welcome to the real Fort Jackson, you scumbags! You have thirty seconds to secure your bags and report to those Round Browns out there on the field. Move now!" There was a huge cluster of confusion on the truck, recruits grabbing the wrong bag and running on the field near a drill sergeant. Once the dust settled, the drills started yelling and maneuvering us into some sort of formation. We were doing either push-up, sit-ups, jumping jacks, and deep knee bends. Finally, a sergeant with sense said, "Drill sergeants, get them into formation."

Once we were in formation, the sergeant said, "When I call your name, you will move over to your platoon." He said, "There are four platoons. I will start with the First Platoon." The sergeant said, "Oh, by the way, you are no longer a recruit. You are now a trainee, moving forward. Kinsey, Moose M., you are in First Platoon."

At the conclusion of filling all the platoons, the sergeant said, "Enjoy your stay here at Fort Jackson, South Carolina." His final words were "Platoon sergeants, take over your platoons."

My drill sergeants were named Staff Sergeant (SSG) James and Sergeant First Class (SFC) Duffy. Drill Sergeant James said, "Grab your bags and follow me!" We walked to our barracks, and Drill Sergeant James said, "This is your home for the next six weeks, and you will keep it clean like Mommy kept your house cleaned." He said, "We only clean before and after training, so what does that tell you, trainees? A lot of late nights!"

The barracks were built prior to World War II, and we still used them for living quarters for basic training. They were two stories high, open bays, with an office on one end and a shower and toilet on the other end. They could house up to thirty soldiers on each floor. Drill Sergeant James told us, "Move inside the building! Your bunks have been preselected for you. Find your bunk and install your linen and stand by your bunk. You have ten minutes, go!"

At the end of the ten minutes, Drill Sergeant Johnson and James approached the door and there was a loud and thunderous "At ease" let out by one of the trainees. Everyone immediately stopped what they were doing and came to the position of attention. Drill Sergeant Johnson said, "Carry on" and everyone relaxed.

Drill Sergeant James said, "Okay, everybody moves over to Private Dawson's bunk. When you get up in the mornings, your bunks must be made prior to exiting the building. I am going to demonstrate to you how to make your bunk." He and Private Dawson made the bunk, and it looked tight. He said, "You don't have to bounce a quarter on it, but it will like good." Drill Sergeant James briefed us on the dos and don'ts of the barracks.

After the briefing from Drill Sergeant James, we were released to retire for the night. Lights were out at 9:00 pm. We awoke the next morning to metal trash can lids being banged together by Drill Sergeant Johnson. It was 4:00 am. "Get up! Get up!" said Drill Sergeant Johnson. He said, "You have thirty minutes to make your bunks and be at my PT (physical training) formation."

We all finished our bunks and went to the PT field for the morning physical training. We started out with warm-up exercises, and we then began calisthenics. After about twenty minutes, we formed up on the side of the road to start running. We ran for about fifty minutes. You could tell the trainees that were not athletes in school. They were dropping out of the run-in volumes. We decreased our speed to keep the stragglers close to us during the run. We finally reached our starting point near our barracks, and once everyone regrouped in formation, Drill Sergeant Johnson said, "Everybody will pass our end-of-cycle PT test or remain at Fort Sill until you do."

The people that dropped out needed to put in practice in the evenings when our training was done for the day. The first week of basic training was mostly learning military customs and traditions, rank and insignia, placement of rank on the uniform, and perfecting our marching movements. The second week, we moved into caring for our M-16A1 Rifle.

I remember one incident where we were on the dry fire range, and I forgot and left my weapon in the rack on the range, and I was supposed to have it with me always. One of the company drill sergeants yelled from the base of the firing line, "Who owns weapon number 28?"

I said, "Private Kinsey, Drill Sergeant."

He said, "Come here, Private."

When I reached the drill sergeant and saw what he was holding in his hand, I was in shock. The drill sergeant said, "You know, Private Kinsey, if I were the enemy, you would be dead right now." With a loud yell, he said, "Get down in the low-crawl position, trainee, and head for the chow (food) line!"

After about twenty minutes of low-crawling, chow was over, and the drill sergeant said, "You were so slow, you missed chow." He said, "Get up and get back with your platoon!"

I went back and rejoined my platoon, and the guys said, "Man, you missed chow."

I said, "Yes, and I am starving."

My weapon was glued to me from that day forward. When we returned to the barracks that evening, Drill Sergeant James said to us, "Every one of you are going to Egypt when you graduate!" Egypt and its neighbors were in a huge dispute during this time. We didn't know any better, so we were writing home saying we may be going to Egypt.

The third week, we began our Basic Rifle Marksmanship (BRM) training and certifications. I was one of three soldiers in our 58-man platoon to become a fire expert with my weapon. It was a great feeling seeing that, after leaving my weapon behind caused me to low-crawl a tenth of a mile and I missed my lunch. It came through in the end for me.

We also took individual pictures during this week of training. We marched across the post to the media center. The platoon stopped at the center, and we entered the building one at a time. As we entered the building, you would take off your utility top and head gear. You would then put on a dress green coat and tie for pictures. Your utility pants and boots would remain on during the time you take your picture. Once I finished my picture, I took off the coat and tie and ran back to our formation. It took about forty-five minutes to complete our pictures, and we moved back to our barracks. The fourth week, we went to the hand grenade and M-60 machine gun range. Our platoon did very well in those two areas as well. Week 5, we took our end-of-cycle test, drill, and ceremony (marching) evaluation, and the physical readiness test. The platoon again did well on those tests. The last week of basic training was makeup testing and preparing for graduation.

Advanced Individual Training

Upon graduating from basic training, I boarded a plane for Lawton, Oklahoma. Destination: Fort Sill for field artillery training. Only a few in our platoon went to Fort Sill. We arrived there the third week in September, and nights were already getting cold. I was in Fourth Platoon and my drill sergeant was Sergeant First Class Jolly. When got there, we were prepared to see drill sergeants like we did at Fort Jackson.

The environment at Fort Sill was much different. All the drill sergeants did was take us to our barracks and to and from our job specialty training. Monday morning, Drill Sergeant Jolly Showed up for PT, and once it was over, we were responsible to go to the training area and meet the sergeants that were training us.

At the first formation, the sergeant asked, "Who in this platoon have a valid driver's license and can drive a stick shift?" I was the only one who raised a hand. The sergeant looked at me and said, "What's your name, Private?"

I said, "Private Kinsey Sergeant!"

He turned to me and said, "Private Kinsey, you are now our company commander's driver, and I want you to report to the motor pool right now."

I went to the motor pool, and the motor sergeant checked my license and he had an M-151 Jeep ready for me to drive. He said, "Private Kinsey, you will be driving for Captain Black."

I signed out the vehicle and went to the company and waited on the company commander to come out of his office. As he approached the vehicle, I got out of the Jeep and rendered him a hand salute, and he returned the salute. He looked at me with much amazement. He said, "Good morning, Private Kinsey."

I said, "Good morning, sir."

He said, "Few new soldiers can drive a stick shift, Private Kinsey."

I said, "Yes, sir, I learned while working on the farm, and my dad had a stick shift."

He said, "Where are you from?"

I said, "I am from Norman Park, Georgia, sir."

Captain Black said, "Where is that about? Macon or Atlanta?"

I said, "We are about 60 miles above Tallahassee, Florida, sir."

He said, "Okay," and continued to direct me to the training site. Once we reached the training site, Captain Black said, "Private Kinsey, you can go ahead and join your platoon until I get ready to go back into garrison (main post)."

I went over to the platoon, and we were training on the M-109 Howitzer. It is an artillery piece. It fires almost 100-pound shells. The firing sequence was very simple. The rounds for the gun are about 30 feet behind the gun. The ordinance team would take the round out of the crate and set it upright. The fuse man would set the timed fuse per the fuse setting received from the chain of command. The officer would double-check the fuse setting prior to the round being carried to the gun. Once the fuse setting was cleared, the round would be taken to the gun for loading. The round would then be placed in the loader-rammer for seating in the breach block. The loader would open command lift the automatic loader and the pushrod would seat behind the shell, and it would move the shell forward with force and properly seat the shell in place in the breach block. Then, a bag of blasting powder would be positioned behind the shell. The number of bags of powder would depend upon the distance the shell would be fired. Once the shell is seated and the powder was in place, then the breach block is closed. The number 1 man would then hook up the lanyard to the firing pin. When the number 1 man is given the command to fire, he will pull the lanyard, and the tank will fire, sending the shell down range.

I do remember one incident that has stayed with me throughout my military career and life. Private McCrary and I were stationed inside the tank. McCrary oversaw the loader-rammer. We had fired about four shells, and on the fifth shell, it happened. The shell was properly seated in the tube of the gun, and it was time for McCrary to position the powder behind the shell. He placed the powder behind the shell and simultaneously lifted the loader-rammer, and his left arm was still inside the breach block. When the loader-rammer followed his hand up into the breach block, he yelled, "Help me!" I immediately stepped over to where he was and helped pull his arm back out of the breach block. His hand did not look good. There was blood everywhere. We immediately called for a medic.

We wrapped his hand and arm up in some towels and rushed him to the hospital. I couldn't believe what I saw. I thought that he was going to lose his hand. After Private McCrary was taken to the hospital, we continued training. A week went by and we heard nothing about Private McCrary's health. Three weeks went by and no one said anything about Private McCrary. We never heard of McCrary again while we were in Fort Sill.

One of my friends in the Fourth Platoon was Art Ross. Art was from Medford, Ohio. He would often talk about back home as many of us would. Many of us guys would keep in touch with each other for a few years, and we would just lose contact with each other almost as fast as we became friends. We continued training, and we graduated on November 20, 1973. My orders had me going to Eighth United States Army Republic of South Korea.

After graduation, I returned home on leave. I had an opportunity to visit some of my friends that didn't venture out like Robert and me. They were either working in the fields or in one of the local plants. Some went on to college, and some just left the area in hopes of finding better jobs than what Moultrie had to offer. I opted to go into the military after my daughter Cassandra Irene Turner was born. I have some friends that elected to stay in Norman Park and help run the family farm. Ed Norman and Earl Stephens comes to mind. Some, on the other hand, went to college and returned to our school system as teachers. Jill Middlebrooks Stuckey, Bobby Jean Ruark Key, Ginger Baker Horne, to name a few—all great people. On November 30, 1973, I was promoted to Private E-2.

First Time Overseas

After vacation, I boarded a flight for Kimpo, South Korea. This was my first duty assignment. I arrived at Camp Corner, South Korea, on December 15, 1973. When I left Southwest Georgia, it was about 65 degrees. When I got off the plane in Kimpo, it was in the 20s.

Camp Corner is the army's in-processing point for all soldiers entering the country. It's located in Seoul, South Korea, the country's capital. Seoul is located about 60 kilometers from North Korea's border, or the Demilitarized Zone (DMZ). North Korea sits below its allies, China and Russia. Therefore, it was important for the United States to keep a good number of our troops on the ground in that country.

As a part of me in-processing, I went through administrative and financial processing as well. A private (E-1) pay was $288.00 per month before taxes, and after taxes, it was $251.00. I knew that my mom and dad needed some financial help, so I took out an allotment for $200.00 per month for them. My check each month was $51.00. That averages out to about $12.75 per week. All I needed was personal items (toothpaste, razor blades, soap to wash my clothes, and deodorant) during the month, which came to about $8 or $9 dollars per month. I didn't smoke or drink alcohol, so I could save some of the money that I kept each month also.

After a couple of days waiting on my assignment within South Korea, I received orders assigning me to the 110th Military Police Company in Camp Ames, South Korea. It was a classified assignment in South Korea. The unit was guarding classified materials.

This was a time when the "cold war" was a tremendous threat to United States and our allies. The priority during those years were to fight the battle on another continent and not our own. I reached my unit. SSG Bridgewaters was my platoon sergeant. SSG Bridgewaters had one of the privates in the company take me around Camp Ames to in-process there as well. I had to travel to Camp Casey to get my field equipment (TA-50). The TA-50 consisted of coats, thermal cold weather boots, thick trousers, thermal underwear, entrenching tool, wet weather gear, mosquito head nets, sleeping bag, and much more.

Once I returned from Camp Casey, I was issued my local gear, which consisted of an M-16A1 rifle and an M-1911A1 .45 caliber pistol. Those weapons were signed for but only issued for duty or in the case of an emergency. After completing my in-processing, I was now ready for work. We worked twelve-hour shifts. If you worked the gates, all your time was spent at the gate. If you worked in the towers inside the maximum security area (MSA), you worked six hours in the towers and six hours in the guardhouse as a backup force. If you were dog handlers, then you patrolled the inner and outer perimeters periodically from the guardhouse. It was one of the most intense assignments that I ever had in the army.

The enlisted soldiers would do different things to relieve the stress because of the possibility of us having to defend the site or receive the orders to engage the enemy from our site. Some new privates would come to us clean-cut kids right out of high school, and within a year of duty over there, they were either drinking or smoking or, in some cases, both. You had to be very strong-willed to overcome some of the influences from other soldiers. Being away from home and the stresses from the job were sometimes overwhelming. There were a few of us that managed to hold on to the reality that we would go back home the same condition in which we came. Many of us either signed up for taekwondo (martial arts) or made model planes and cars to pass the time in a more meaningful, diplomatic way. I saw a lot of soldiers get in trouble over there, either through drinking alcohol or selling things illegally on the black market.

There was a national curfew over there during the cold war period. Military and civilians had to be off the streets at 11:30 pm each night. If you were caught on the streets after that time, you were taken to jail. The top black market items were American cigarettes, Jack Daniels liquor, American beer, and a host of other American products, including ox tails. When you sign into your unit, you are issued a rationed control plate (card). You were only allowed a certain number of items on that card per month, such as two bottles of liquor, two cartons of cigarettes, or two cases of beer per month. There were soldiers in my unit receiving Article 15s (non-judicial punishment) and, in some cases, court-martial (judicial punishment), equivalent to a felony. Some soldiers were court-martialed out of the army from there because of the black market.

We did have a small theater on our post. The movie started at 7:00 pm each night. If you arrived about twenty minutes early, they would play National Football League previews. When the movie started, the national anthem would play, and all soldiers would stand for the duration of the anthem. The military payback then was very low for soldiers.

The army and other branches of our military were asking soldiers to take care of themselves and their families with $62.75 per week. It was extremely hard on the soldiers that were married. That's part of the reasons why some of our soldiers were selling things on the black market. You couldn't blame the Korean nationals because if the soldiers didn't sell to them, then they couldn't get the items. The other reason was that they wanted to party more and took a chance on adding to that cause. I was too afraid to get into trouble. Guys would ask me to buy things on my plate for them, especially when they found out I didn't put items like that on it. Eventually they realized that Private Kinsey was not going to ruin his career for them.

The Korean people are a very kind and polite group of people. They love their country. Their law dictates that every abled male will serve in their military, the Republic of Korea Army (ROCK Army). They must serve at least twenty-six months in either the ROCK Army or Koreans Augmented to the United States Army (KATUSA).

When the Koreans marry and have children, they pray that one of their children is a male. Korean custom is that once the parents can no longer work or provide for themselves, the son provides for them. This holds true in most Asian nations, especially China, because of the massive population and population control law. Couples in China are limited to one child per family. China also has a very high mortality rate among female births. The Korean society treats their elderly with the utmost respect. Almost every shop, store, or almost anywhere you go in Korea, if a male in his mid-twenties or older is there, then he will probably tell you that he was a sergeant in the army. It is a very patriotic country.

During the summer months, the farmland outside of Seoul harvests tons upon tons of rice. The rice paddies are flooded with water. This makes it difficult for the army to train away from garrison during the summer months in South Korea.

This time in South Korea, there were very few civilian-owned automobiles. You would see some black sedans on the road, but those were mostly company-owned vehicles. They have a great massive bus and train system in Korea. Taxis were and still are a major part of their transportation system as well. Ginseng tea is another farming product that the Koreans grow, and it is very profitable. Today they export just about anything one can think of.

The gate guards would start their tour of duty with checking out an M-16A1 rifle and twenty-round clip of ammunition (ammo) from the company arms room. The guard would then move to the guard shack for inspection by the sergeant of the guard. The sergeant of the guard would either release you because you were not prepared for guard duty or send you to perform your duties. If you were not prepared for your duties, you were sent back to correct whatever was wrong during the inspection. Your tour of duty on the gates was to ensure you only allow authorized personnel into the MSA. The guys that occupied the towers were searching and scanning for people trying to gain unauthorized access to the MSA. The gates were the best duty because in the winter the gates were much warmer than the towers. The towers were very cold because they only had a very small space heater in it. You had to dress as if you were in the field on maneuvers. On April 1, 1974, I was promoted to Private First Class (PFC) E-3.

Reassignment and Vacation

About halfway through my tour at Camp Ames, some of the soldiers at our location were selected to fill vacant positions at Alfa Battery in Incheon, South Korea. The duty was the same. Alfa Battery had a lot of soldiers rotating back to the States with new assignments. About fifteen of us were reassigned to Incheon. Alfa Battery was just off the Yellow Sea. I had already applied for mid-tour prior to our transfer to Alfa Battery. My vacation was coming up during this transition. I got authorization to depart the country and return to my new duty station in Incheon. I was taking a military airlift command flight. This was a free flight to Moody Air Force Base in Valdosta, Georgia. I signed out of my unit at Camp Ames and signed in at the transition point at Camp Casey. I left all my gear there at Camp Casey prior to departing the country. My girlfriend was back home with Danny, and she was pregnant with Dedric. My dad was a big proponent of marriage, and I decided to get married when I returned home.

I boarded the flight for back home. We had our first stop in Yakota, Japan. The plane landed in Japan, and we all deplaned. When it was time to re-board the plane, there was a service member from a base in Japan that had an emergency and needed my seat, and I was bumped off the flight. The next flight leaving Japan was in three days.

The first day, I decided to see what Japan looked like. I walked off base and was in total shock at how different things were compared to the United States. The first thing was the automobiles; they drove on the opposite side of the road. Their steering wheel is located on the left side of the car. After observing this amazing discovery in a new land, I walked on toward a pastry shop. I was just as amazed at the cleanliness of the streets and of the sidewalks. I didn't see dirt or paper anywhere. Inside the bakery just floored me at the spotless walls, floors, windows, tables, and machines. I looked in one of the corners of the shop, and there was a soda machine about 5 feet high and about 2 feet wide. I got change from the lady in the bakery to put in the machine. She said it cost 30 yen per can. I took the change and put in 30 yen and pressed

Coke, and a canned Coke came out of the machine. The Coke looked like it was about 1.5 inches in diameter and about 5 inches long. There was maybe 6 oz. of Coke in the can.

I didn't want to venture too far away from the base, so I went back to the military airport to check on different flights going to the United States. I stayed on the base for the remainder of my time in Yakota. On day 3, I was departing Japan for home, and after hanging around the airport for three days, I was more than ready to go. We landed in California, but we were only there for a short time, and the plan was back in the air again. We stopped at Tinker Air Force Base in Oklahoma, after the plane's captain came over the intercom and said that there was a slight problem with the plan. As I was coming down the steps of the aircraft, I saw that the engine housing on the left side of the plan had folded back across the engine. That was enough to change my plans. I caught a cab to the civilian airport and got on a plane to Atlanta. I called my dad to ask him if he could pick me up in Albany. He said that he would be there. I waited about three hours in the Atlanta airport prior to flying to Albany, Georgia. Albany is about a 40-minute ride from Norman Park.

The plane arrived in Albany, and Mom rode with Dad to pick me up. This was the longest I had ever been away from home, and Mom and Dad were very glad to see me. We all talked at great length about South Korea all the way home. Over the next couple of days, some of my buddies stopped by to see me. I only had a week at home because of being bumped off my fight in Japan, so I didn't go out to visit anyone. I got married to Opal D. Croft. We were expecting Dedric McLoyd Kinsey on September 6, 1974. Two days later, I was on a plane heading back to South Korea.

Back to the Land of the Morning Calm

Once I was back in Korea, I was faced with new challenges. New unit, new chain of command, and new peers. I returned to Camp Casey and awaited orders to Incheon. The next day the orders came through, and I was on my way to my new assignment. I arrived at Alfa Battery and was assigned to the enlisted barracks. The next day I in-processed through the orderly room and the company first sergeant introduced me to my new platoon sergeant and platoon leader, Sergeant (Sgt.) Jackson and Lieutenant Paceli.

Sergeant Jackson took me to the guard shack and introduced me to most of the platoon. The guys were relaxed and content with their duties. This was very different from my previous assignment. Camp Ames was an army post where we had a post-exchange (PX) store and a movie theater. We had formal inspections, and your uniforms had to be excellent in appearance.

At Alfa Battery, it was a very small site. All we had was a mini PX about the size of a construction worker's office and a mess hall and barracks. The guard shack and the MSA were about an eighth of a mile from the barracks. I was immediately placed in the work rotation and started at the gate.

The first day I was on duty, I showed up at the guard shack about thirty minutes early, and the outgoing shift was very surprised. One of the guys coming off duty said, "Hey, this turtle is thirty minutes early." He went on the say, "You will change once you've been here for a while." Another said, "Hey, look at his uniform. It's pressed and starched up." I didn't say too much. I just went inside and waited for the sergeant to get there. There were twelve of us per shift for the gates and the towers. At 6:00 am, only two had showed up, and I could see about three of them walking toward the guard shack. The sergeant himself showed up at 6:05 am. The last guard reported in at 6:22 am. We had no formal inspection, we were only briefed on our general orders and deadly force. Somehow, I think that if I wasn't there, they wouldn't have been briefed at all. We were then released to move to our guard post.

I reached the gate that my partner and I were to occupy, and the guards were upset because we were late in relieving them. I told the guards that people showed up late for duty. After they left, my working partner said, "Hey, man, why are you all starched up today? Are you trying to make an impression on someone?"

I said, "No, I dress like this for duty all the time."

He asked me if I had performed this type of duty before.

I said, "Yes, I am transferring from Camp Ames, which is located south of here."

He said, "How long have you been in country?"

I said, "I leave this country for stateside duty this December." I told him that I had about five months left in country. He said that he had about three months left before it is time for him to rotate back to the States. I asked him why the Sergeant of the Guard (SOG) would allow the guards to be late for duty. He said, "Sergeant Jackson is one of the boys."

I said, "One of the boys, what do you mean?"

He said, "We party together. You know, we go to the ville together."

I said, "Okay."

He said, "You are a PFC already?" I said that I had gotten promoted prior to leaving my unit at Camp Ames.

He asked me where was I from in Georgia, and I told him, "Norman Park." Of course, he didn't know where it was, and I told him it was about 60 miles above Tallahassee, Florida. I could tell that he was making a mental picture of where I was from when I mentioned Tallahassee. He said that he was from Spartanburg, North Carolina. We continued to talk about our tour in Korea and about home. At lunchtime his relief showed up, but mine didn't, so as I waited, the lieutenant came by and asked if we had been to lunch, and I told him that I was still waiting on my relief. Lieutenant Paceli left and went to the guard shack, and a few minutes later, my relief showed up and he was twenty-five minutes late. This sort of thing was commonplace in this unit. I couldn't believe that these guys got away with not taking their job seriously. The Noncommissioned Office (NCO) leadership in this unit was very poor and had not been challenged. Part of the reason was that the NCOs went out drinking with the lower enlisted, and there was no respect for the NCO's rank. The platoon sergeant would allow the privates to be loosely supervised by the other sergeants. I had not seen this in my unit at Camp Ames. Staff Sergeant Bridgewaters was all about the business of doing our job and executing that duty correctly.

At that time in my career I wasn't sure what to do or what to say or to whom. I didn't want to get anyone turned against me because I was new and wanted to make a difference in the company. So I said nothing to anyone. I just kept coming to work early and not complain when someone didn't relieve me on time.

Apparently, some noticed because the lieutenant promoted me to corporal (CPL) E-4. The rest of the privates were either E-2 or E-3s, and they were furious. They approached me, of course, and not the lieutenant. "Why were you promoted over these privates that outranked you?"

I said, "I don't know!"

That evening, the lieutenant held a formation to address the platoon. The very first thing he talked about was my promotion. He said, "I was given one slot for E-4, and I selected Private First Class Kinsey for that slot, and I will explain to you why. Corporal Kinsey comes to work about thirty minutes early every day. His uniform is always cleaned and pressed. He has never complained to me about being left on the gate for sometimes hours prior to being released to go to lunch. He has never been late relieving the gate guards for lunch. I understand that he never goes to the village to party to the point of getting into trouble; in fact, I have never heard of Corporal Kinsey going to the club, and one reason is that he asked the platoon sergeant to put him on the night shift the rest of his time in South Korea. Lastly, Corporal Kinsey takes his job seriously, as all of you can attest. Promotions following the grade of E-2 are based on performance, and that's how I promote my soldiers." The lieutenant closed with, "We need more soldiers like Corporal Kinsey who are willing to do their job to the best of their ability and ask for nothing in return."

After that formation, people stopped giving me a hard time, not that it mattered to me anyway. I was doing what I was taught to do by Staff Sergeant Bridgewaters and back home. To me, being on time, working late, doing the best at whatever job was given to me were all better than cropping tobacco and bailing hay back home in the middle of summer.

My Tour of Duty Did Not Prevent World Events from Continuing

The next week was a big week for boxing because Muhammad Ali was going to box Big George Foreman for the heavyweight title in Kinshasa Zaire, Africa. They started the broadcast at about 10:00 am on the AFKN radio station. We couldn't get the play-by-play commenting off the radio, but rather the end-of-rounds highlights of the fight. I think 99 percent of all listeners had picked George Foreman to win the fight. George was such a strong, punishing fighter. I saw him hit Joe Frazier so hard in a fight that it lifted Joe in the air. There were many people saying the fight wouldn't last five rounds and Muhammad Ali would be knocked out by that round. Most Americans wanted to see Muhammad fall to George Foreman. The ring announcers would say at the end of each of the rounds that Muhammad was hit numerous times, and he is still standing. Then the eighth round came, and when the announcer came back at the end of that round, they were shouting, "He did it! He did it! Muhammad Ali has just knocked out George Foreman."

Who would have thought this would have happened? No one in this building was convinced that Muhammad Ali could beat George Foreman. This was one of those events where you look back and say, "I know where I was when Muhammad Ali knocked out George Foreman."

My summer jobs were more demanding than standing at a gate ensuring that only authorized personnel gained access to the MSA. Days later, one of my coworkers did acknowledge that I was doing a good job. I got a call one day at the orderly room, and it was Robert Davis, my friend from back home. He had finished. His AIT (Advanced Individual Training) was in Camp Red Cloud, South Korea. Camp Red Cloud was north of Incheon. I decided to travel up there to visit him. I left Incheon early in the morning to avoid the curfew. Camp Red Cloud was about three or four hours away, and that is because of the transportation. Riding the taxi, bus, and the train, I arrived there a little after noon.

Camp Red Cloud was about the same size as Camp Ames. Robert and I met at his barracks. He and I had not seen each other since boot camp. He did not leave Fort Jackson; he stayed there and trained to be a mail clerk. I told him that I traveled halfway across the country to be a canon cocker (field artillery crewmember). We talked mainly about back home, family, and friends. He seemed to like his assignment very well.

I left from visiting Robert and headed back to Incheon. I had to get my uniforms ready for work the next day. The following weeks, I began to see some change in some of the guards. Their uniforms were looking a lot better, and they were showing up for work on time. Some of them even visited me in the barracks, and we talked and played spades.

One of the guys asked me, "Why don't you go to the club?"

I said, "I don't have time for the club."

He said, "All you do is stay here and listen to Casey Kasem on the radio."

I said, "Yes, you're right, but Casey Kasem is not going to take my money from me." I told him. "I don't have to pay for a cab to listen to Casey; I don't have to buy liquor or beer to listen to him."

The guy said, "Yes, but you can have a good time at the club, if you know what I mean."

I said, "I am here to work, not have a good time and spend all the money." I asked the guy, "How many times were you late for work because you stayed overnight in the ville and had to wait until the curfew lifted and you couldn't get to work on time?"

He said, "A few times."

I said, "Who knows, that may be the reason you haven't been promoted, coming to work late."

He said, "But I need that sometimes to help me pass the time until I go home."

I said, "That's why I reach out to Casey Kasem and the American Top 40 and Gladys Knight, Neil Young, Elton John, the Temptations, Van Morrison, Bob Dylan, and others to pass my time."

After that conversation, we kept playing spades. December was around the corner, and I was ready for it to arrive. I started out-processing around the end of November. I turned in all my gear, and the final week in the country, you had to return to Camp Corner for final out-processing. I left Alfa Battery around the tenth of December, heading for Camp Corner. I reported in and immediately began to out-process up there. The main thing you had to clear at the transition point at Camp Corner was the rationed control plate. You must have that plate in hand, and it must not be overused for the big-ticket black market items. I have seen guys return to their unit until an investigation was completed, and they were either cleared or abuses were found. If abuses were found, you are sent back to your unit until it was determined how much abuse took place. Minor abuse resulted in an Article 15 non-judicial punishment, or if major abuse was found, it could lead to a court-martial. Every soldier entering Camp Corner was reminded of that initial briefing entering the country, and it was that if you don't have that rationed control plate when you get ready to leave the country or you have abused it, don't plan to go home on your permanent change of station (PCS) date. Mine checked out perfectly, but unfortunately, many other soldiers were being flagged because of violations.

Even though I knew nothing was wrong with my card, I was still nervous about the whole system. I got up early on the morning that I was leaving and packed my clothes. I decided to eat breakfast that morning. As I was walking up the hill toward the mess hall, a soldier was approaching me, and he looked like he was wobbling or staggering as he walked. By the time he had reached me and I could look him in the face, his eyes went skyward, his head went back, his right leg couldn't find the ground, and he went down right in front of me. I immediately yelled for help and kneeled next to him and turned him over on his side and just held him down until help arrived. Several soldiers ran over immediately and began working with him. I knew immediately that it was a seizure because of no muscle control. His body had gone into spasms. The medics arrived and took over and thanked us for helping until that arrived.

I went from there on to the mess hall to eat breakfast. After breakfast, I went to the exit point to be picked up and taken to the airport for my flight home. I said my goodbyes to the guys that were left behind until their flights were available. Leaving an assignment is both good and not so good. Not so good because you are leaving a part of your fraternity behind. Good because you are heading home to see family and friends.

Fort Hood, Texas

My next assignment was the Second Armored Division at Fort Hood, Texas.

Fort Hood is a United States Army post located in Killeen, Texas, which is about 60 miles north of Austin, the state's capital city. The post is named after Confederate General John Bell Hood. He commanded a Texas brigade during the Civil War.

Camp Hood opened in 1942, and it was established to accommodate testing and training for armor units. In 1942, Camp Hood had over 42,000 troops living and training there. The most famous soldier that lived and trained on Camp Hood was Elvis Presley. It was reported that Elvis would receive three to four bags of mail per day. He arrived on March 28, 1958, and departed for Germany on September 19, 1958. When I arrived at Fort Hood, there were over 50,000 soldiers assigned and First Cavalry Division, Second Armor Division, Third Corp, and Third Brigade ("Grey Wolf") were the major units on the post. Fort Hood was and remains the largest military installation in the United States.

My stay at home was very brief, I only took a two-week vacation because of taking mid-tour leave from South Korea. I decided to take my family with me to Fort Hood and find an apartment once I reach Killeen.

When I arrived, we immediately went to the post guesthouse. I picked up a Killeen newspaper and began looking for rental houses in town. I found one outside the city and called the owner, and we set up an appointment for 8:00 am the next morning.

The next day, I signed into my new unit at about 6:00 am. The staff duty NCO told me what unit I was assigned to and where it was located. I immediately drove to the unit and talked to my new company first sergeant (1SG). 1SG Lemann and I talked about me in-processing the following day. He also said that my rank of corporal would have to come off; all the E-4s there were specialist fourth class. The 1SG gave me the rest of the day off to sign for the apartment and get the lights and water turned on.

I left the orderly room and drove near a town called Coppers Cove, Texas. I arrived at the owner's house and knocked on the door. When she opened the door, she looked like she had seen a ghost. I said, "Ma'am, I am Mose Kinsey, the person that talked to you about the rental that you have." I don't think she was prepared to see me because of her mannerisms and body language. Once she regained her composure, she said to me, "We have already rented it to someone."

I said, "Thank you, ma'am," and went back to my car and left.

I stopped at a gas station when I made it back to Killeen. I went inside to pay for my gas, and I began talking to the owner about me just arriving in Killeen and needing a place to stay. The owner said, "If you can get by with a one-bedroom, I have one available?"

I asked him if I could look at it, and he said, "Yes, let me get the key." He returned with the key and said that the rent for the place is $75.00 per month and that the utilities are normally between $35.00 and 45.00 per month. I said okay. He gave me the keys and the address and began to explain to me where the apartment was located. I found the house and looked at it, and I was okay with the small place under the circumstances. I went to the guesthouse to pick up the wife and return for her inspection of the place, and as I suspected, it didn't pass with her. I began to point out the pluses versus the few minuses, along with her not working, I could overcome her opposition to the apartment. We would have to put a bed in the living room to accommodate the boys.

We went back to let the landlord know that we wanted the apartment, and he said that he was pleased with renting it to us. We left there and took care of the utilities and moved our belongings into the apartment as well as shopped for groceries. The next morning after morning formation, my platoon sergeant allowed me to start in-processing. My first stop was finance. I was still getting paid as an E-2 because I was so far away from Camp Casey each time that I was promoted, I never turned my orders in for the wage increase. My pay was still $51.00 per month, and Mom was getting $200.00 per month. The finance sergeant gave me a hard time for not turning in my orders, but they back paid me anyway. My back pay was about $600.00. I changed my mother's allotment from $200.00 per month to $50.00 per month, and I would have about $275.00 per month after taxes for me and my family to live on. It was still about a sixth of my pay that we would have to miss out of our budget. I was willing to make that sacrifice for my parents. They did their best at raising us as kids, and looking back, I wouldn't have wanted it any other way. We challenged ourselves with a very strict budget to master.

With the extra money from back pay, we got off to a decent start with the apartment and other expenses. After the first six months, I started to fall short of cash by the end of the month. I would tell the guys that lived in the barracks, that if they needed someone to pull their duty over the weekend, I would pull it for $10.00. The guys that partied on weekends would always look me up prior to the weekends to see if I would pull their duty. I would pull about two soldiers' duty each month, and that would help me stretch my pay and not overrun budget.

I didn't have insurance on my car for two reasons. One, it was not mandatory by the law at that time, and two, I just couldn't afford it. The kids were not school age yet, so I didn't have to worry about school clothes and other school expenses. I didn't have to pay childcare because the wife didn't work. It was extremely hard to stretch the cash each month to make the budget work. One month I had the pay for a part on the car, and it threw me far behind budget. I had to pawn my high-school ring to help put food on the table for the remainder of the month. I couldn't afford to get it out of the pawnshop, so to this day, I have been without it. Those were very tough times for me and my family.

I was assigned to an 8-inch field artillery firing battery in the Second Armored Division. General George S. Patton in World War II commanded this division. To my surprise, a General Patton still commanded the unit. His son has rose to the rank of general and is commanding his father's old unit. This was a huge part of American history whereas a son of a United States Army general followed the same career path as that of his father. I personally felt that it was a privilege to serve in that unit with General Patton's son.

Shortly after arriving to my unit, I was summoned to the 1SG office. I couldn't figure out what the 1SG wanted with me prior to reaching his office. Most of the time, it was not a good experience having to go to the 1SG office. I made it there, and I knocked on his door, and he said with a very loud voice, "Enter!" I walked in and said, "Specialist Kinsey reports as requested, 1SG."

He replies with "At ease, Specialist." 1SG Lemann said, "Specialist Kinsey, the military police came by my office and said that someone left their windows down and keys in their ignition out in the parking lot. Do you happened to know who drives a 1968 Dodge Charger?"

I said, "Yes, 1SG, it's me."

He said, "You are looking to lose that car to a thief. People steal, you know."

I said, "Yes, 1SG, it won't happen again."

I went back to where my platoon was training. My platoon sergeant wanted to make me the number 1 man (runs the firing operation on the gun) on one of our main guns, and that was primarily because I was a specialist in rank. I didn't feel that I should be put over someone already in the platoon even though they may be of lesser rank. The platoon sergeant insisted that I take over that position, and I finally said okay. The number 1 man is second in command on the gun, which makes this a very important position within the platoon.

After several weeks, one of the guys in the platoon seemed as though he was upset at something. Whenever we began training, he seemed nervous about something. He would make sarcastic remarks at things that didn't make sense. I had never worked on an 8-inch gun before, but I was catching on very quickly. We were doing a dry fire sequence, and the guy made a comment that I was too slow and I should be off the gun so that we could fire faster.

The other guys said to him, "Hey, man, give him time. You couldn't shoot that fast your first time out either." That response irritated him, and he got worse. I ignored him the whole time. I just tried to stay focused on what I was doing on the gun.

At the end of the day, one of the guys caught up with me on the way out of the motor pool. He said, "Specialist Kinsey, don't listen to him, man. He is jealous that you are taking over his spot on the gun."

I said, "His spot?"

He said, "Yes, he was in trouble for possession of marijuana and lost his rank. That's why he is an E-2 with over four years in the army."

I said, "I guess that does make sense, don't it."

The guy said, "Don't let it get to you."

I said, "I won't."

A few weeks went by, and he was calm with trying to provoke me into a verbal confrontation. Then one day we had returned from a field training exercise, and he and I ended up at the wash rack at the same time. He had a broom pushing dirt and water back into the trench drain, and I had a shovel, shoveling the dirt over into the drain as well. Suddenly he just started in on me saying that I was too new to be made the number 1 man on our gun.

I said, "Hey, man, someone had to."

He said, "It shouldn't have been you because you just got here. You haven't been in the army two years yet. A lot of soldiers in this platoon has been here longer than you. Why did SSG Charlton give the job to you anyway?"

He just kept going on and on, and I just closed my eyes and gripped the shovel in my hand as tight as I could get it. I thought to myself, "Hit him right across the face as hard as you can, and that will solve this issue." Then I thought about my family being here and me getting into this type of trouble. I opened my eyes, threw the shovel down on the wash rack, and walked to our equipment storage area (Conex) and located our platoon sergeant and told him that I would like a transfer and the reason.

I said to the platoon sergeant, "If I remain in this platoon, I am going to get into some trouble, and it almost happened today."

My platoon sergeant talked to the 1SG, and I was one of the guys that started up the first 8-inch field artillery battery in the First Calvary Division in Fort Hood, Texas.

First Cavalry Division, Fort Hood, Texas

We made that move in the summer of 1975. About 30 percent of the soldiers in each 8-inch field artillery firing battery were transferred to the First Calvary Division. Along with new equipment came much field testing and maintenance of that equipment. We trained in the field with this new equipment quite extensively. We would leave for the field on Monday morning and return on Thursday evening, and Fridays were reserved for cleaning and maintaining the guns and equipment.

It seems that God always has things planned for me. To my surprise, my platoon sergeant volunteered as well. So did some of the soldiers in our previous platoon back in the Second Armored Division. Many of us wind up back in the same platoon under SSG Charlton as our platoon sergeant. SSG Charlton was all about hard work and dedication to the platoon; everything was about the platoon, not an individual. If you couldn't work as a team, SSG Charlton would tell you quickly, "I don't know if you belong in this platoon."

SSG Charlton was also family oriented. He himself was married and had children, so he knew and understood how to handle problems when soldiers came with issues in that arena. He was with us in the fields every week just like everyone else, so there was very little complaining about being away from family. Apparently, there were problems with some of the soldiers' wives calling the company and using various reasons to see if they could get their husbands brought back in from the field after they deployed.

I remember one incident with me that happened in that year. The wood-frame house that I was raised in burned, and I was in the field and no one notified me that it had happened. I returned from the field and my wife asked me, "Why didn't your unit let me talk to you?"

I said, "You can't just call to talk to me while I am in the field."

She said, "Your mom and dad's house burned very badly, and everybody was calling to find out whether you could come home and help with that."

The next morning at work, I complained to my platoon sergeant that I was called while out in the field, and no one reached me for an emergency.

He said, "What was the emergency?"

I said, "My parents' house burned down Monday night, and my family called for me."

He said that he would talk with the 1SG and find out what happened and why I wasn't notified. A few days went by, and the 1SG sent for me to come to his office. I reported to the 1SG, and he said, "Come go with me. We are going to talk to the company commander."

We went across the hall to CPT Dukes' office, and I knocked on his door, and he responded with "Enter!" The 1SG and I went inside the door, and I said, "Specialist Kinsey reports as requested, sir!"

He said, "Stand at ease, Specialist Kinsey." CPT Dukes said, "I heard what happened to your parents' house, and I am sorry it happened." He said, "There was a mix-up in getting your wife's information out to the field so that we could notify you of what happened. We are not sure right now where the breakdown happened."

CPT Dukes said, "We do get a lot of wives and girlfriends calling to get their soldier out of the field."

I said, "Sir, I was in South Korea for a year without my wife. Going to the field for three or four days is nothing to me." I also told him that my sisters and brothers have taken care of everything, and that I was fine. The 1SG and I left Captain Dukes' office, and I returned to my platoon.

I began enrolling in college courses at Fort Hood. Florida State University had a satellite campus there, and I attended it when possible. The army paid 90 percent of my tuition, and I paid for my books out of pocket.

I started off with taking general subjects such as English, math, and history. That was one benefit that I certainly wanted to take advantage of just in case I didn't make the army a career. My three years in the army were rapidly ending. July 1976 was when my term of military service expired. Captain Dukes had already stopped by in the motor pool and talked to me about reenlisting. I was still undecided whether to stay in or leave. I talked to the reenlistment NCO, and he told me that I could go into another job skill if I wanted to. I said, "Okay, how about REDEYE (heat seeking missile)!"

He said, "Yes, you qualify for air defense that MOS, which is 16S."

I said, "Go ahead and put the paperwork together, and let's get it done."

He said, "Six?"

I said, "Six?"

The reenlistment NCO said, "Yes, when most soldiers reenlist, normally everyone take six years at a time. That way, you only should reenlist two more times and you are at twenty."

The summer of 1976 was full of tragedies and celebrations. Palestinians hijacked a plane loaded with 258 people on board in Greece and landed in Entebbe, Ugunda. Israeli commandos stormed the plane and rescued them. An earthquake in Tabgshan, China, killed 655,000 people. Sara Jane Moore tried to assassinate President Gerald Ford and was sentenced to life in prison. Ted Turner purchased the Atlanta Braves for $12 million dollars. Steve Jobs formed Apple Computer. We celebrated our 200 years of independence from Great Britain, and we printed the $2.00 bill. The price of gas was only 59 cents. Cuban heavyweight fighter Teofilo Stevenson won his second straight Olympic gold medal in boxing. We all witnessed Sugar Ray Leonard defeat opponent after opponent to win the gold medal in the welterweight division.

Meanwhile, back at Fort Hood, Texas, we celebrated our 200 years of independence as well. General Julius Becton had a huge picnic, and Jeanie C. Riley performed her big hit, "Harper Valley PTA," for the soldiers. As these events were happening, I was wondering where I would be assigned next if I reenlist.

One of the things that I regret about my assignment at Fort Hood was that before I left home for the military, I had bought a 1968 Dodge Charger, and when I brought my family to Fort Hood, I had the Charger with me. When I found out that I was going to Panama after my AIT, I decided to get a family van to accommodate the size of our family. Orenthal Juan Kinsey was born December 20, 1975. The family was growing rapidly. The upside to this family growth is that we had more space. The downside to this situation is that I lost my best friend, my Dodge Charger.

Reenlistment, New Job Skill, and New Assignment

I finally did reenlist for six years and go into the air defense field. Three weeks later, I received orders reassigning me to Fort Bliss, Texas, for the army's Short Range Air Defense (SHORAD) course.

Along with the MOS change, I received another duty station, the Republic of Panama. All I knew about Panama was that ships traveled through it from one ocean to the other. I went to the post library to look it up in an encyclopedia; the computer age was a few years away. There I learned a little about where it was located, its people, tropical climate, Sandblast Indians, the Canal Zone, and other important facts of the country.

I reported for training in February 1977. My orders assigned me to an AIT course. I remained in the unit with the new trainees just coming out of basic training. The drill sergeant gave me my own private room so that I wasn't with the trainees. I drove my vehicle to training, and they accommodated it for me as well. When we had formation, I was always positioned in the rear.

There were a lot of characters in that class. I remember one the privates in our platoon, who was already in his early thirties coming into the army. He said that he was a cab driver in New York. He told us one story of Colonel Sanders, the Kentucky Fried Chicken colonel, being beaten up and robbed by some New York gang members. We didn't know if he was lying or telling the truth, but the way he told the story made us want to believe him. During breaks and down time, he was the comic relief that we needed to help us through the training.

We trained on the Vulcan Gun, the Chaparral Missile System, and the Stinger Missile System. The Stinger was replacing the Redeye Missile System; both were man-portable. It could be fired from the shoulder of the gunner, and it is highly maneuverable. All the systems were very easy to operate in training. There was a group us wanting to live fire the Stinger missile. Each cycle's top graduate fires the Chaparral, and the runner-up fires the Stinger missile. We all knew that if you received a "no go" on any test, it may put you out of the competition for the top spot. The runner-up is typically the soldier that misses only one task.

There were four or five of us in the running for the top graduate spot. With two weeks left, it was just three of us left with perfect test scores. I wanted to deliberately fail a test so that I could come in second and fire the Stinger missile, but I was afraid that the other guys would test out perfectly and that would leave me with not firing a missile at all. So I kept passing the tests as they passed them. I was hoping one of the guys would fail two tests and that would give me a cushion to fail one and be in second place. Unfortunately, it didn't happen. With two tests left, I passed the first one and the other soldiers failed it. After that, I reluctantly went ahead and passed the final test with a perfect pass score for the cycle. I ended up the top graduate of the training cycle and had the privilege of firing the Chaparral missile.

The Chaparral was a very highly technical missile system that was mounted on a track armored carrying system. The mount was like the inside of a cockpit of an aircraft fighter. It had many gauges, electronics, and many toggle switches. You used the hand controls to maneuver the missile rails and to engage and fire the missiles. The Chaparral was the most challenging system to track a target; lock in on it and engage it and hit the target. To SHORAD soldiers, it's a very big deal to live fire a Chaparral Missile System. About 98 percent of all soldiers that work on the system don't get an opportunity to live fire one. I am very proud to be one of the few soldiers to have fired the missile system.

Several big historical events took place during my training at Fort Bliss. The army post practically shut down for seven straight nights. Alex Haley's movie, *Roots,* was playing for a week. The movie was the talk of everyone that knew it was playing. It was a movie that, once in our time, had everyone talking about race in America. People who have read about America's history now had a chance to see and talk about some of the most regrettable times in America.

Another powerful event that took place during this time came from an unlikely place in America. A man was executed by firing squad. The State of Utah sentenced murderer Gary Gilmore to death by firing squad. Gary decided that he would oblige the State of Utah by accepting the date of his termination and by not appealing his sentence. Gary relayed through his attorney that he would not object to the date set forth for his execution. Many people in America couldn't believe that Gary would go through with it because 99 percent of murderers don't want to die themselves. Gary Gilmore proved to the world that he was not a coward.

Firing the Chaparral missile was the culmination of a very long training cycle filled with soldiers that worked very hard to succeed. We would have training sessions at night, and guys wouldn't go out because they were determined to pass the course. Air defense is a small branch within the army, and our job is to protect fellow soldier and their units against enemy air attacks.

Fort Kobbe, Panama

After a brief leave with family back home, I was on a flight to Panama. I arrived in Panama in April 1977. My new unit was the Combat Support Company (CSC) in an infantry battalion. Our unit consisted of Mortar Platoon, Communications Platoon, MAN Portable Air Defense System (MANPADS) Platoon, and Maintenance Platoon. We supported the Grunts in the line companies. CPT Burton was our company commander, and he was all about work and no play. Air defense soldiers were new to the infantry units, and we were very short of MANPADS soldiers; however, we were beginning to enter the country. Our platoon sergeant was SSG Sermons, and our section sergeant was SSG Monds. Both came out of the infantry line units to establish our MANPADS platoon. SSG Sermons and SSG Monds were Redeye sergeants; the rest of us were Stinger-certified as Redeye was being phased out of the army's inventory. Our platoon had about ten soldiers upon my arrival in Panama. SSG Sermons appointed me as a team chief within the platoon. A MANPADS team consists of a team chief and a gunner/driver. Each team had an M-151A1 Jeep, trailer, and basic missile load of six to include your individual fighting equipment.

The Republic of Panama is in Central America, below Costa Rica and above Columbia. The Kuna Indians were the original inhabitants of Panama prior to the Spanish arriving.

The Kuna Indians mainly live on the San Blas Island, but throughout Panama as well. They are not very tall, and their traditional dress and jewelry is nothing short of amazing. When I arrived in Panama, their self-appointed leader was Omar Torrijos. Torrijos was the leader of the Panamanian National Guard, which is the country's primary defense force for the country. The Military National Guard leaders mounted a coup and installed Torrijos as its official leader of the country. Torrijos was considered by most countries a dictator because of how he gained power.

A few years prior to my arrival, Torrijos filed an official request with the United State Government requesting the Panama Canal

Zone be returned to the Panamanian government and its people. The negotiations were increasingly intense as time went on.

Torrijos announced that if the Canal Zone would go back to the country, then he would resign as its leader. The United States Senate would vote on the deal later. The United States was awarded the zone for engineering the waterway that crosses the country so that ships can cut off thousands of miles of travel by just journeying through the locks across the isthmus. The politics of this country had nothing to do with me, I was there to assist in protecting the country as a soldier in the United States Army.

Our small platoon was made up of men from across the United States. Sergeant Jiminez was from California, Sergeant McInnis was from Alabama, Sergeant Mansford was from Washington State, PVT Mitchell #1 was from North Carolina, PVT Mitchell #2 was from Kentucky, PVT Adamson was also from Kentucky, PVT Coleman was from Texas, PVT Brevard was also from Washington state, and I was from Georgia. We trained together for more than six months before another soldier came to our platoon. PVT Bevard was my driver/gunner. He was a good soldier, and he was very dependable. When we went to the field, there was nothing to worry about. PVT Bevard would have everything we needed to sustain us the duration of a field training exercise.

When the unit was in garrison, PVT Bevard believed in partying. Our platoon was very cohesive and, for the most part, we hung together most of the times when we were off duty. We trained separately from the rest of the company, except physical training (PT) and company-related training. We would have company formation at 6:00 AM for PT. After the formation, the 1SG will release the company for PT, and we would conduct PT by platoon Monday through Thursday, and on Fridays, we would conduct PT as a company.

We would often be finished with PT by 7:00 AM; between 7:00 AM and 8:00 AM is personal hygiene and breakfast, and there would be an 8:00 AM work formation. From 8:00 AM to 5:00 PM, each platoon is responsible for their training for that day. At 5:00 PM, the final company formation of the day is held by the company 1SG. We sometimes would leave the company area for training.

As an air defense platoon, we had some very critical skills that we must master. Map reading is one of those critical skills, and we would often check out our vehicles from the motor pool and go to different locations that had previously been assigned to each team to find. The team would take their grid coordinates and move to their location by utilizing their map sheet and wait on the platoon sergeant to verify that the team was in the correct location.

Map reading is very critical to us as MANPADS platoon members. One reason is that if a team is protecting a critical asset such as an armor or infantry unit and team is not in their correct location to engage the enemy aircraft, then the enemy aircraft will conduct a successful air strike on our soldiers. We must be positioned so that we can engage the enemy before it engages our soldiers. Secondly, if we are not sure of our location, then we could be in enemy territory or run the risk of being captured by the enemy. Another critical task for our teams is aircraft recognition. As a MANPADS platoon member, we must be able to identify aircraft both friendly and foe. We don't want to engage a friendly aircraft.

During some of our training, we do manage to add a little flare to the mission. We sometimes meet at the same location for lunch and pull out our canned meals (C-rations) and eat the most wonderful meal in Panama. One location we all loved to meet and have lunch was called the French Cut. The French started digging the canal, but they lost so many workers to malaria and yellow fever that they stopped. The Americans took over and went a different direction. Soon after the United States started the canal in 1903, Doctor Gorgas, an army doctor, was instrumental in combating the spread of malaria and yellow fever by mosquitoes by emptying their main breeding grounds such as swamps and ponds, and this allowed Americans to finish the canal in 1914. Our platoon would set up for lunch, and some of the guys would dive off the cliff into the water and pull oysters from the rocks and bring them back to us for lunch. We cracked them open and put either hot sauce or salt on them or whatever each person wanted on the oyster. We would just open the oyster up, put some hot sauce on it, and let it slide down our throat. This is obviously something new and the crowd knew it. I had told them that I had never had oysters like that before. They would hand me an oyster and watch me gag the thing down, and they would just laugh uncontrollably.

After they picked themselves up off the ground from laughing so hard, they'd say, "Hey, that one didn't go down the way it should have.

You must eat another one to pass the test." Finally, I said, "Guys, you all start downing them. I have eaten enough for one day." It was a fun lunch, although I turned out to be the platoon's entertainment for that day.

After all the lunchtime fun, we continued training the rest of the day, and we returned to garrison and stored our equipment and awaited the 1SG's 5:00 pm formation. The end-of-day formation was for the company 1SG to disseminate important information to the platoons from the higher commands such as upcoming events or activities. One day out of the week, we would have "motor stables" (motor pool maintenance of all company vehicles). During this time, we would pull Preventive Maintenance Checks and Services (PMCS) on all platoon vehicles. If there was a vehicle in your platoon that was inoperable (deadlined), it was reported to the motor sergeant so that it would be given attention as soon as possible. A deadlined vehicle means that your platoon is not fully combat ready for your portion of the company's mission. This meant that the company had less air defense coverage of being protected against enemy air attack.

The infantry had only two vehicles in their company, the company commander's and their 1SG's. The infantry travels very light; they walk everywhere their mission takes them. They are truly a dedicated branch of soldiers. They are the backbone of the army when it comes to fighting on the ground. Those guys have the utmost respect from the other branches of the army. The Vietnam War showed us that the highest casualties in war come from the ranks of the infantry soldiers. I must add a caveat for the marines. They too are highly respected among all branches of military services. Our own infantry, army rangers, special forces teams, the marines' infantry and recon units, the navy seals, the air force, and all other branches of Delta Forces are very highly prestigious units that many service members attempt to triumph, but very few achieve such an accomplishment.

Three days in the week was dedicated to platoon training. The final day of the week was dedicated to company-directed training. Our company training schedule ran six weeks in advance. Each year our battalion would conduct an Army Training and Evaluation Program (ARTEP). The ARTEP would rotate each year from a conventional ARTEP to a counter-guerilla ARTEP. During the conventional ARTEP, our platoon was allowed have our vehicles to set up critical asset defenses for the units that we were protecting. During the counter-guerilla ARTEP, we traveled on foot with the infantry soldiers in the jungles. We conducted short- and long- range patrols just like the infantry soldiers. We slept on the ground and pulled security at night as well. If the infantry walked twenty kilometers a day through the dense jungle, then we were integrated into their platoon also.

The walking, patrolling, and the jungle didn't bother me; what did was the possibility that I may wake beside a boa constrictor or a bushmaster snake the next morning. Nights were almost impossible to get any sleep because of the noise on the jungle floor. You hear things walking very close to you, noises in the trees near you, and you hear things crawling. My imagination just went completely wild during these times when we were in the jungles. I had to be tired to get any sleep while I was in the jungle.

The mosquitoes were a different set of issues. Once we went into the jungles, it was a battalion rule that your shirt sleeves had to be rolled down, and gloves are worn while on a field training exercise. This rule protected the soldiers from a lot different things, as well as the mosquitoes. When we signed for our field gear at supply, we were issued a mosquito head net and a mosquito bar for field use. I remember one of the first of many field training exercises I went on in the jungles. We were out for about three days, which was very brief for some of the trips we took over the years that I was stationed there. We were deployed as a static asset-type defense for our company. This meant that we would be providing air defense coverage with overlapping protection from one team to the next. The umbrella of coverage would extend at least five kilometers beyond the critical asset or unit being protected. My team provided the northern coverage while the other teams were implemented to provide complete overlapping air defense coverage for the company. My gunner was set on a hill about six kilometers forward of the defended unit. The location was ideal for an air defense fire team. We were on a hill for maximum observation and 360 degrees of air defense coverage. However, the mosquitoes were relentless in their pursuit of us. We had our sleeves down, gloves on, and our mosquito head net on, and they were still all around us as if they were waiting on an opening so that they could get to our skin and take a bite. We didn't have to use our Inert (dummy round) Missile for practicing engaging aircraft. We were only set up to simulate proper overlapping fire coverage. We were glad that we didn't have to take off our mosquito head net or we would have been bitten beyond recognition. The engineers sprayed for mosquitoes every evening back in garrison, which included the post housing areas. Spraying helped keep the mosquito population down somewhat.

On August 20, 1977, Dwayne McLoyd Kinsey was born in Vereen Memorial Hospital in Moultrie, Georgia. Later that year, I was recommended by my company commander to go before a promotion board for the rank of sergeant. The board convened and I passed the board, and I was put on a waiting list for promotion to sergeant. Promotions to sergeant and staff sergeant are local promotions provided you passed the board and meet the point score cut-off that the department of the army sets based on the need of your specific job skill army wide.

For example, the army may have 10,000 infantry soldiers on the waiting list for sergeant. Each soldier has a cut-off score after the promotion board, and this is based on certain criteria, such as points of the board, PT Test, BRM score, military education, civilian education, army correspondence courses, and awards and declarations. The maximum a soldier can earn is 1,000 points. If a soldier scores less than 450 points coming out of a promotion board, then that soldier is disqualified to sit on the promotion list; that soldier failed the promotion board. He or she could reappear in front of a future promotion board. The soldiers that meet the minimum score will be added to the waiting list army wide by MOS. If the infantry waiting list score for the month of October drops to 650 points and 4,000 infantry soldiers have at least that many points accumulated, then all 4,000 infantry soldiers are promoted to sergeant that month.

The army can control the number of soldiers promoted to those ranks by either raising or lowering the points in each career field each month. Promotions at the senior enlisted ranks are awarded differently from those of the junior NCOs. Sergeant first class (E-7), master sergeant/first sergeant (E-8), and sergeant major/command sergeant major (E-9) are all centralized promotions. This means that only your personnel files are sent each year to a board being convened by lieutenant colonels, colonels, command sergeant majors, and a general officer to determine what junior-grade NCOs will be promoted to senior-grade NCOs. You do not represent yourself; only your files represent you in front of the most critical eyes in the military. Example, if the air defense branch has

800 SFC E-7s being considered for eight E-8 promotions army wide, then that board is responsible for selecting those eight soldiers from the field of 800.

There are many items that do not need to be found in your records at that level or you will be passed over for promotion. Some are DUI, continued writing of bad checks, non-judicial punishment (Article 15), domestic violence, poor annual evaluations, current photo of individual in dress uniform not present, wearing the wrong awards and declarations, and others. It is very critical that soldiers view their individual microfiche at least six months prior to the promotion board convening.

Once I was promoted to sergeant, I was at a crossroad. Do I continue socializing with my buddies that were privates? Do I turn off the switch and just flat out tell them that I could no longer socialize with them because of my recent promotion to sergeant? I did realize through our constant classes of leadership training that there had to be a change in relationship for me and the soldiers that were subordinate to me within my platoon. This was a very difficult situation because these guys knew everything about me because as buddies, we talk about any and everything together. No stones were left unturned when it came to sharing information with your buddies. Fortunately for me there were no bad stones to look at when one was turned over. I didn't smoke or drink, nor was I a partier.

The toughest thing for me was losing the closeness of the guys within the platoon. What I decided to do was to slowly withdraw myself away from the closeness of the group. I would concentrate more on company and platoon policy and enforcement of policy to let them know that I was changing. This was done gradually. I made myself less available for socializing with them as a group. I started asserting myself increasingly as events and opportunity presented. I began teaching classes that the platoon sergeant and the other sergeants in our platoon were teaching.

Within six months the transition was complete, except one challenge from my driver/gunner. He and I were close because of the nature of our job, but one morning he tested our friendship. It was about five minutes from the 1SG's morning formation. I went to check our soldiers because I didn't want to see them late for the formation area. As you would have it, one of them was in bed sleeping and recovering from a mid-size hangover from the previous night downtown. I went into his room and I yelled at him to get up and that he only had five minutes to formation. He rolled over and said, "F--k you, Mr. New Sergeant!"

My initial reaction was to throw him out of the bed and on to the floor. I didn't I stood there for a moment astonished. I regained my composure and walked closer to the bed and said to him, "Private, I am going to imagine I didn't hear what you said, but if I hear it again and you don't get up out of this bed and head downstairs to our morning formation, I am going to go to SSG Monds (our platoon sergeant) with a formal complaint of insubordination and I will ensure that you receive an Article 15."

He jumped out of bed and got dressed for PT and came to the formation. Later that day, he and I were in the motor pool working on our vehicle, and I brought the subject up. I said, "What was that this morning, Private?"

He said, "Oh, I was still drunk from last night."

I said, "Private, you are in my platoon, and you and I have been good friends since we have been in Panama. Don't let my promotion cause friction between us because this morning will not happen again." He apologized and said that it wouldn't happen again. We continued to talk about personal issues that were troubling him, and I gave him some advice on how to cope with those problems, and in the end, we managed to understand each other again. He was a very good soldier as well as a friend, and I think he allowed jealousy to enter his mind, which offset his normal way of thinking. The private had always followed my orders when I was a specialist. He and I had a long talk, and we both concluded that his insubordination had nothing to do with my promotion. He was okay after that situation, and he was soon back to normal.

The most shocking news of 1977 happened on August 16, when Elvis Presley died at age forty-two. Our platoon was conducting motor stables, and a few of us were up around the conex and one of the communication (commo) guys came from the motor sergeant's office and he said, "Elvis Presley just died."

We didn't believe him. I said to him, "Man, get away from us with another Beatles hoax."

One of our soldiers turned on his radio, and it seemed like the entire world was in mourning. It was true. Some of the movies that I watched as a kid upstairs in the Colquitt Theater were Elvis Presley movies. Elvis Presley was larger than life; he was the legend that got rock-n-roll jump started for all Americans.

Primary Noncommissioned Course (PNOC)

I left Fort Kobbe to attend BNOC at Fort Davis, Panama. Fort Davis was on the Atlantic side of the country. PNOC was a basic leadership course for sergeants. There we learned basic first aid, map reading, land navigation both day and night, patrolling techniques, and much more. During the land navigation training, our group were dropped off about ten kilometers from the base and we were to navigate back.

Land Navigation Exercise

We arrived at our location, and we immediately began to shoot our asthmas given to us to get us back to the base camp. There were six of us in our team. We sent out our point man, and we had our compass men shoot their asthmas as they moved forward. We were doing well during the day, but once night hit us, we were not sure of ourselves. One of the things that we failed to remember is that when you are moving through the jungles at night, the point man tends to always move to the right as he is walking. We did not factor this into our movement plans, which did throw our line of travel off. We thought we were still on the right path to reach our destination at 10:00 PM that night. Our journey would last much longer than the projected time of completion. It was already 11:00 PM, and we missed our transfer point in which we were to be picked up and taken back to our base camp. We were off course and some of the soldiers had already begun to wonder if the group was lost or if we were just slightly off course.

At 12:00 AM, there was great concern that we are now off course a lot more than was suspected initially. The soldiers were still calm and working together as a unit. 1:00 AM and the last flashlight was passed up to the point man over an hour ago, and he constantly reminded us that the batteries were very low and that he could barely see in front of him. 2:00 AM and the point man can no longer see in front of his face to use his machete to cut the wild vines. I gave the order to continue our path, but each soldier had to grab the person's web belt suspenders in front of him as a precaution. I was in the middle of the team, and I can only hear the machete cutting the vines up front. I can no longer see the ranger eyes in the back of the soldier's helmet in front of me. This was the darkest I have ever witnessed in my life. We could hear water slamming against the shore, but we didn't know how far away it was. The area that we were operating in was very wet; the water was standing about two inches deep, yet we could still hear the waves slamming into the shore. It was 3:30 am and the sounds were getting louder as we continued to move forward. The sound of the machete stopped, and before I could say anything, the entire group moved forward because of us holding onto each other's web belt suspenders. We caught the point man from falling off a cliff. We continued to hold on until the point man was lifted back up on our path. I ordered the men to move back about fifty to seventy-five feet and drop rucksacks (backpack) for the night. We just formed a circle and we tried to get whatever sleep we could get under the circumstances.

The sounds of the ocean waves pounding the shorelines woke me up. It was around 6:50 AM and daylight was creeping in, so we could finally see down in the jungle. I sent two soldiers in the direction of the sounds of the water pounding the shorelines, and the rest of us walked back toward the cliff that almost injured our point man. We reached cliff, and it was about a twenty-foot drop-off. With him not being able to see the bottom of the cliff, he could have been injured very severely. After seeing how deep the drop-off was, we moved back to our break area where our rucksacks were located and waited for the two soldiers that investigated the water sounds. A few minutes later, the two soldiers returned with good news; we were only about 200 meters from the hardball road that will take us back into our base camp.

We secured our rucksacks and proceeded to the hardball road and on into our base camp. We made it back in our base camp just in time for the first training briefing of the day, and we were expected to be moving out for the day's training within the twenty minutes. We had enough time to grab breakfast and head out again. We were looking forward to the end of the day so that we could get some badly needed rest for our group. The final week of our training, we had a field training exercise that the devil must have put together. We had to launch an ARB 15 boat in the Chagres River, rappel 80 feet down a cliff, and build a poncho raft and cross the Chagres River.

Boat Capsizing Exercise!

As we prepared to travel to the Chagres River, we were nervous and afraid of the shark-infested waters, and the thought of us capsizing a boat in that water made us all somewhat skeptical and uneasy about this event. The group navigated to the point where the boats were located. We got the boat and entered the water and began to paddle toward the Atlantic Ocean. Maybe a mile away, we could see the opening of the Chagres River that leads into the ocean. I looked around at the soldiers, and I could see them looking at the water as if they were trying to locate a shark.

The instructor said, "Okay, gentlemen, we are far enough. Let's capsize the boat right here, because I don't want to get too close to the mouth of the river."

There was recent sighting of sharks there, and that is a recipe for disaster. There were about ten or eleven of us on the boat with the instructor, and he seemed kind of nervous himself. Half of us got into the water, and the other half stayed on the boat and began to tie off ropes on the left side of the boat.

Once the ropes were tied off on the left side of the boat, the five soldiers stood up on the right side of the boat holding onto the ropes, and as they stood straight up and went over backward off the right side of the boat, the boat came up and over, turning it upside down in the water. Once the boat was upside down, we then had to get it back upright so that we could get back in it and move back to our start point for the next group. To get the boat back upright, five soldiers stood on one side of the boat with their ropes in hand and ready to lean backward and pull the boat back upright. The only difference is that we placed a soldier on the other side about midway, and he held onto the side that he was on so that when the boat rotated back over, the soldier would be lifted out of the water with the boat and he would land inside the boat, then he could pull the rest of us back into the boat.

Once this was done, I felt very confident that we could do almost anything. We paddled the boat back upstream to our starting point so that other groups could start and complete this task.

Poncho Raft Exercise!

After returning the RB 15s, we continued with our regularly scheduled training. The next event that we were going through was the poncho raft. Prior to the poncho raft, we had to navigate 10 kilometers to the river falls so that we could rappel down the cliffs to the Chagres River. Once we made it to the falls, the instructors began setting up the rappel stations so that we could rappel down the cliff to the Chagres River. After about two hours, the site was ready for rappelling. I approached the rope with my Swiss seat (a rope tied around the buttocks and the waist to form a seat) already secured with a snap link. The instructor waved for me to get into his line. I walked up to the start point, hooked my snap link in, and turned and faced away from the downward view and began to step backward down the cliff. I continued to walk backward down the hill until my body formed an L-shape. I had the rappel rope in my hands, and I looked at the instructor for further instructions. The instructor said, "Hey, guys, this one is ready."

He then turned to me and said, "Go!" I jumped away from the cliff and pushed my right hand away from my body that was securing the break rope to allow me to drift down the cliff. After drifting a few feet down, I would bring my right hand with the break rope back behind my waist, which would slow or stop my descent. I would then repeat that procedure until I reached the ground. After everyone rappelled down the cliff, we gathered at the side of the cliff. We waited on the instructors to assemble for the next event. Once the instructors were on the ground below the cliff, they began classes on how to prepare a poncho raft and swim across a river. I am a weak swimmer, but there were guys here that were panic swimmers. I watched them during practice drills wearing life preservers back at our base camp, and they were panicking just getting into the water with their vests on. It was a chore for the instructors to get them to calm down while in the water. They were mostly afraid that their heads would go under water. After working with them for quite some time, the instructors managed to get most of them into the water without panicking. They were paired up with strong swimmers prior to us leaving base camp. By doing this, it will increase the chances of everyone making it across the river without drifting too far downstream or reaching the mouth of the river, which empties into the Atlantic Ocean.

After that block of instructions and safety briefing, we were ready to construct our poncho rafts and enter the river's swift current. Sgt. Wesley Williams was my swimming partner. He too was a Stinger team chief for MANPADS. He was stationed at Fort Davis, which was located on the Atlantic side of the country. Fort Davis was near the city of Colon. Fort Kobbe was near Panama City on the Pacific side.

My swimming partner and I began to button up our ponchos together. We placed our M-16s about 18 inches apart and pointed it in the same direction. We then began to put our rucksacks in the middle of the M-16s and our boots as well. We placed other gear into the poncho raft also. We sealed off the raft as best as we could for the journey across the river. My main concern was my swimming partner, whether he could get the raft across the river, because he was the lead man on the raft, and the raft would be strapped to him for pulling. I was a strong enough swimmer that I felt that I could get myself across, but I knew I couldn't push the raft enough to help him get it across the river. I asked him prior to us getting into the water, did think he could make it without my help? And he said, "Yeah, I got it, Kinsey."

We could see from standing on the bank that the current was swift and that we would have a tough time landing on the spot that we were projected to land on. The instructors signaled to the groups that were on the bank that it was time to enter the water and start our crossing mission. We were the fourth team to cross, which meant that we had an opportunity to watch other teams cross. This also gave us a chance to see how swift the current was in the river. A team of strong and weak swimmers went first, and it was not good. The strong swimmer made it across the river just slightly below their crossing point; however, his partner landed about 700 or 800 feet below their target point. I am thinking, man, I know I can beat that.

My team was now in the water and holding on to the grass shrub around the bank and waiting for the signal to go. We got the signal, and we took off. I tried to help push the raft until the current got stronger, and I let go of the raft and started swimming on an angle up and over to the left of the bank across to the other side of the river. Thinking of sharks possibly approaching me from behind actually made me swim faster. Williams reached our target point, and I was about 75 feet swimming in below his spot. It was fair to say that our team did very well. Sgt. Williams did a great job with pulling the raft all the way across the river by himself, but I was proud of myself for landing not too far away from him on the shoreline. By now team one's missing link (the soldier that drifted 800 feet beyond his target point) had now caught up to our main staging area where the rest of the teams stood.

The good news was that he made it across safely and without incident. We all were proud of him because he didn't give himself any credit or confidence that he would make it across the river. As he approached us, we were cheering him on, and finally he gave us all a big smile. That made our day. We took a lunch break, and we were on our way back to our base camp. Once we crossed the Chagres River, we knew that we had made it through the course and everything left was just a formality. We went on to graduate that Thursday and headed back to our units. The course had given us a great amount of maturity and confidence that was needed to lead a team or squad. I arrived back to my unit to the tune of "Give him more classes to teach now that he has been trained." I was ready to accept those new duties and responsibilities.

Prepared for the Worst (the Treaty)

Meanwhile, the country was being deeply enthralled in politics because of the Canal Zone situation. The nation's leader and dictator, Omar Torrijos, wanted the United States to relinquish control of the canal by the year 2000. The United States did not want to return the canal zone to a dictator so a deal was prepared. If the Senate ratified the treaty, then Torrijos would resign and there would be an election for the next president of the republic. President Nixon and Ford talked to Torrijos and wanted the treaty, but at that time Reagan and Carter opposed the treaty. Once Carter was elected and looked further into the substance of the treaty, it is believed that this is part of what changed his mind and support of it. Several weeks prior to the vote by the United States Senate on the Canal Zone Treaty, my unit received orders to move to Balboa Mountain and to remain there as a backup force if needed to help defend the safety of the locks.

There are three locks (Miracles, Gatun, and Pedro Miguel) that soldiers were strategically placed to maneuver ships through the canal from one side of the isthmus to the other. Everyone throughout the world knew that if one of those locks become inoperable, then the entire waterway would be shut down. The locks were designed to raise and lower ships so they go from one ocean to the other. Some units were placed at and around the locks two weeks prior to the Senate vote. My company went the Balboa land area and set up. We were phased completely into the infantry unit that we protected against air attack. We were no longer air defenders; we were now poised with protecting the waterways to keep the ships' traffic going through the canal.

An engineer company had gone ahead of us to cut out a landing strip so that we could rappel into our position. CSC arrived at our location by helicopter, and all soldiers and equipment rappelled on the mountain and moved on into our positions. Our platoon did travel together as a platoon, but we were quickly integrated into the infantry patrolling duties. Time, we set foot on the ground, we were installed into an infantry squad and were on patrol. We began with short-range patrols, and they eventually ended up as long-range patrols. Day patrols were not so bad, but flashes of the patrols in PNOC started to enter my mind. These infantry guys in our company were much more experienced in patrolling than the guys in my PNOC class, and it showed once we began to move and maneuver down into the jungle.

We would navigate out about four or five kilometers and back without getting lost. We continued to patrol and plan our strategy for responding to riots in Panama City if possible. About two weeks prior to the vote on the treaty, we stopped the patrolling and waited for a call to go secure the locks. Things were very intense during that time. The day of the vote, we thought for sure it wasn't going to pass, but it did, and the natives were dancing in the streets. Fireworks were exploding everywhere. The people were celebrating all over Panama. The next couple of days, we began to move back to garrison as things began to settle down in the cities of Colon and Panama. The treaty would allow Panama to take over full control of the Canal Zone by December 31, 1999. The decision to relinquish control of the canal back to the country where it's located will be debated for years to come.

Coach Kinsey

The Youth Activities department representative got ahold of me and asked me to volunteer my services to coaching youth on Fort Kobbe. I agreed to start off coaching soccer. We would play the kids from the surrounding bases—Howard Air Force Base, Rodman Marine Barracks, and some teams from Fort Clayton over in Panama City. Brian was one of the forward on the team, and he was awesome. His dad was a helicopter pilot for the army, and their family lived on Fort Kobbe.

Shane, the son of SGT McInnis, a sergeant in my platoon, was one of my defenders, and he too was just awesome. Most of the players were new to the game of soccer. My son, Danny, was our goal keeper. Danny had very good lateral movement and could jump very well. I just built the team around those athletes. My son, Dedric, was a forward, and he had decent skills as well. We had dribbling drills, kicking drills, passing drills, heading drills, and throwing drills, and we could fill in the other positions by observing the other kids executing those drills.

Once we started practicing, the kids improved very quickly. Our first game would let us know where we needed to adjust on our field positions. We played a team from Howard AFB first, and we beat them by 6 goals, and they didn't score a goal against us. We were very surprised that we won that game so easily. The next game was the same, and not a goal scored on us. Danny learned the goalie position very quickly, and he took pride in not letting a ball get past him. Shane McInnis was very big and tall, and we used him on defense. When the ball came to him, he would run toward the ball, and the other team members would move out of his way and just let him kick the ball down the field. Well, Brian would run the down the ball and dribble it to the goal and fire it in. We played the Iguanas from Rodman Marine Barracks next, and they played us hard. We beat them 2-0, and it was hard to score on them. Danny met a huge challenge in that game; he stopped 8 shots that came at him very hard. Goalies on other teams wouldn't have made the stops that Danny made playing the Iguanas. We went on through our schedule undefeated. In the playoffs, we knew who we had to beat them to win the tournament. It came down to us and the Iguanas.

The game started off very slow. The defense on both teams were very much alive. The lost period was just as tough, but about two minutes prior to the end of the game, we finally scored a goal.

They marched back down the field and fired several hard shots at Danny, but he caught them, thus winning the game 1-0. The kids had an undefeated season and won the playoffs. The kids on Fort Kobbe were very happy that they beat Howard AFB at something. I think that this team won the hearts of all the kids on Fort Kobbe because each time I coached a team, it seemed like every kid on Fort Kobbe signed up to play. I continued coaching the kids on Fort Kobe until I left for my next assignment.

Jonestown, Guyana

There were other world events that required our assistance and fast. There were reports coming out of the States that something horrendous had happened in a country near Panama called Guyana. We knew that we would be involved somehow because the country was so close to Panama, but not exactly what.

The mission finally came, and it did involve one of our units on Fort Kobbe. The unit was A Company (Airborne) that got the call to deploy most of their unit to Jonestown, Guyana. The rest of the battalion assumed that it wasn't a big deal, but A Company found out otherwise.

Jim Jones was an evangelist preacher who had a history of unorthodox and very controversial way of practicing religion. After receiving much criticism from people outside his church, he decided to move his congregation so that they would have to answer to only him. They bought a spot of land in the jungles of Guyana. There, they would live as a commune and raise their children and practice his religion without outside interference. Many of his followers were very unhappy there, and they expressed that in some of their mail correspondence to friends and relatives back in the States.

This prompted a United States congressman to come investigate the situation. Congressman Ryan did fly into Jonestown, and he talked with Jim Jones about the concerns of family members back in the States. Jim Jones decided to let some of his followers leave the commune with Congressman Ryan. Before Congressman Ryan and his group reached their plane, Jim Jones gave the order to his security group to terminate each person that left the camp and all of Congressman Ryan's group as well. Jones then ordered the group to prepare a cyanide drink for the entire camp. Jones, however, died of a self-inflicted gunshot to the head.

A Company was deployed to Guyana with the prospects of recovering around 200 or 300 bodies, along with some survivors. When they arrived and started to search for bodies and dig mass graves, they discovered that the count would be much higher than anticipated. Women and children were lying in the open, and graves were filled.

Increasingly bodies were being found as the search continued. When the search discontinued, there were 908 dead and just a few survivors that fled for their lives down in the jungles. After recovering the bodies and returning to Panama, the soldiers underwent a debriefing, and those that wanted it went through counseling. This was indeed a traumatic event for many young soldiers that went on that trip to Guyana. A Company performed fantastically given the extraordinary task at hand. As far as Jim Jones was concerned, some people are so dedicated to Christ that every now and then, they may follow a false disciple and believe that he is a true follower of Christ.

Panama Bridge Incident

My family and I decided to go shopping over in Panama City for the evening. We visited several stores and were very pleased with the prices. The kids enjoyed it because it was something different to do. We finished shopping and left to travel back to Fort Kobbe, and we had to cross over the Canal Bride. The bridge is extremely high, and as we were going over the bridge, everything seemed good with the van. We made it to the top of the bridge. I pressed the brakes to get ready to ride them down the other side of the hill, and I had no brakes. I thought to myself that I couldn't let anyone in the van know that I have no brakes or it will be a widespread panic going down this bridge. I moved my left hand over to the lower left side and underneath the dash and placed my hand on the brake lever and grasped it firmly and gently pulled on it until it contacted the brake pads on the wheel of the van. I could feel the hand brake grab the brake pads, and I could also feel the van react to the handbrake. I slowly looked around to see if anyone noticed me pulling on the hand brake. No one said anything, so I continued to pretend that everything was okay. The van started to speed up going down the hill, and again I moved my hand over to the hand brake and pulled on it slightly so that no one would notice. I kept my hand on the hand brake all the way down the hill, and no one said anything.

Once I reached the bottom of the hill, I felt a lot better, but we were still about six more miles from home. We continued toward home, and we came up on the front gate entrance to Howard AFB, and it was there when I broke the news of the brakes. They became very angry with fear because I traveled over extremely high bridge without brakes.

I said, "No one ever noticed anything, and I just kept going because I knew that all of you would panic like you are doing right now." We made it home, and I asked a soldier that worked in the motor pool to help me fix the brakes. Once the brakes were repaired, no one was afraid to get into the van anymore. This was one of those situations where it was best to withhold bad news until the situation got better.

Relax with a Reel and Rod

Some soldiers choose different ways of how they relax or wind down from the rigorous military training we conducted, especially in the jungles of Panama. I chose to go fishing with my buddies. Sergeant Manford asked me if I like fishing, and I said that my dad and I fished all the time when was a kid. He asked me if I wanted to go fishing with him.

I said, "Yes, but where would we go?"

He said, "There is a place past Rodman Marine Base not too far from one of the locks." We both agreed to leave at 6 am the next Saturday.

That Friday afternoon, I went over the Morale, Welfare and Recreation Office and picked up a canoe and loaded up on top of my van. The next morning, I left home about 5:45 AM and went by Manford's house and picked him up, and we headed to the fishing pond. We stopped a little way away from the pond area and bought some minnows from some of the local kids. Manford said, "Don't get too many minnows because you will probably catch a fish with each minnow you buy."

I said, "Are you sure about that? I have never caught a fish with every piece of bait that I bought before."

We went on our way for a few miles, and we arrived at the fishing pond, and we took the canoe off the van and lowered it into the water and off we went. I got out a minnow and put it on my hook and cast it out there, and no sooner did it hit the water than I got a bite. I pulled on the reel, and I could feel the weight of the fish, and I began to reel him in. When it reached me in the canoe, I was very surprised at how big the fish was. I secured the fish and rebated my hook with another minnow and recast my reel. Again, I had a bite and pulled the reel, and another fish was heading about to be pulled into the canoe. I had bought two dozen minnows, and I caught twenty-four fish. They ranged in weight from three to five pounds. The best catch for me ever.

We loaded up the canoe and headed back to Fort Kobbe. I got home, and the kids could not believe that I caught that many fish. The fun part was cleaning them.

The next Monday back at work, Sergeant Manford tells everyone in the platoon that I was an expert fisherman. I said, "It was like shooting turkeys in a pen."

The second trip that Manford and I made to the pond was a little scary. We had been fishing for about twenty minutes, and we were close to the bank and Manson got a bite. The fish went into the direction of the bank and got tangled up near the bank. We moved the canoe close to the bank, and he decided to sit on the side of the canoe and then all in one motion, we both went overboard. The boat just flipped over, and I went straight to the bottom of the pond. I stopped breathing and remembered once I touched the bottom of the pond. I jumped upward and reached my arms out, feeling for the canoe. When I reached the top of the water, I was reaching for the boat, and my left hand found the boat. I just grabbed it and held onto it. The canoe was upside down, but it had air trapped under it, and it continued to float.

Manford came up before me, and when I saw him holding onto the boat, he immediately said, "Kinsey, hold on to the boat and I will get on the bank and pull the boat onto the bank."

Once I reached the bank, we looked around the pond area and tried to find our equipment before we put the boat back into the water.

Manford said, "Kinsey, we are going to have to put the boat back in the water to get back on the other side of the pond."

I said, "Okay let's do it."

After we reached the other side of the pond and loaded the canoe back on the van, we headed back home. We did return to the pond to fish but didn't return with a canoe anymore. We returned in a flat bottom boat, a boat that we knew wouldn't capsize.

The Race That Shocked the Battalion

On August 20, 1979, Falisha Michele Kinsey was born in Gorgas Hospital in Panama. Once a year, our battalion would have an Organization Day for the soldiers. This was a huge picnic with food, drink, and fun events for the soldiers. There would be several events the soldiers could participate in to help build morale. One such event I entered was the 60-yard dash (YD). No one knew that I ran track in high school and had ran the 100 and the 200 YD. Specialist Lewis from Headquarters Company was a star football player in high school prior to entering the army, and he was quite fast. Alfa, Bravo, and Charlie Companies had some fast runners, and they were saying how they were going to show Specialist Lewis who was the fastest runner in the 60 YD.

The guys in my platoon knew that I could run fast because of seeing me run while playing on softball team and the flag football team, but they had not once seen me put on a pair of running shoes and run for time. The talk of the entire battalion was how the runner from Headquarters Company could beat everyone by running backward. The guys from my company put the word out that we had a secret weapon. Obviously, no one listened. It was now the day of the race and the Headquarters fans were even more confident that their runner would beat anyone on the track. They chanted for their runner while the rest of the fans remained silent.

We went to the starting blocks and waited on the starter to fire the gun. I had been listening to the starter's rhythm of his count prior to firing the gun. My plan was to time the starter's rhythm and anticipate the firing of the gun. His rhythm was very fluid and rapid. One word following the next without hesitation (ready, set, bang). The starter began his count with "Ready, set," and on "set," I started out of the blocks. By the time the gun went bang, my feet were starting to leave the starting blocks and no false start was applied to race.

They say by the time the Headquarters runner or any other runners came out of their starting blocks, I was already 5 yards down the track. I finished about 7 or 8 yards ahead of the Headquarters runner. All of the Headquarters fans were in shock and disbelief. You could hear some of the crowd saying, "Did you see that."

The Headquarters runner did come over to me and congratulated me. He asked if had run track before, and I said yes. He said, "I thought so" and turned and walked away. This one occurrence holds that the old saying is still true that "you can't judge a book by its cover." The Headquarters runner suffered a little ego damage that day, but eventually he accepted the fact that he lost to a fellow runner. He also knew that I was not one to brag about beating him. When soldiers approached me about beating him, I would always say, "I was just lucky."

Now time was winding down for me in Panama. In a few months, I would be leaving for my new assignment at Fort Bliss, Texas. About a month from leaving the country, I took my van to the port and shipped it back to the States. It would arrive in Charleston, South Carolina, while I was on vacation. After almost four years in Panama, I saw a lot of changes in the military and in the world.

New Assignment: Fort Bliss, Texas

We arrived in the United States on November 20, 1980. The family stayed at my mother-in-law's house (Mrs. Flossie Croft) while I caught the bus to Charleston to pick up the van.

The van had served its purpose for the family while we were in Panama. I had converted it into a taxi for the kids that I coached. I took out all the seats and put benches on both side running from front to back so that I could carry the entire team to either practice or a game. The kids on my team would all meet at my house over in the housing area, and when I made it home from work, they would all load up in the van and off we went to the game. A lot of parents got off from work at different times, so it made it very convenient for them and the team. Also, none of the kids would be late to a game. When I arrived at home, all fourteen or fifteen kids would burst out of my front door and head straight for the van. I would not be surprised if some of the kids on my teams back then didn't have pictures of themselves in the van in their homes as adults today.

Unfortunately, I had to buy something that would take the family to El Paso, Texas, without breaking down, so I had to buy another vehicle to travel to Fort Bliss. Those kids are probably some of the brightest individuals in our society today wherever they are, because they were the most respectful and kindest kids you would ever want to meet.

While we were on vacation, the most tragic news of the new decade appeared—John Lennon was murdered. It was the same feeling I had when Elvis Presley died; the news was not believable at first. I thought it was a mistaken identity and that it was probably someone else. I grew up knowing the Beatles. There was Beatlemania, and John played a huge role in the group's success. No one wanted to hear that one of them was gone. It was truly a sad day in America when John Lennon died. My vacation had ended, and it was time for us to leave for El Paso.

Fort Bliss is a United States Army post located in Texas and New Mexico. Its land area is about 1,700 square miles, and it is the second-largest U.S. Army installation in the country. It was established in the mid-1800s as a Southern outpost due to the constant Indian raids, which led to garrisons being frequently moved. When the American Civil War began, the Department of Texas ordered the garrison to surrender Fort Bliss to the Confederacy. The Confederacy used the garrison to launch attacks into New Mexico and Arizona. In 1878, the Ninth Cavalry was sent to Fort Bliss, thus finally establishing it as an army post. Its mission in part was to provide the U.S. Army with missile and anti-aircraft defense capabilities. Two of its main missile test sites are White Sands Missile Range in New Mexico and McGregor Range at Fort Bliss.

I arrived at Fort Bliss on a Sunday, and I got a room for the family at the post's guesthouse. The next day, I signed into my new unit, and the division decided to put me in the student battalion, and they further assigned me to the noncommissioned officers' cadre on Biggs Army Airfield at Fort Bliss.

I reported in the next day, and I was told by the sergeant that I would be one of two NCOs running the 16S (Stinger) Basic Noncommissioned Officer Course (BNOC). Once I had signed in, the sergeant gave me the rest of the day to get my family settled into the Fort Bliss area. I went to sign up for on-post housing, and I found out that the housing waiting list for a four-bedroom house was about six months. The sergeant gave me a list of approved landlords in the area. I found a three-bedroom house about six minutes from work. We moved in the next day. My wife enrolled the kids in school and I was ready for work.

The Redeye course was being phased out, and the Stinger track was being implemented. The problem was that there were no lesson plans for the new course, and it was the new instructor that was Stinger-certified that had to put them together. That meant me and someone else. When I made it to the NCO Academy, the 1SG introduced me to two Chaparral instructors, SSG MCcabe and SSG Hicks. SSG Hicks was also Stinger-certified, and he and I would be the two 16S instructors for the academy. Since I had not gone through BNOC myself, I went through the Chaparral course, which was ran by SSG MCcabe and SSG Hicks. Upon completing this course, SSG Hicks and I were free to work together on the 16S course. We worked on the lesson plans and setting up the course over the next six months. After the completion of the course lesson plans and curriculum, I went through a three-week instructor training course at Fort Bliss.

Once I completed that course, we got all the logistical planning accomplished then we were ready to start the course up. The course started on schedule, and it was quite effective. Students and outside instructor's feedback was very positive for the program. The disinterested inspectors who evaluated us were very pleased with the content of the course.

We averaged about ten students during a four-week training cycle. These are sergeants being prepared for promotion to staff sergeants. They learned how to deploy a MANPADS section either as a critical asset or implement them into a convoy. Map reading, aircraft recognition, and leadership training are keys to the success of a MANPADS section. Sergeants and all students had to excel in those tasks prior to graduation. MANPADS BNOC at Fort Bliss was the only one in existence in the army, so we received students from military installations overseas and the States for training each cycle. Anonymous feedback from our students helped us gauge where the program stood and what we needed to do to make it more challenging for the students in the future. The program produced many professional soldiers who went on to have great careers in the army.

Continued My Civilian Education

While at Fort Bliss, Texas, I could continue my schooling. I enrolled in El Paso Community College and was awarded an associate's degree in liberal arts in 1982. It's not that often that soldiers have an opportunity to continue their education. Some soldiers take advantage of it, and many do not. I knew that there would be other opportunities for me once I completed my military career and have a college degree.

Attending college while on active duty is a challenge. I had only one vehicle for the family, so I needed other transportation to and from work. I didn't want to leave the family without transportation should something happen to one of the kids. I found a KZ200 Kawasaki motorcycle to ride to work and to school. I bought the motorcycle and studied for and passed the test for motorcycles. I drove the motorcycle to work even on rainy days. I drove it during the wintertime because it didn't get too cold in El Paso during the winter. I also drove it to the college campus downtown in El Paso, which was a challenge. The campus downtown was off the Interstate 10 freeway, and it was nerve-racking. There was about a ten-mile stretch on the freeway that I had to travel, and it was tough riding down the freeway when a big rig passed by. That little KZ200 was being pulled all over the road when a big rig passed by me. It was great cheap transportation and very easy to operate and park. I loved that little bike.

It doesn't rain in El Paso that often, but that day it rained, and it stopped before I left work, and I thought it was okay to ride and would miss the rain. I took off for home, and I was riding over on Railroad Street, and it had poured rain for it seemed like hours. As I was on the road, a big rig was coming toward me, and the biggest gathering of water in one spot of the road was between me and him. As the big rig approached me, I braced for the water, and as it flew in my path, I was drenched from neck to toe. I did have my helmet on, and that played a huge role for my head not getting wet.

The bike was one of the main reasons I could get to school and graduate. I remember, I also wanted to improve my chances when it was time for my records to be viewed for promotion. My advice to all soldiers is, if you plan on staying in the military, don't settle with just being a sergeant. Be the best sergeant in the army, and you must work hard at being far above your peers.

Very few people knew that I applied for flight school back in the early '80s. A friend, Sergeant Tomlinson, at the NCO Academy and I applied at the same time. We both waited until we received our associate degrees from El Paso Community College, and we began testing for flight school. We both passed the basic piloting skills test as well as the instruments test. We both were very excited to be so close to completing our packets for flight school.

The next and final hurdle was the surgeon's flight physical. We went on the same day to take the physical. The exam took most of the day, but the hearing exam was supposed to be routine, but not for me. I failed the first test. My high-frequency hearing hovered around 55 decibels, and the maximum allowable was 25 decibels. The doctor said for me to come back the following day and that most people do better the second time through.

I went in the next morning and went through the exam again, and the results were the same. So, the doctor took me through a voice test where he would call out names to me, and I would repeat what name he called out to me. Again, I didn't pass the test. The doctor recommended that I get a good night's sleep and cover my ears on the way in the next day for the final test. Meanwhile, Sergeant Tomlinson was done, and his packet was being forwarded for review by the Department of the Army for flight school selection board.

I returned the next morning, ready to go through the final tests. I went through and again the results were the same. I just couldn't get the score low enough to get into flight school, and I had to face reality. The years at Fort Hood firing those tanks without earplugs hurt my chances of becoming a helicopter pilot.

A year and a half after Sergeant Tomlinson and I applied for flight school, he returned to the NCO Academy wearing his flight uniform, and he was being stationed right there at Fort Bliss in the Third Air Cavalry Division. I was proud of him, but at the same time I felt a little sad for myself because I didn't make it. Maybe those were not the plans that God had for me.

As my military career progressed, I felt that this indeed was the best path for me in the army. Another friend of mine at the academy named SFC Albert Totten was a good golfer, and he asked me if I would like to go golfing with him and some of the other instructors on Saturdays when we were off duty. I said yes, but I have never played before. He said, "Don't worry about it, we will teach you how, it's easy."

I said, "I don't have clubs," and he replied, "You're in luck. My wife bought me a new set and you can have my old set."

I said, "Okay."

We met at the Fort Hood Country Club the next Saturday we were off duty. Totten said we will start off at the driving range so we can practice hitting off the tee. He showed me how to hold the club so the ball wouldn't slice left or right, and he gave me pointers to help my game in other areas prior to teeing off. The outcome of the game was very predictable on my part in that I played very poorly; however, I came away enjoying the game. I had no idea that I would develop such an intense interest in the game after just one time on the course.

We would play at least two to three times per month, and my game gradually improved over time. After about nine months into my learning the game, I came very close to matching several of the guys' scores. One of the guys in our group made a comment. He said, "Hey, we have created a golfing monster here." Then he turned to me and said, "That's a good thing."

In early 1983, two sergeants came through the 16S course that I knew from being stationed in Panama. Sergeant Reilly and Sergeant Adorno were PFCs when I was in the Stinger Platoon of combat support company at Fort Kobbe, Panama. They were very dedicated soldiers who took their jobs very seriously. I was not surprised at seeing them come to the program. As privates, these soldiers, under the guidance of their team chiefs, Sergeant Manson and Sergeant Mc Innis, learned their job very thoroughly. The soldiers in the Stinger Platoon always trained hard and often. Prior to my leaving Panama, Reilly had already won the Soldier of the Month award within the battalion. The Soldier of the Month award is given to a soldier in each battalion level command that demonstrates those skills that set them apart from their peers such as military history, military customs and courtesy, leadership, job skills, current events, etc. When I gave a block of instruction within the platoon and PFC Reilly didn't quite understand it, at the end of the session he would always ask me to further elaborate on the subject. I liked those qualities in him. He displayed a career soldier's mentality.

I was nearing the end of my tour of duty at Fort Bliss and the NCO Academy when I decided to volunteer for drill sergeant duty. It took a lot of thinking because once a soldier goes on drill sergeant status, the world as they know it vanishes. They are tied down to their unit practically the entire time they are on the trail (drill sergeant duty). My friends said, "No way, don't do it."

SFC Totten said, "You will only see trainees for the duration of the time you are on the trail."

I told myself it's a challenge that a lot of people don't want to accept. I filled out the packet, and I pondered on it for weeks, and one day I went to the kitchen table, picked up the packet, and had it sent off for approval. After a week passed, I began to have regrets on signing up for the job.

Three weeks passed and one day at work, I received a phone call, and the 1SG called me into his office and said, "SSG Kinsey, you have a phone call from the drill sergeant branch."

I took the phone, and the sergeant on the other end of the phone said, "Congratulations, SSG Kinsey. You have been selected for drill sergeant duty. The reason I called you personally is to talk with you about a possible assignment at Fort Benning, Georgia. Would you be interested?"

I said, "Well, I only live two hours from there. I guess I can."

He asked me when I would like to start Drill Sergeant School. School, he said, would be at Fort Benning, Georgia, and there is a cycle starting up in late October and will be finishing up in January sometimes. I said to him that October would be a good time to go.

In two weeks, I had orders for me to report to Drill Sergeant School at Fort Benning, Georgia. I thought, Wow, I am leaving Fort Bliss.

The next several months prior to departing for Fort Benning gave me some time to reflect on my current assignment, where it started, and where it is now. SSG Hicks and I got the 16S track off the ground and running like a charm. Sergeants are coming in from all over the world just to attend our track. It was what we needed for the 1980s, and it worked very well, and everyone was proud of it.

It gave me time to reflect about some good and not-so- good things about my assignment at Fort Bliss, Texas. I remember after graduating from El Paso Community College, I wanted to get a class ring. Well, I was going to a mall to order one from a jeweler. My daughter, Falisha, wanted to go with me to the mall, and I said okay. We arrived at the mall and went into the jewelers store, and inside the mall they have many animated attractions to catch the eye. They were sizing me for the ring, and Falisha was standing beside me, then I turned around and she was gone. I looked outside the store and saw nobody, and I began to panic. I looked toward the east end of the mall and only saw the animated attractions as far as the eyes can see. I was going into a panic mode, and I started to run to the front of the store. My mind was saying, "Where is she? What if someone had taken her? Do I have time to find her before she is taken from the mall? If only I had paid more attention to her while we were in the store . . . Should I call the police or keep trying to find her? What if, what if, what if?"

I have now passed about seven different businesses en route to the front of the mall. As I approached the front of the store, I saw two little old ladies with a little girl in tow heading to the customer service department with Falisha.

I reached them and said, "Hey, that's my daughter. We were in the jewelers, and she wandered off."

Falisha turned around after hearing my voice and yelled, "Daddy!" She was now crying up a storm.

The ladies said that she was wandering down the center of the mall, and they asked her, "Where is your mother?" and she said, "She is at home." And then they asked her, "Are you with your dad?" and she said "Yes." They then asked her, "Where is your dad?" and she said, "Here." They also asked her "Where," and she said, "I don't know," and that's when they decided to take her to customer service to locate me.

We left immediately for home. Falisha was the baby of five siblings, and she was the only girl. So Mom was quite upset that Dad had lost the baby in the mall.

Ronald Reagan was elected president of the United States in 1980. The United States Military benefited during that time because President Ronald Reagan signed into law the biggest military pay hike on record (10 percent). It was across the board, all ranks, all military branches, and I didn't have to pawn things out of my house or borrow money from a friend to put food on the table for my kids the last three or four days of the month. It didn't take us out of poverty, but the soldiers who had families and stuck to their strict budget did a lot better paying bills and feeding their families. He allocated more funds for the military budgets so that we could modernize somewhat, buy spare parts, and function as military units. We, like other motor pools, had deadlined vehicles and most of the time didn't have parts available to fix our vehicles. After Reagan was elected, that changed.

I am a Vietnam era veteran, and my years of service came in the '70s, '80s, and '90s, and we were not thought of as heroes. The Vietnam War and politics kept us on the sidelines without much progression. Police officers and firefighters protect our communities, the military protect our country, but we were looked at last when it comes to pay, benefits, recognition, and service to our country during that time frame.

It was time for me to report to my school assignment at Fort Benning, Georgia. The Drill Sergeant Course was from October 1983 through January 1984. The decision was made to leave my family at Fort Bliss until I completed the course.

Fort Benning was named after a Civil War general, Brigadier General Henry L. Benning of the Confederate Army. Fort Benning was built in 1918 and was the home of the infantry. During the 1980s, Benning was a Training and Doctrine Command (TRADOC) post. The 197th Infantry, Infantry Basic Combat Training units, OCS Airborne School, Third Ranger Battalion, Drill Sergeant School, Bradley Fighting Vehicle course, and other training units were at Fort Benning at that time. Dwight D. Eisenhower served at Camp Benning in December 1918 and left in March 1919. Lieutenant Colonel George C. Marshal served as assistant commandant of the post in 1924. He became the army chief of staff during World War II. Marshall is the author of the Marshall Plan and won the Nobel Peace Prize in 1953. The country's last five-star general, Omar N. Bradley, commanded the post from 1941 through 1942. Fort Benning is in Columbus, Georgia, and it sits on the border of Alabama.

I arrived at the Drill Sergeant Course at Fort Benning and began training. The course was very intense and detailed. We had to execute marching movements through words to explain to a trainee how to execute a specific movement. For example, the movement "Right face," once you give the command, you would have to explain to the trainee through a series of counts how the body is positioned. Right face: While standing at the position of attention, the head and eyes are looking straight ahead. Lift the heel of your left foot and the ball of your right foot, keeping your hand and arms next to your sides with your fingers and thumb curled and alongside the seam of your trousers. Twist your upper body while using your feet. Turn 90 degrees to the right, and bring your left foot alongside your right foot and resume the position of attention.

It was very difficult to do at first, but once you got the hang of it, everything flowed very well. We went through everything we were expected to put the trainees through while on the trail. We went to the obstacle course and the confidence course too.

One of the events on the confidence course was a thirty-foot-high ladder that we all had to climb. We had to master the ladder because as a drill sergeant, if your platoon comes through and you have a trainee that can't make it over the top, you must go up and assist him in going over the top of the ladder. If a person doesn't look down while executing the obstacle, it wouldn't affect them. Looking down reminds them that they are in the air, and the trainees that are afraid of heights will freak out. The drill sergeant often will go up the ladder himself and talk the trainee on up and over the top and back down the obstacle. Most of the time, a classmate would stop at the rung just under the top one and just freeze. They don't move and don't say anything. The drill instructor would go up to him and say, "What are you going to do when you have a trainee stuck on the second-from-the-last rung and can't get over the top? Are you going to call the fire department or are you going to get him down yourself?" The drill instructor did have to get some of our classmates over the top of the ladder and that didn't help their chances of graduating.

The gas chamber was another challenge for a few of my classmates. That tear gas would bring you to tears no matter how you prepared for it. We were lucky that we didn't have guys running into pine trees near the chamber when that exited the room. Most of the guys were in a straight run from the chamber because your eyes were burning so bad. We went through bayonet as well as pugil training. We had sergeants dropping out left and right, and I finally asked one of my classmates why we were losing so many people.

He said to me, "SSG Kinsey, did you volunteer or were you drafted to attend?"

I said, "I volunteered."

He said, "Kinsey, not very many infantrymen volunteer to come here because you will never see your family."

I knew that some of the guys could have made it over the wall on the confidence course and other could have done the drill movements, but they seem to not want to pass them. We started our class with around forty-plus soldiers, and we were down to about twenty-eight just four weeks into the program. I was not infantry; I was air defense, and I had to learn infantry tactics because we were keeping the trainees for thirteen-week cycles, which included their Advanced Individual Training (AIT). When we combine basic combat training with their AIT, we call it One Station Unit Training (OSUT). I studied a lot of extra hours learning the trainee handbook or Blue Book to teach my trainees. We had to learn patrolling techniques, movement to contact, suppressive fires, and many more infantry techniques. Well, we graduated twenty-seven drill sergeant candidates in our class. I was being assigned to Delta Company Ninth Battalion Second Infantry Brigade (D 9/2) Harmony Church. Upon graduating from Drill Sergeant Course, I left Fort Benning and traveled back to El Paso, Texas, to move my family back to Georgia.

On the Trail (Drill Sergeant's Duty)

The family moved to Cusseta, Georgia, during my vacation time between duty stations. I reported into D 9/2 orderly room and talked to 1SG Hendrix. I was assigned to Fourth Platoon, and my drill partner was SSG Bowers. SSG Bowers had broken his leg in airborne school, which is located across the post. There were four platoons per company, five or six companies per battalion, five battalions on Harmony Church, and five Battalions on Sand Hill at the time. D 9/2 were only able to provide two drill sergeants per platoon. So, it was just me and SSG Bowers. SSG Bowers could do some of the paperwork for the platoon. Other than that, it was me and fifty-eight trainees.

I came to the platoon while they were in their fourth week of training. I lived about twelve minutes away from the company area. I would set my alarm clock across the room on a dresser, and it was set to go off at 3:30 AM. Once the alarm clock goes off, I would get up, put my physical training uniform on, and grab my battle dress uniform (BDU), boots, and gym bag on the way out the door to my truck. At about 3:38 AM, I would be on the way to the company area. I would pull up in the parking lot and walk to the barracks and enter my office, and it would be about 3:56 AM. I would walk to the trash can and take the lid off and begin to bang it against the can to get the maximum amount of sound as possible. I would yell, "Get up, trainees, you are now sleeping on my time, and I don't like it when you are sleeping on my time.

"If you don't hit the floor in thirty seconds, you will be rewarded with an additional hour of PT today."

Once the trainees are all out of bed, I begin to walk up and down the open bay area introducing myself as their new drill sergeant. I am sure they didn't know what to expect of me because I came in breathing fire. The platoon was just about to enter the BRM phase of their training. Then, they will enter the machine gun and hand grenade training qualification training. The platoon was traveling a while to and from the Malone ranges. When we returned to the barracks in the evening and after the dinner meal, we would continue to train for the next day's event or task. BRM training is probably the most complex training for a trainee because there are so many working parts that must be done at the same time or one after the other to get a good shot. I bought a BB rifle to help the trainees practice because most trainees have never fired a rifle in their entire life up to that point. I would utilize our upstairs open bay area; on one end, I would put up a chair with a sleeping blanket and a bull's-eye target. The trainees would get in the prone position with the BB gun. I would have them lie facing the target, spread their feet shoulder width apart, place their non-firing elbow on the floor with their non-firing hand underneath the hand guards, then put their firing elbow on the floor in a comfortable distance apart from the other, place the firing hand on the pistol grip with the lower three fingers and thumb wrapped around it and the forefinger placed alongside the bolt housing pointing at the target. They would place the butt of the weapon in the pocket of the shoulder to help cushion the recoil. The trainee would place his nose to the rear and slightly touch the charging handle. Looking through the rear sight aperture and locating the front sight post, line them up so that the front sight post is center mass of the rear sight aperture. Before the trainee shoots, he must take in a slight breath of air and hold it (the body would want to move for over eight seconds), and while holding his breath, he would squeeze the trigger (if the sound of the round exiting the chamber is a surprise, the trainee will hit his target). Cocking one of the legs will also relieve pressure from the stomach area and make breathing easier.

    The trainee performed superbly on the firing line. We had the most expert firers within the company. The infantry drill sergeants couldn't understand why an air defense drill sergeant's platoon could outshoot them. I didn't let on to the other platoons that I was training my trainees in the barracks at night. My goal was to win Honor Platoon of the cycle. The Honor Platoon marches first during graduation. Our platoon went on to win the Med-cycle Test award, PRT, Drill and Ceremony award (D&C), and the End-of-Cycle Test, thus winning Honor Platoon.

Private Baez

The second training cycle was one to remember for me as a drill sergeant. We graduated the first cycle on Thursday, and our second cycle came in on Monday. We got a call from the reception station about 4:00 PM alerting us that the buses had just left and were en route to our company. Once notified that the trainees were on the way, all drill sergeants in the company came out on the PT field and awaited the bus arrival. As the buses pulled up, all the trainees saw were drill sergeants all over the PT field.

I walked up to the second bus and said, "The last one out of this bus owes me a hundred push-ups." As you probably know by now, it was not a casual conversation. I went around the bus to one of the windows and jumped up on the window, and it just shattered. Glass flew through the bus, and trainees were exiting the bus everywhere. They opened the rear door and began piling out of the bus. I noticed one soldier that looked like a butterball. He was about five feet tall, and he weighed around 250 pounds. I yelled at him, "Son, I know you didn't bring that much weight here to Fort Benning. I want this one in my platoon. He will leave one hundred pounds here at Fort Benning."

As the dust settled down, the four platoon sergeants lined up so that we could receive our assigned recruits, and everyone became quiet. I was about to receive trainee number two, and the administrative clerk said, "Baez, Antonio," and to my surprise, all the drills started chanting, "Short round, short round, short round." It was the trainee that I had pointed out as a butterball. I could see the look on his face that he knew that he was in trouble. After the roll call and the platoons were being released to their drill sergeants, I walked over to Baez and said, "You are in for a very long cycle, trainee."

I moved the platoon to the barracks and briefed them on the dos and don'ts of the platoon. I gave them time to set up their bunks and settle in. The next morning was a big test for Baez. We headed out to PT, and I explained to the platoon that we must function as a team. If someone falls out of a PT run, we will return the formation around, go back, and pick up the team member to ensure that the team member makes it back to garrison. We conducted our stretching, calisthenics, and began our run. Shortly after we started the run, Baez began to fade slowly to the rear of the formation. I turned the platoon around, and we circled Baez and just slowed down and ran a shuttle run so he could keep up with us. We made it back to the PT field about five or six minutes longer than we probably would have if we had not picked up Private Baez. I released the platoon to go and conduct personal hygiene, clean the barracks, eat breakfast, and be ready for training within one hour.

We departed for training on foot (marching). As we were walking with our rucksacks, Baez would slowly drift to the rear of the formation. I would have two trainees get behind him and push him at the same pace we were marching. The trainees in our platoon said that Baez had stopped eating sweets and bread in the mess hall. At week 4, we had to send Baez back to supply for another refit for his uniform. At week 7, Baez was falling out of the five-mile marches but not by much; he was improving every day. At week 9, Baez had to go back to supply again for a refit of his uniforms.

The big test for Baez was yet to come: it was the twelve-mile road march from one of the Malone ranges. I told Baez that he had to make the road march or be recycled to another company until he could make it. By now, the entire platoon had bought into helping Baez graduate with their class. He turned to me and said, "Drill Sergeant Kinsey, I'm going to make it." I said to him that the entire platoon, including myself, will be pulling for him. We finished training about 4:00 PM, and it was time to begin the big march. I turned to the platoon, and they had already gathered around Private Baez, giving him a pep talk. I told the platoon that everyone must finish the march within the proper time or they will not graduate with their class.

I considered Private Baez's eyes and told him that "Every trainee in this platoon, including myself, wants you to finish this march with the platoon and to be a part of the best Honor Platoon that has ever passed through D 9/2."

Private Baez shifted his eyes from mine and relocated them on the platoon and simply said to his peers, "I'm going to do it." I positioned him just behind the platoon guide-on carrier. We started the road march, and the trainees were looking very good for the first five miles, but as we began to hit the seven-mile marker, Baez began to fade. He drifted from up front to about five feet behind the last man in our platoon. Ten miles into the march, Baez faded a little more, and I went back there and talked to him. I told him that all his peers were counting on him to finish with them. He was too tired to talk, but he nodded his head as if to say, "Drill Sergeant, I'm going to make it."

We crossed the finish line, and Baez was within five feet of our formation, which was within the distance of allowing him to complete the task. The road march was documented in his files as a completed task toward graduation. The entire platoon formed around him and congratulated him for pushing his body to the limits so that he could continue training with them. On graduation day, Baez's mother and sister arrived, and neither of them could recognize him at first because he had lost so much weight. Private Baez told his mother that he wouldn't have made it through training if Drill Sergeant Kinsey wasn't patient with him. He thanked me and his platoon for helping him make it through training.

Private Baez lost a total of 78 pounds. I told Baez and his family that it wasn't me or his platoon; it was his determination and refusal to quit or give up on himself. He made up his mind at the very beginning of the training that he would not quit this program. Private Baez truly earned the respect of his peers and instructors alike through his willingness to shed weight and keep up with his platoon physically to graduate with his class.

Time for the Kids

The stories I had heard about drill sergeant duty prior to applying for it was officially true. The extremely long hours, no time for family, 126-plus-hour weeks, physically demanding, mentally challenging, ultra-stressful, mother, father, doctor, postman, police, judge, jury, coach, nurse, and about fifty other hats a drill sergeant wears. When you are on drill status, you are not allowed vacation during cycles nor any other time off unless you are off from the previous night's duty.

When I did have a day off, I would spend that time with the kids. I would take them to the theater to watch a movie. I would take them in the seating area and seat them, and Danny (the oldest) and I would go to the counter and get everyone popcorn and a soda. Falisha would always want to sit next to me during the movie. They would sit there and watch the movie and eat their treats and not make a fuss at all. On the way back home, we would talk about the movie and the next one that we would like to see based on the previews that we watched. I bought them a go-cart to ride also. We would go to an area where the rangers did their water survival training.

There was an asphalt road over there, and at one point it made a complete circle, and that's where we rode the go-cart. I would have them take turns driving it at a slow pace until they learned how to control it. The older boys, Danny and Dedric, learned to maneuver the cart very quickly. Dwayne and Orenthal were still trying to master entering a curve and slowing down so that they could make the turn without sliding off the road. Falisha was very cautious and slow because she didn't want to overturn the cart.

After our second or third visit to the training area, the whole group was now very confident in driving the cart. We started off well. Everyone was riding very carefully, and after a while, I noticed that they were getting faster and faster. I began to tell them to slow down as they were cranking up the speed prior to entering the turn on the road. After a while, they started to ramp up the speed again, and before I had a chance to say anything, Orenthal was entering the curve so fast.

I yelled at him, "Take your feet off the gas and turn!"

He entered the curve, and as he turned and backed off the gas pedal, it was too late. He began to slide sideways into the woods and the brush. We could see him bouncing and kicking up pine cones prior to disappearing in the thick bushes. We all ran to where he was, and he walked out the bushes laughing, and everyone chimed in, and we just started laughing. We knew when he walked out of the brush laughing that he was okay. After that episode, I gave them a safety talk about riding too fast on a go-cart and how Orenthal was very lucky that the cart didn't flip over on him and injure him very seriously. I couldn't help but think that there was a talk among them about who would have the fastest lap of the day when we returned to ride the go-cart. Accidents do happen, but when there is horseplay involved, then there must be consequences.

When I returned home from work one night, I was told that the window in one of the boys' room had been completely out! I asked them what happened, and no one owned up to what happened to the window.

I said, "If no one wants to tell me what happened, I guess everyone has to pay for it." I knew that they had been playing in their room, and one of them broke it somehow. Well, all four of the boys got the belt. They never confessed who broke the window until years later. Apparently, Dwayne and Orenthal were playing in the room, and Dwayne pushed Orenthal, and he went backward through the window and broke it, completely out. The playing in the house led me to purchase a small travel trailer and set it up in the backyard so that they would have something to play in outside the house. The travel trailer helped them make it through the summer without seeing the belt again.

Airborne School

At the end of the fourth training cycle, our company had three weeks before we picked up the next group of trainees, and our 1SG asked us if anyone wanted to attend airborne school during that cycle break. Four of the cadre volunteered to go, and I was one of the four. Airborne school at Fort Benning hosts students from all over the world and from all branches of service. We had a rare opportunity to go and earn our jump wings. We started school around mid-April 1985.

I want to share an excerpt of A Parachutist's Creed: "I realize that a parachutist is not merely a soldier who arrives by parachute to fight, but is an elite shock trooper and that his country expects him to march farther and faster, to fight harder, to be more self-reliant than any other soldier. Parachutists of all allied armies belong to this great brotherhood."

The first week of airborne school was very intense. In the morning of training, we began with what the cadre explained as "break area procedures." This procedure consisted of hundreds upon hundreds of push-ups. As we were doing push-ups, the cadre would walk from soldier to soldier asking them if they wanted to quit. The soldiers would respond with "No, Sergeant," and they continued to drill us. We were drilled for about forty-five minutes before I heard the first soldier say, "Yes, Sergeant. I want to quit." The cadre would zero in on a soldier that had stopped executing the push-up, and they would ask him or her if they wanted to quit. After this ended, we ran for a mile and if anyone fell behind more than four feet from the running formation, they would have to leave the course and return to their unit.

We also had to execute seven chin-ups from a dead hang on the chin-up bar. If you can't complete the seven chin-ups by the end of the three-week course, then you will return to your unit without jump wings.

After PT, we began training for the day. The first week is called Ground Week. My unit was the Forty-second Company Fourth Airborne Training Battalion, Fort Benning, Georgia. LTC Leonard B. Scott was my battalion commander. He was also a Vietnam veteran who wrote a book called *Charlie Mike* on his experiences of the Vietnam War.

During the first week on instruction, we trained on how to exit the aircraft. We used a mock door representing the aircraft in flight. We would stand in the door, keeping the head lowered, placing the hands on the reserve chute, and jump up and away from the aircraft. The 34-foot tower helped us master those skills. We practiced our landing skills by utilizing our five points of contact of the body: the feet, the calf muscle, the thigh muscle, the buttocks, and upper back muscle. The students that successfully completed this week of training could move into the tower week of training. The second week of training became more intense than the first week. The PT was even more intense, the chin-ups ramped up, we ran two miles and no one could be more than four feet behind the formation or go home. We had to prepare for the 250-foot tower jump. The 34-foot tower was still used during this phase of training to help us master exiting the aircraft while in fight. The suspended harness and swing landing trainer assisted us with our landing techniques. On Friday of week 2, we ran three miles and everyone had to be within four feet of the formation. If you completed all tasks satisfactorily, you could move into jump week. I passed all tasks during week 2 and was feeling happy and sad at the same time. I was glad that I had finished the rigorous training that all parachutists go through, but simultaneously I felt that going up into an aircraft to jump out of it with a parachute was a little bit dangerous. We went home for the weekend and that was all I thought about, whether the chute would malfunction. I said to myself, I have completed all this painful training and I haven't jumped from a single aircraft. At week 3, we had to complete five jumps successfully to earn our jump wings.

I returned on Monday morning for PT and to complete the third and final week of airborne training. We began our training learning the different chutes that we would be utilizing during the jumps. The T-10B chute and the MC1-1B chute were the chutes that we would be using for our jumps. We would also jump from a C130 aircraft, which is propeller-driven, and a C141 jet. The difference between the two aircraft from a parachutist view is that in the C130, the jumper must jump up and away from the aircraft when exiting. The C141 is a jet, and a jumper must be ready as soon as they reach the door of the aircraft because it sucks you out of the aircraft. Once you count to four, your chute should be open. My chute should always be open when I reach the count of three. We jumped from 1250 feet to 2000 feet.

Around 1:00 PM, we moved to the airstrip on the tarmac and waited for the next aircraft take us up and get that first jump accomplished. The aircraft arrived, and we boarded it and sat along the wall. No one said anything to anyone. One of the guys in training with us was all mouth in training, but up in the air with his static line hooked up, he was the quietest person on the plane. We were nearing the drop zone when the doors of the aircraft opened and the jumpmaster said, "Two minutes." The talkative soldier in training was vomiting everywhere. The jumpmaster at the door said, "Stand up." He immediately said, "Hook up." We hooked up our static lines on the wire. He then turned to the student in front of him and he said, "Stand in the door." The jumpmaster immediately focused on the light on the door. When it turns green, that's the signal to go. The green light came on, and the jumpmaster said to the first man in the door, "Go." Everyone behind the first man continued to move toward the front door to exit the aircraft.

When the red light comes on, the jumpmaster will stop and halt all soldiers from jumping because we would then be normally at the end of the drop zone (DZ). When I hit the ground, I began to shout like everyone else, "I made it!"

On my third jump, I hit the ground a little hard on my calf muscle, and it was very sore, but I wasn't going to tell anyone because I didn't want to be kicked out of jump school, especially after three successful jumps and only two more to go to complete the course. I couldn't imagine going back through the first two weeks all over again. I did complete my last two jumps to earn my jump wings. Jump school was quite an accomplishment for me. It was a huge challenge for all of us. We graduated on May 10, 1985. The four of us from D Company 9/2 are still drill sergeants, but now we returned as paratroopers.

On Monday evening the following week, we picked up another cycle of trainees. About halfway through that cycle, I received orders sending me to Fort Bliss, Texas, for Advanced Noncommissioned Officer Course. Prior to departing for school, the battalion had learned that two SSGs in the battalion had made the promotion list to SFC. The battalion command sergeant major (CSM) said that no one from Delta Company had made the list. I was sort of disappointed that I didn't make the list. As the day went on, I started thinking, I am in an infantry battalion, not an ADA battalion, and what if the list that was viewed did not have air defense soldiers on it.

I decided to call the air defense branch to find out whether anyone in the Air Defense MOS at Fort Benning made the SFC list and, more importantly, me. To my surprise, I was on the list. I immediately called my 1SG to let him know that I made the SFC list, and that I was not an infantryman and that's why no one would know that I was on the list. I was very happy that I made the list. Promotions at SFC, 1SG, and SGM levels are all centralized promotions, meaning that your records go before a panel that consists of CSMs and colonels, and is chaired by a general officer, and the board is conducted at the Pentagon. It is very prestigious to earn a promotion through that system because only the top soldiers in the U.S. Army are promoted on to the senior ranks.

After the completion of another honor platoon cycle, I went to El Paso, Texas, for school. In the Air Defense ANOC, we learned air defense tactics and how to deploy an air defense platoon. We also went through two weeks of Nuclear Biological Chemical (NBC) training, and the students in the class that scored 100 percent during this section in the class would be awarded a certificate in NBC training. After those two weeks, I was one of those very few fortunate students to earn the certificate in NBC training. That portion of the course was very intense and technical, but a few of us survived.

I returned to Fort Benning after competing ANCOC at Fort Bliss and was glad to be back. My family life was not good at this point in my career. I was very dedicated to the military, and between being on the trail and the military schools I attended, there wasn't much time spent at home. The time I did have free was spent with the kids. As I returned to Fourth Platoon, my drill partner (SFC Mitchell) was looking forward to my return so that he could get somewhat of a break. I knew how tough it was to run a platoon alone.

No sooner had I returned to Benning, than I received orders sending me to the United States Army Recruiting School at Fort Benjamin Harrison, Indiana. I thought, "Oh no. Another very demanding job, virtually no time for family again."

So far in my career, I had never turned down or tried to get out of an assignment, and I wasn't going to start then. If the army wants me to recruit, then I will be the best recruiter the army must offer. You are talking about going from the frying pan into the fire; this resembled that scenario to a tee. Drill sergeant duty is practically 24/7 as for as time spent with the trainees, and recruiting is almost the same, plus 2000 percent more stress. In recruiting, you must change your leadership style. You are no longer an authoritarian leader. Now, you must master the art of persuasion. You can't say, "Son, go down to the recruiting office and join the army now!" As a recruiter, you must ask them to join. Civilians don't react to a sergeant's voice like a recruit or trainee.

I was glad that the school was several months away so I could still perform my duties as a drill sergeant for a little while longer. I had set a personal goal for myself to accomplish, and that was to win Honor Platoon the entire time that I was on the trail. So far, I had won every cycle's Honor Platoon award. This cycle would be my sixth in a row that I have won as a drill sergeant. As far as anyone knew, no one in Delta Company has ever won six Honor Platoon awards. The only one I missed was when I was attending ANCOC at Fort Bliss, Texas.

I got to the point that trying to be the best platoon in the company helped time pass a little easier. My thoughts were that if I must be here with the trainees, I might as well put my time to good use. Instead of being in the drill sergeant's lounge, I was always in my barracks training my trainees. At the end of cycle 2, PFC Coutemarsh told me that all the other platoon trainees called my platoon "Kinsey's Kids." The reason is that my platoon rarely went to the PX or wandered outside the barracks because we were always training. Coutemarsh said, "We would always look out the window, and the other platoon trainees would be outside pointing at us as if we were behind the iron curtain."

PFC Coutemarsh was one of my huge success stories. He came to us while applying for Officer Candidate School (OCS). Coutemarsh had a bachelor's degree from a school up in Massachusetts. When his training class graduated, he went across post and reported to the OCS staff to begin training toward becoming an army commissioned officer. I remember being out on one of the Malone ranges with my platoon, and my company 1SG came out to the range and said that he came to pick me up to go back into garrison because Coutemarsh was about to get pinned his lieutenant's bars and he wanted me to be the first enlisted soldier to salute him.

The company 1SG said, "Coutemarsh told the general that he wanted Drill Sergeant Kinsey to salute him and no one else." The 1SG said, "That boy got everybody at Fort Benning looking for you, and the general is waiting."

The 1SG and I arrived, and as we were walking up, I scanned the crowd. There had to be over a thousand people there, and all one thousand had their eyes on me. They wanted to know who Drill Sergeant Kinsey was. I looked over at the graduating cadets, and there was Coutemarsh standing at parade, waiting for me to move forward. I walked over in front of him and stopped and came to the position of attention and rendered a hand salute, and Lieutenant Coutemarsh came to the position of attention and returned the salute, and then he handed me a silver dollar, thus completing the army tradition.

He said, "Remember, I asked you if you would be the first enlisted soldier to salute me."

I said, "Yes, I remember, but I didn't know when you would graduate."

He introduced his wife and family to me. They were very nice people. After meeting and talking with his family, I understood why he was such good man and soldier. I said goodbye to Lieutenant Coutemarsh and his family prior to leaving to go back and rejoin my soldiers in the field. If Lieutenant Coutemarsh maintained that compassion for his soldiers, then he was going to become a very successful army officer.

The 1SG took me back to the field to rejoin the company and my platoon. My drill partner thought that it was very thoughtful of one of my former trainees to honor me in that manner. I said to him, "Yeah, he is a truly a good soldier."

We completed our training in the field and moved back into garrison. And yes, we did finish that cycle as honor platoon. All the drill sergeants in our company didn't leave the trail under good conditions. The job was indeed very high speed, and the hours a drill sergeant put in each day and week was unconscionable. Despite the long hours, the time away from family, mental and physical demanding schedule, and broken marriages, a drill sergeant must still perform his or her duties in a military manner and always in the highest level of professionalism. If not, you will fall hard.

There were some stories that were very surprising to me from other companies and battalions, but I will dwell on what happened at Delta Company 9/2 during my tenure as a drill sergeant.

Second Platoon came in from the field, and one of their drill sergeants' wet weather top came up missing. He called for a platoon formation and asked his platoon if they had they seen his wet water top. The platoon trainees did not know where the drill sergeant's top was located. He dismissed his platoon and called the platoon guide over and told him that he must collect enough money from the platoon to buy him another wet water top. The platoon guide, not knowing that the drill sergeant was breaking army policy by taking money from a trainee, did what he was told. The platoon guide went ahead and collected as much money as he could to replace the wet water top as directed by his drill sergeant. The platoon guide turned in about $50.00 to purchase the drill sergeant's top.

The platoon guide was not just an ordinary platoon guide. This trainee was a student at Texas Agriculture and Military (Texas A&M) from Bryan-College Station. He was in a special program wherein he could go to basic training and AIT during the summer and still go into the United States Army as a commissioned officer. Well, the platoon guide knew that this was not what he was being taught at Texas A&M. So he went to the senior drill sergeant and reported what the drill sergeant had asked him to do. The senior drill went to the company commander and reported the incident to him. The drill sergeant was charged with taking money from a training for personal use. The drill sergeant was a career soldier with nineteen years in the army. The company commander elected to punish him under the non-judicial punishment code (Article 15). His punishment was a disqualification from drill sergeant duty and forfeiture of pay, and he was asked to file for retirement as soon as possible.

Drill sergeants are there to train new recruits and mold them into soldiers that will always carry out their mission with the utmost pride and professionalism. A dishonest drill sergeant is ineffective in carrying out this mission for the army.

Another case in my company was when we were on the Hand Grenade Course. We had different classes going on prior to sending the trainees to execute a live hand grenade throw. We had to teach them the proper throwing techniques. The holding area is just prior to sending them to the start point. The cadre were standing behind the trainees at the holding area. As we were observing the trainees, two of them left the holding area and went to use the wood line near the impact area

(Exploding Hand Grenades). One of the First Platoon drill sergeants went to retrieve them from the wood line, and when he returned with them, he was yelling at the top of his voice. He was cursing them like two sailors at a bar. The problem was that an inspector from another unit was on the range with us and observed the drill sergeant cursing the trainees. The inspector left the range, and within thirty minutes, a major from the Judge Adjutant General's (JAG) office was present and asked to see our company commander and the drill sergeant. We summoned the company commander and they talked. After a few minutes, the drill sergeant was called over to see them both. The conversation was very short, the drill sergeant left the range with our company commander, and they followed the JAG officer back into garrison.

By the time we completed training and returned to our company, the drill sergeant had gotten all his gear and was out of our company. The last we were told was that the drill sergeant was transferred to another company while awaiting punishment. Trainees can be frustrating at times because of some of the things they do, and that is why they are trainees. They don't know any better. Again, leaders must handle very intense and dangerous situations with calmness and professionalism. We are there to train, lead, and protect our trainees. We are not there to abuse them in any way. Their moms and dads entrust us with their sons and daughters' lives, and they want us to be a positive example for them.

We had a serious incident in one of our earlier cycles where our company was tasked with an experiment the army was conducting. It was on water purification. The test was to see if soldiers in the field would fill up their canteens with water from a pond or stream if it was flavored. To make drinking the water more enticing, the trainees were issued flavored water purification tablets to drop in their canteens when it was time to fill it up with water. They were issued different flavors the morning of the experiment: grape, cherry, orange, and strawberry. It was late spring in the month of May time frame, and it was hot and muggy at Fort Benning. We were moving through the woods practicing our patrolling techniques at a good speed, and we stopped at a pond to fill our canteens, and everyone seemed normal with no complaints. The trainees all went and filled their canteens up and dropped their flavored tablets in in their filled canteen. At about 2:00 PM, one of the trainees yelled, "Drill Sergeant Kinsey, Private Ladowski is down!"

I immediately radioed Senior Drill Sergeant Kinman to meet me with the truck on the hardball road near our training area. I left Drill Sergeant Hiles with the platoon and took Private Ladowski and put him in the back of the truck, then Drill Sergeant Kinman drove off to Martin Army Hospital. While Drill Sergeant Kinman drove the truck, I loosened Private Ladowski's clothing and boots and tried to get him to respond to me. He would just groan. I took out my canteen and began to give him water. He was dehydrated to the point of heat exhaustion.

We made it to the hospital, and the medics were waiting for us. As soon as we arrived, they put in an IV and took him away and into a room a waiting. Drill Sergeant Kinman and I waited to find out about Private Ladowski's condition. After about thirty minutes, they came out and told us that he was going to be okay and that he was suffering from severe heat exhaustion. They said that they were going to keep him overnight. We were very relieved and glad that Private Ladowski was going to be okay.

On the way back to the company, I checked his canteen, and it was full of water. We assessed that he was not drinking the flavored water. We realized that some of the trainees wouldn't drink the pond water even though it was disguised through flavoring. They would not drink that water under any circumstances. We halted the water purification testing immediately. We would not continue the test for fear that other trainees would do the same as Private Ladowski and others in our company.

Ladowski was from Massachusetts, and this time of year it's still a little cool, but in Georgia, it's hot and muggy in early May. His not drinking water made him a prime candidate for heat exhaustion. This was a lesson learned for everyone. The trainees should have said that they couldn't drink the water, and for us, we should not have assumed that every trainee would drink the water. We should have asked for volunteers to participate in the experiment and to check to ensure that our trainees were drinking water, whether it was flavored pond or regular water. Private Ladowski had a temporary setback for a few days, but he did graduate as an infantry soldier.

One of the most unbelievable events in American history happened during the time I was on the trail. The space shuttle exploded in midair, and I just couldn't believe what I saw. Family, friends, colleagues, peers, and fans were in total disbelief that this was unfolding in front of them. The flight seemed so routine when it launched. The nation's first teacher in space was an extraordinary partnership with NASA. I traveled to Washington, DC and to Arlington National Cemetery to see their gravesite, and it's a very chilling experience. You tend to relive that moment in time once you approach the gravesite and view their pictures. It was an incredibly sad that day for all Americans.

My time on the trail was ending. It was time for me to go to the recruiting course at Fort Benjamin Harrison, Indiana. I would leave my family in Cusseta until I return from school. One of my best friends from childhood was stationed there, Robert Davis. Robert and I enlisted together and went to basic training together. When I arrived, he came over to the student battalion, and we caught up on what was going on back home. It was great having a little downtime from the trail. School was a breeze for me, and before I knew it, school was over and it was time return to Fort Benning and wait for my new assignment on recruiting duty.

Recruiting Duty

Three weeks after returning to Fort Benning, I received orders for the Los Angeles Recruiting Battalion. I immediately called the battalion sergeant major (SGM) and asked to be assigned outside of the Los Angeles area. The SGM said that he would see what he could do. A week later, I received a phone call from SSG Michael Boatwright, station commander for the New Hall Recruiting Station. He said, "Welcome to the New Hall Recruiting Station." I introduced myself and asked him what it was like there. He said, "It's sunny California and the gunslingers are alive and well."

Gunslinger was the self-appointed name given by the recruiters in the station. It fitted well considering that this town was where William S. Hart lived. He was involved in the spaghetti Westerns that we saw on television during my childhood. The local high school was named in his honor, William S. Hart High School. I told SSG Boatwright that I would be out there within three weeks. We moved to California for recruiting duty. We moved to Edwards Air Force Base, California, which was about forty miles north east of New Hall.

There were already three recruiters in the station (SSG Boatwright, SSG Morrow, and SSG Powell). I was SSG Powell's replacement. He had requested a transfer to another recruiting station down in Los Angeles. He went to the Glendale Recruiting Station. The station had three high schools in its jurisdiction: Sargus High, Canyon Country High, and Hart High. I was assigned to Hart High after SSG Powell left. I also had to assume SSG Powell's Delayed Entry Program (DEP) recruits. These are the people who have signed up to go into the army but have not left for their training. My responsibility was to ensure that these DEPs don't incur any law violations, don't become overweight, and more than anything else, they must ship. We had our DEPs come in once a week to ensure that they were still motivated to leave on time and were within the army's height and weight standards. SSG Powell had two DEPs that he had not seen in over two months, and that made me feel very uneasy of being assigned his DEPs. One of them had moved out of the area, and I had no clue what he looked like. The other DEP, SSG Powell, I could never catch at home; he worked at Magic Mountain. Magic Mountain was Los Angeles' state theme park, and a lot of teenagers work there.

The recruiting station was shared between all four major branches of military services. The army, air force, marines, and navy each had offices in the same building. We were members of the San Fernando Valley Recruiting Company, and Captain Phyllis Spivey was our company commander. Our Military Entrance Processing Station (MEPS) was located downtown Los Angeles in Englewood.

The first thing I wanted to do was get all my new DEPs in, introduce myself to them, and start seeing them once a week until they ship. I got ahold of the one that moved out of the area (Steve Huizinga), and he agreed to come to the recruiting station the next Saturday morning to talk to me. The other one (Robert Sanchez) that was missing in action, I couldn't reach him by phone. I had to go by his house around 11:00 PM to catch him home. He too was working and could not be reached. I introduced myself and explained to him that I needed to see him every week prior to him going to MEPS. It was done; I had contacted all five of my new DEPs, and they were going to meet me on Saturday.

On Saturday, all the DEPs showed up except Steve. I went ahead and weighed in everyone, and all but one made weight, and if I had to guess who wouldn't make weight, it would certainly be Robert Sanchez. Robert was just three weeks away from shipping and he was 17 pounds overweight. I told him that he must meet me every morning at 7:00 AM at the recruiting station for morning PT. I told him that he could not eat any more sugar, and had to slow down on the carbohydrates and drink plenty of water. Steve Huizinga called me and said that he got called in for work and said that he was sorry for not making it, but he would come in on Monday morning to talk to me.

Monday morning at 7:00 AM, Robert did show up, and he and I exercised and ran for about a mile initially. I conducted phone power (called high school graduates) between 9:00 AM and 10:00 AM. Steve came in at 10:30 AM, and he and I mapped out our plan for him to make his ship date. He was not overweight and still wanted to ship. He was trying to pay off some bills prior to going in the military.

Our plan was for me to meet Steve at MEPS upon his ship date. His parents were going to drop him off at MEPS. I felt a lot better about the recruits that we already had in the pool, but I have not yet put a person in the military. Those recruits belong to someone else, not me. I would have phone power of the 5:00 PM for high school seniors.

First High School DEP

I got a kid to come into the station that went to Hart High. His name was Ken Chapin, and his dad was a retired lieutenant colonel in the air force. He and I talked for over an hour, and his heart was set on being an air force firefighter. Well, the air force couldn't get the job for him right after graduation. I asked him, "What if the army can guarantee you the job and you will leave within a month of graduation?"

He said, "I would go into the army if you can do it, but you must talk with my dad."

Ken was very popular at Hart High School. He was on the diving team and was very good, but he wanted to be a firefighter. Ken set up a meeting with me and his family. I went over to his home and introduced myself to his father and him likewise. He said that he was fine with him going into the army if he gets what he wants, and he wants to be a firefighter. His dad said that if he could remember, Ken has always wanted to be a firefighter.

So I closed with, "If we can't get him the job as a guarantee, then I will bring him home without him signing up."

The next day, I went by Hart High School to introduce myself to the school counselor, Mrs. Paul. The meeting went fine until I asked to see Ken Chapin, and she snapped. "What do you want to see Ken for?"

I said, "I need to ask him some questions. I found out that we are going to send him to MEPS next week."

She said, "He's going into the army, Ken Chapin?"

I said, "Yes, ma'am, he is going in as a firefighter."

"The army has firefighters?" she asked.

I said, "Yes, ma'am. They protect our military installations against fires." I said, "We are just like any other community. We have firefighters, police, doctors, and lawyers."

She looked at me in amazement and finally regained her composure and had her runner locate Ken and had him come to her office to see me. Ken stopped by, and I explained to him that he needed to bring his birth certificate and Social Security card with him next when I pick him up to take him to MEPS.

Mrs. Paul said to Ken, "Sergeant Kinsey said that you are going to be a firefighter."

He said, "Yes, ma'am. I hope to be leaving early summer."

We both left at that point. I went back to my office and started calling follow-up prospects until the end of the day.

The next morning, Robert showed up and he said, "Sergeant Kinsey, I am sore all over." I said, "That is to be expected; you will feel better in the coming days."

We continued our workout routine, and Robert was fine. I told Robert that we would weigh him in after the first week of workouts. On Saturday, Robert weighed in, and he had lost two pounds. We were both very happy, and I told him that he must continue working on losing the weight. On Sunday, I took Ken down to the hotel in Englewood, next door to the Forum where the Lakers basketball team played. The bus would pick him up the next day and take him to the MEPS station for a physical and get his job guarantee. The physical would take him most of the day, and he should arrive at the counselor's office for his job around 3:00 PM. I left my office in New Hall about 2:00 PM to be there for his job. I got there, and Ken had already seen the counselor, and Ken told me that they couldn't get the job for him.

I told him to wait on me in the waiting room while I go talk to the counselor. I went in and talked to the counselor, and I told them that the kid was not going to enlist for anything but firefighter. I told them that I had already talked to Captain Spivey about it, and she said that we shouldn't have a problem.

The counselor said, "Okay, give me time to hit the ROCK (Exception to Policy) and see what I can do."

It is now 5:00 PM and the counselor has not given me any news, and at this point I am very disappointed that we may not be able to get him the job. A few minutes later, the counselor came out and said, "We got it, but I won't have it in a contract form until Tuesday because all the systems are now closed."

I said, "No problem, Ken, you all right with that?"

He said, "Yes."

We left for Ken's house, and my biggest obstacle now was to convince his dad that he has the job. We made it to Ken's house, and his dad was waiting for us to get there. We went inside, and I began to explain what happened about the no-written contract, but he does have the job.

His dad simply said, "No contract, he won't ship."

I left and went home. The next day, I was on the phone with Captain Spivey, the counselor at MEPS, and anyone else that would get me paperwork guaranteeing Ken that he was going to be a firefighter. We finally got it through the counselor's office, and I went and picked it up and took a copy to Mr. Chapin that evening.

Mr. Chapin said, "I am impressed by the army sergeant. You said that you were going to make it happen, and you did."

I said, "Yes, sir. We guarantee all our jobs. It's just that some are a little difficult to acquire than others." I told him that I could place people in the infantry, armor, and field artillery all day long, but some of our more technical and rare jobs are much harder to obtain.

Ken was one of the most significant DEPs I had in the pool. He was from Hart High School, which is famous for sending 95 percent of its students on to college. Most of its juniors and seniors drove to school in expensive cars. They lived in Valencia and New Hall, where a typical mortgage could run you about $2,700 plus per month, and this was in 1986. His name was mentioned often in conversation when I was conducting phone power with high school students.

First Female High School DEP

I began calling off my female name list, and a student named Rachael Middison agreed to an appointment. She came in, and we talked about the medical and administration fields, and she said that she would take the ASVAB test just to see if she would qualify. I knew if she went to Hart High, she would pass the ASVAB. I decided to give her the practice ASVAB in our office, and she did very well on it.

Rachel was friends with another DEP (Sarah Winston) that SSG Boatwright had put in. On the day that Rachel was going to MEPS, Rachael asked us if Sarah could go with her, and we said yes. We decided to take Rachael down in the evening so that she could take the ASVAB test that evening and the physical the next morning. Everything went well with Rachael as we predicted She did very well on the ASVAB test, and she scored very well in the areas she needed to get either one of the jobs that we had discussed that she wanted.

Later in the evening, Rachael came out of her physical with no problems and it was time to look for a job for her. She decided that she would go into the administration field. The counselors got her the job, and Rachel was happy. We returned to the recruiting station later that evening from MEPS, and Rachel and Sarah went home.

On the upcoming Saturday, all DEPs were to report to our office for updates and weigh-ins. All my DEPs showed up except Steve. I knew that Steve would probably not make it due to the distance and his commitment to meeting me at MEPS on his ship date. Robert and I continued to exercise each morning to help him lose weight. The DEPs were starting to ship, and I began to relax a little because if one doesn't ship, I must replace them. With everything going as I hoped with Sergeant Powell's DEPs, I must continue to enlist people into the army myself because I get no credit for the DEPs of Sergeant Powell.

Army Ranger

I called up a graduate named Greg Masada. He agreed to an appointment at the station. He and I sat down and discussed how we would sign him up as an army ranger. I asked him if does he have what it takes to become an army ranger, and he said yes. I asked, "Why do you want to be a ranger?"

He said, "Those guys are tough."

I said, "Yes, and those guys go through a lot of tough training that you may not be able to go through."

He insisted that he could go through the same training without any problems. I tried everything I could to talk Greg out of enlisting as an army ranger. We went to take the ASVAB test, and he scored in the 70s on the test, which will easily qualify him for Ranger School. I asked him if he had been to college, and he said, "Yes, but I want to be a ranger." He also said that he and his dad got into it, and he kicked him out of the house.

I asked, "Why did he kick you out of the house?"

He said, "Well, I wrecked several vehicles that he bought me. The last one was a four-runner. I just rolled it not too far from my house." Greg also wanted to leave right away.

I said, "Okay, Greg, we need to get your birth certificate and Social Security card for your enlistment."

He said, "I need to call my dad and ask him to leave the door unlocked so I can get my documents." Greg called his dad, and his dad agreed to leave the door open so he could get his personal information.

The next day, Greg was dropped off at the recruiting station, and he and I left for his house. I drove several miles outside of New Hall, and finally we turned up a driveway that was quite long. As we were coming up to the house, just off to the left was a helipad, and about 300 or 400 feet from it was a recreation house with pool tables and a swimming pool on the other side. The main house was directly in front of us, and it was one of the biggest mansions I had ever seen.

I asked, "Are you sure we are at the right place?"

He said, "Yes, my dad is a heart surgeon, and he flies to work to Los Angeles every day."

I said, "Why didn't you just go to college and stop partying and trashing your vehicles?"

He said, "I don't want to go to college. I want to do something different."

I asked, "Does he know that you are going into the military?"

Greg said, "Yes, and in fact, he suggested I go into the military for now until I make up my mind as to what I want to do as a career." He was staying with a friend and needed some money to help pay them for staying there, and he asked me if I would buy his guitar.

I said, "Your guitar? I don't know how to play a guitar."

Greg said, "Sergeant Kinsey, you can learn or just sell it to someone else."

So, I did give him a $100 for the guitar and to this day, I still have Greg's guitar. We did get Greg to Army Ranger School as an enlistment guarantee. Greg did ship, and I never saw him again. There are many reasons soldiers never see their recruiters again. I hope Greg did well with the rangers and in the army.

Robert and I were on our fourth week of working out and trying to get him prepared to ship. He has now lost twelve of the seventeen pounds that he needed to lose to ship. We both were very happy. Steve Huizinga did ship on time, and Julie I had not heard from in a few weeks. Ken was at every DEP function and was ready to go. Meanwhile, SSG Boatwright and SSG Morrow had motorcycles, and they were hinting at maybe I should get one. I asked them if they knew of anyone that may have a used bike, and SSG Boatwright said, "Yes, I know just the guy. SSG Brawley, the company trainer."

I called SSG Brawley and asked him about his bike, and he said, "Yeah, I have a Honda 750 I will let you have for $1,200."

I said, "I will buy it." I picked it up and took it out for a ride, and it rode very good. Occasionally, we would shut down the station during lunch and go riding in the mountains. It was a great stress reliever to hop on your bike and just ride. It helped me also when riding to and from work; the gas bill went down.

The Harsh Reality of Los Angeles

I had an applicant who moved to New Hall, but he used to live in South Central Los Angeles and we had to go down there and get a police check on him. SSG Morrow and I went down there to get the police check. We entered the area, and I knew that I was in a different world when I looked around and saw that police officers had pulled over a car and the occupants of the car were sitting on the ground handcuffed with certain valuables on the top of the car. Not a block away, I saw police officers rushing into an apartment building and bringing out residents of that apartment and putting handcuffs on them and placing them on the ground.

As we approached the building, we had to go through a metal detector. This was quite different from New Hall. When you see a police officer in New Hall, they are normally just passing by. It was also different from the little town of Norman Park that I left behind a few years earlier for economic reasons. Being in this environment made me feel that I had to be on my guard always for safety reasons. I found myself constantly looking around and scanning everyone who approached me for guns. Walking from my car to the police station was a walk of constant observation of the area. We acquired the police check and left for New Hall.

As we were leaving the police station and driving back through the neighborhood, that feeling returned. I looked over at SSG Morrow, and he looked terrified until we reached the freeway. Once we were on the freeway, SSG Morrow said, "Wow, did you see how busy the police were down there?"

I said, "Yeah, they were very busy."

He said, "Man, I am glad to be heading back to New Hall."

I said, "Yeah, we are very lucky to be stationed up there."

He said, "I don't see how the guys down here do it."

The names Compton and Carson are well known for gang violence throughout Los Angeles and the United States.

I remember watching the news one evening, and the Cripps and Bloods were in a shootout, and close to twenty young men were killed and many others were wounded. It was one of the worst shootouts that Los Angeles has had with the rival gangs. About a week later, I was carrying an applicant to the hotel, and on the freeway I saw one of the most astonishing things ever: Eleven hearses one after the other going down the freeway, and each one of them had a blue bandana in the right rear window blowing in the wind. It was one of the gangs burying their young. There was a constant stream of vehicles following the hearses. Gang violence represents a good portion of deaths in Los Angeles each year; thus this was a sad week in the city's history.

SSG Boatwright's Worst Nightmare

In the meantime, back at the station, some good and bad news were called in from the company commander. The good news was that SSG Boatwright made the promotion list, and the bad news was that he had to pass the Army Physical Readiness Test (APFT). As soon as I hit the door from MEPS, SSG Boatwright said, "SFC Kinsey, I need your help."

I said, "Sure, what can I do to help?"

He said, "You must get me to pass the APFT."

I said, "Do you see that thing in your right hand?" He said, "What, this?" (Pointing to his cigarette that he was smoking.)

I said, "Yes. You must reduce the number of sticks that you smoke every day. You must start eating healthier and you must work out with me and Robert every day."

He said, "SFC Kinsey, that's why I am a career recruiter. I don't like working out."

I said, "If you want to be promoted, this is what's going to do it for you."

He said, "Okay, let's do it."

I said, "Okay, I will see you at 7:00 AM."

He said, "In the morning?"

I said, "Yes, in the morning!"

He nodded his head backward and forth, indicating agreement with me. The next morning at 7:00 AM, Robert and I began our workout routine, and about twenty minutes later, SSG Boatwright showed up. We stopped training, and I asked him, Was he serious about working out, and he said yes. And I said, "Why are you late?"

He said, "I got a slow start this morning."

I looked at him and said, "We are finished," and Robert and I left. I went to the Racket Club to take a shower and get ready for work. I went to the recruiting station a little to 8:00 AM, and SSG Boatwright was already there at his desk. I walked in, and he got up from his desk and walked to mine and he stood there and said, "SFC Kinsey, I apologize for this morning, and I promise you tomorrow morning, I will be on time."

I simply said okay and started pulling out my planning guide. Later that day, he came over to my desk and said, "Hey Kinsey, everything all right?"

I said, "Yes, I am fine."

He said, "Hey, I am going to be on time."

The next morning, I drove up at 6:50 AM, and he and Robert were waiting for me. He said, "See, I told you I would be here."

I said, "Outstanding." I said, "Okay, let's go to work."

We started off with stretching and then push-ups, sit-ups, side-straddle hops, and finally what everyone hates, the run. I told SSG Boatwright that we were going to start him off with one mile, and he wouldn't have to run the entire mile. He had to run, walk, run, and walk the mile. The run would be a very slow shuffle, and the walk had to be at a brisk pace. We started off running a very slow shuffle, and SSG Boatwright made it about 100 feet before stopping.

I told Robert to continue his routine while I work with SSG Boatwright. I said to him, "Hey, Boatwright, you don't have to run right now, but you must continue walking even if it's not at a brisk pace. Just keep walking."

He said, "Kinsey, I don't know if I can do it."

I said, "You are the best recruiter in this battalion. You are not going to let a little workout beat you? Look what you have waiting on you after you pass the APFT. You will have SFC E-7. Man, that's hard to make in our MOS." I said to him, "Come on, SFC Boatwright. You can make it, you can do it, it's easy."

He started walking, and we walked the entire mile. He was gasping for air, and I repeatedly told him that he could make it. We reached the office, and he was more than exhausted. He was outright beaten physically. I told him to make sure that he drinks at least four glasses of water before he comes back to work.

I arrived at the office about 9:00 AM, and Boatwright arrived about 10:30 AM and he was walking very slowly. He reached his desk and the first thing he pulled out was a cigarette and he lit it up and began to smoke.

I said, "How many have you had today, SSG Boatwright?"

He said, "If I hadn't met you this morning, I would have had about four by now, but I have been hurting so much since then that I have only had one today."

I said, "That's good, just get up from your seat every once in a while and walk around the station so that you can loosen those muscles so that you will be ready for our workout tomorrow morning."

He said, "Okay."

The next morning, he did show up on time. This time after the warm-up exercises, we started walking first so that he could build up to the run. He still had an extremely hard time getting through the mile. We continued this routine for several weeks, and he finally began to show some progress. He could run-walk a mile within twelve minutes. It would have been awful on the APFT, but for him and where he came from, it was great news. In the third week, we were down to ten and a half minutes. The time to beat for his age was two miles within sixteen minutes and fifty-five seconds. Running two continuous miles was another feat that we must accomplish. In the fifth week, we started running and walking two miles, and we had a little minor mental setback. His mind was telling him that he couldn't do it. I had to dangle the carrot back in front of his face. I reminded him of what the promotion would mean to him and his family, not to mention the prestige of being a senior noncommissioned officer. He began to refocus on why we were doing this hard work. After three weeks of this two-mile routine, I decided to time him. I ran with him during the timing to help motivate him to stick with the two-mile run. We started off and he seemed to be doing good but at a slow pace. We made it to the finish line in eighteen minutes and forty seconds. We had two weeks to get him ready for the APFT. We continued to work out and the closest we could get him to the time was eighteen minutes and twenty-five seconds.

The day of reckoning was finally here. All the recruiting stations met at our company location to conduct our annual APFT. We all got on the track, and everyone knew what was at stake for SSG Boatwright. He must pass the APFT, or he wouldn't be promoted to SFC E-7. I decided to risk me not passing the APFT to help SSG Boatwright pass his so that he could earn his promotion. We started off again a little slow on the run. I kept telling him that we were a little behind time. I was constantly talking to him to keep his mind off the run. We crossed the one-mile marker at eight minutes flat, which gave us a little cushion.

I told him that we were forty seconds behind and that we had to make it up during the second mile. I tried to keep him on the pace that we were on, but it was very difficult because he started to tire and slow down. I began to lean into him as far as talking to him. Trying to keep him motivated was getting harder. His body was telling him to stop, but I kept telling him not to listen to it. I was running alongside him, letting him know that if he fails, I fail, and that we were in it together. He didn't stop, he just kept going and going, and as we reached the finish line, Captain Spivey yelled out sixteen minutes and ten seconds.

He said, "Hey, we did it."

I said, "Yes, you did it, you passed the test."

The entire group came over and congratulated SSG Boatwright on passing the test and earning his promotion. Captain Spivey got everybody together and said, "Congratulations to SFC Boatwright on passing the APFT and earning his promotion." She also said, "I want to give a special thanks to SFC Kinsey for whipping his station commander into shape so that he could pass his APFT."

The Gunslingers

Robert Sanchez and the rest of SSG Powell's DEPs have all shipped by now. We had a great year of recruiting at our station. It was almost time for our annual banquet. At the end of each recruiting year, the battalions have banquets, and they recognize the top recruiting stations by category or size. We already knew that we had won the top medium station for the year based on statistics. SFC Boatwright said, "Let's dress like gunslingers this year."

We went to Glendale and found a costume shop, and they had everything we needed for the role of gunslingers. We were totally decked out in Western wear for the banquet, from our cowboy hats down to the spurs on our cowboy boots. We each had a set of .45 caliber pistols in holsters and the three-quarter trench coat.

On the night of the banquet, we waited until everyone was at their tables before we entered the room. As we walked in, people were going, "Aww, look at them. Where are they from?"

We made it to our table and before we sat down, Boatwright said, "We are the gunslingers of New Hall, the Top Medium Recruiting Station in the State of California." Every table from the San Fernando Recruiting Company went wild. We ate our dinner, and it was now time to receive awards.

Each company under the Los Angeles Recruiting Battalion took turns handing out their awards. It was now time for Captain Spivey to pass out our awards.

Reseda received the Top Small Station award. Lancaster received the Top Large Station award. Captain Spivey said, "And now, for the Top Medium Station, New Hall." The three of us got up and went to receive the award, and the entire building was shaking from the applause we received. People wanted us to stay up there so they could take pictures of us in our outfits. It was such a memorable event that will never forget it.

Time with the Kids

Spending time with the kids after my last assignment (Fort Benning) was always important. We would often play touch football on Sundays.

Sometimes, we would go to the recreation center and play pool, foosball, or ping pong. We were still moviegoers as well. The kids and I would go to a baseball shop. There, you could buy or bid on baseball cards. If you were the highest bidder, then you would win the card. There were some good cards up for bid each Saturday. There were Will Clark, Darrell Strawberry, Dion Sanders, Bo Jackson, and many more from that era. The one that we are most proud of winning is a Ted Williams All-Star card. We have the complete sets of some years still in its original package. Collecting baseball cards was one of the most fun times that we have ever had together.

I remember us driving back to Georgia on vacation, and it took us three days to make the trip. By then, I had gotten a van so that everyone could have travel space. On the way home, we went to San Antonio, Texas, so that we could visit the Alamo. We pulled up to go visit the Alamo, and my initial impression was, "Wow, I thought it was bigger than this." The kids didn't know the difference. They just knew that they were at the infamous Alamo of Davy Crockett. The trip was just me and the kids. The wife and I were separated at the time. Unfortunately, time was nearing an end of our relationship. Being with the kids took a lot worry, stress, and aggravation out of the equation, at least, for me. The kids and I pressed on to Georgia and visited their grandparents, aunts, uncles, and cousins. We all had a great time back home, and after several days visiting, we returned to California.

It was time to refocus on putting civilians in boots. Late in the evening, I began phone power, and I talked to a female from my high school list. Her name was Stephanie Behrens. I asked her what she thought about the military and that Ken Chapin had joined as an army firefighter.

She said, "Ken is going into the army?"

I said, "Yes, he is going to be an army firefighter." I said, "Would you be interested in hearing a little bit more what the army can offer?"

She said, "I don't mind." Then she followed up with, "Can you call me back?"

I called her back about thirty minutes after the initial call. She answered the phone and asked me if I could come talk to her parents. I said, "Yes, when?"

She said, "You can come over at 7:30 PM tonight."

I said, "I will be there."

I looked up her address on my high school female list, and I knew there was something wrong with the way she wanted me to talk to her parents. She lived in one of the wealthiest neighborhoods in Valencia, California. I told SFC Boatwright that I shouldn't go because Stephanie is probably going to UCLA once she finishes high school. He agreed but said, "You should go anyway, because you promised."

I left for Stephanie's house and I knew that this was the wrong thing to do. As I was driving up to her driveway, all I could see was the house. I got out of the car and walked down the sidewalk, and I was now observing the front door. The front door was huge and had so much stained glass that it looked like it could have cost more than what I get paid in a year. I rang the doorbell and Stephanie's mom answered the door. She said, "Would you please come in, sir?"

I said, "Yes, ma'am."

She seated me in the living room and offered me some coffee and coffee cake.

I said, "Thank you, ma'am."

Her husband immediately came out, introduced himself, and sat down. Mr. Behrens explained to me that he worked as an engineer with Lockheed aircraft. We talked about the military for a short time, and the subject was switched to just everyday things. I knew that their plans were for Stephanie to attend college, and they didn't want to sound impolite. As I was leaving, I said to them that I wished Stephanie well in college, and they smiled and said thank you.

South Korea, a Second Tour

As time moved on, I earned my gold recruiting badge within the first year on recruiting status. This was a rare achievement for most recruiters. It normally takes about two to three years to earn the gold recruiting badge. I was sent back to Fort Benjamin Harrison, Indiana, for the Station Commander Course. Captain Spivey appointed me station commander of the Lancaster Recruiting Station.

A lot of things happened over the next three years in Lancaster. The station won Top Recruiting Station, I became divorced, and my oldest brother passed away. I received orders to go back to South Korea for a second time. I didn't dispute or try to change the orders; I just got prepared to go. Departing for South Korea was just a few months away; I had a lot of loose ends to tie up. My kids would remain with my ex-wife until I return from overseas. My oldest son, Danny, enlisted into the army, and he left a month prior to me departing for South Korea. He went to Fort Bliss, Texas, to become a Stinger (Man-Portable Air Defense System) gunner. Danny went into my career field, air defense artillery. I did remarry (Marlee Meadows) just days prior to leaving for South Korea.

I landed at Kimpo International Airport in South Korea on July 23, 1990, and this time it was very hot and humid. The last time I was in South Korea, the president was Park Chung-hee, and he was assassinated in 1979. The president this time was Roh Tae-woo. The North Korean President was still Kim Il-sung.

The two Koreas are separated at the 38th parallel, and the Demilitarized Zone (DMZ) is a neutral point of separation. We were bussed from Kimpo to Camp Corner for processing. I was further assigned to an air defense battery called RC-4, and battalion headquarters was located at Camp Stanton South Korea. RC-4 was about five kilometers just below Munson, South Korea. Munson was on the border of the DMZ. We were as far north as you could go without being in North Korea. RC-4 was a small army post. It had a very small PX, a small theater that seated about eighty people, a mess hall, and living quarters for the soldiers. Our motor pool (vehicle storage area) was at the other end of the small village of Song Do. RC-4 was commanded by Captain Tripp. RC-4 had a Headquarters Platoon, a Chaparral Platoon, a Vulcan Platoon, and a Stinger Platoon.

I was appointed platoon sergeant of Fourth Platoon Stinger. I had four Stinger sections in my platoon; each Stinger section consisted of four Stinger teams; each Stinger team consisted of a team chief and a gunner/driver. My platoon provided an air defense section for the unit that's occupying Warrior Base.

Their mission was to provide air defense protection for that unit while at Warrior Base and to integrate into their convoy when the protected unit departs Warrior Base for garrison back across the Bridge of the Americas. The Stinger Platoon also provides air defense for armor, field artillery, and infantry units when they deploy.

Extreme Hardship for Civilians

Three weeks into my tour of duty, I got a phone call from back home. It was my new wife saying that she was at the Korean Consulate in Los Angeles finalizing her paperwork to come to South Korea. She said, "You need to find an apartment. I will be there in three weeks."

I said, "Okay." I talked to Sergeant Roth because his wife was there. He took me to his landlord, and she (Mrs. Kim) did have an apartment available to rent for 300,000 won or $375.00 per month. Mrs. Kim said that I would have to go into Munson to talk to the electric company and gas company for the gas stove. The heat was through an Ondol system of heating. This system works through heating the floors in the house. The floors are made of mortar, and the warm air passes under the floor, thus heating it. Koreans are accustomed to sitting on the floor, sleeping on the floor, and working and eating at low tables instead of raised tables with chairs. On the outside of the house, the stove box would hold coal briquettes. Windows had to be vented to prevent carbon monoxide poisoning. This led to other technologies to heat other Korean homes. A briquette would last for several hours. The fire box or stove held three briquettes, and they needed to be changed every four or five hours.

Sergeant Roth went with me to Munson to get the electricity turned on and to have the gas company bring out a bottle of gas. The next stop was the phone company because if a soldier lives off post, they must have a phone to be contacted in case of an emergency or a recall alert. Everything was done now a week away from arrival. I found some furniture for the apartment just in time for her arrival.

I cleared it through my chain of command to have my driver take me to Kimpo Airport to pick her up. Kimpo was under two hours away by vehicle through normal travel time. We didn't anticipate the amount of traffic on the road to Kimpo. When we arrived at Kimpo, the airport was closed, and the armed guards were patrolling the entire airport. We weren't sure whether she was on the flight, so we went back to RC-4. When we arrived at RC-4, the sergeant on charge of quarters (CQ) caught me entering the door and said, "SFC Kinsey, your wife called. She is at a hotel outside of Kimpo, and she gave me a phone number."

I called and she gave me directions from the Kimpo Airport. My driver and I left again and arrived at the hotel. She had already been traumatized by the events at the airport. Apparently, she waited for us until the airport closed at 9:00 PM. After the airport closed, the ROK soldiers started patrolling the airport, and they told her that she had to leave the airport. Well, there were several taxi drivers still there, and this one taxi driver came up to her and said that his family had a hotel and that he could take her there until someone would come and get her. We arrived there, and she feared several things that she didn't understand. She couldn't believe that armed soldiers patrolled the airport. She couldn't believe that I was late in picking her up.

I immediately began to explain to her what a real hardship this tour was going to be. I said first, there's no McDonald's down the street; the nearest post exchange (grocery store) is about twenty miles and three bus exchanges away; you can only bring what you can carry on the bus; no television; can't drink the water; soldiers throughout this entire area; constant alerts; house with minimal furniture; when an alert sounds, you must be in RC-4 and go directly to our mess hall for evacuation; and much more. After that ordeal at the airport, it was very easy to explain why the refrigerator was only four feet high, and we were sleeping on a mattress on the floor.

The next day, she was put in contact with Sergeant Roth's wife, and my worries were somewhat over for a while. Meanwhile, I had a platoon to run, and I couldn't have any distraction. We trained practically seven days per week. The first Sunday she was in country, we had an alert (when the alert siren goes off, all soldiers in the village have fifteen minutes to be in the compound [installation], and all soldiers in the installation must be prepared to move to their tactical assembly area within two hours). It was mandatory that all the wives assemble in the mess hall for possible evacuation. Well, about twenty minutes prior to the wives boarding the Humvees and evacuating south to Seoul, the alert was called off. She now understood that the world she left in Los Angeles was nothing compared to the one she had entered. My explanation over the phone in trying to discourage her from coming had now become a reality.

The wives were released to go back home, but the soldiers had to turn in their weapons and ammunition, and we had to move our missiles back into storage.

It was 2:00 AM when I got home. I was up again at 4:30 AM, heading back on post for a 5:00 AM meeting with my platoon just prior to our morning physical training. The North Korean threat was and still is very real up on the border. My platoon was filled with soldiers that either had just arrived in the country or had been in the country for almost nine months. Our training schedule had us training for our annual Stinger certification. The annual Battalion certification would also determine who will fire a live missile during our annual live fire. There are several tasks such as map reading, aircraft recognition, target engagement, and fire commands on the evaluation that determines which Stinger gunner in the battalion will end up in first place and fire the Stinger missile. My platoon did win two of the three missiles that were going to be fired at the live fire range. Our platoon was ecstatic because the RC-4 had not fired a missile in the last four years per statistics. The soldiers were very proud of being a part of a winning team. The company commander praised them with the information, which made them feel glad that they were at RC-4. Some in the platoon were fresh out of AIT, and some had been in the service for a while but all of them worked as a team. That's what winning is all about; working together in a winning effort. Once they get a taste of winning, it became addictive; they worked harder, and they were more loyal to their company and to their platoon.

Next up, we were set to deploy on field maneuvers the following week. The wife wasn't happy that I would be gone for a week, but that's why Korea, for most soldiers, is like serving a hardship tour; wives are not encouraged to come. It is training for war 24/7 without rest or relaxation. The North Korean leader (Kim Il Sung) was very unpredictable, and we just didn't know what to expect of him from day to day.

When we deployed, each Stinger section deployed with the unit that they were defending. Once the company sets up the headquarters section and the company tactical operations center (TOC) was set up, my driver (PVT Cedric) and I began to check on each Stinger section. The field artillery unit out of Camp Casey was the closest protected unit, so we went there to check on our teams. We had all the team locations prior to departing for the field. We reached the location of team 2 of our first Stinger section, and they had not camouflaged their vehicle yet. They pointed out their firing location, but they had not completed their site setup, which indicated that the enemy could locate their position. I gave them some advice on how to get their camouflage nets up faster and more efficiently.

We moved on to inspect the next team's position. The next position we came upon was team 1 of the second Stinger section, and I was faced with the same deficiency; they had not camouflaged their position so that the enemy could not find their position.

The next team I inspected (team 3 from our second Stinger section) did have their camouflage nets up and in place, and they pointed out their firing position but could not tell me their alternate exit route of travel in case of a hasty exit from the enemy.

Finally, I reached team 4 from our second Stinger section, and they were camouflaged well, the firing position was good, and they had a good exit route, but their location was too close to the protected asset. The Stinger team must be far enough, away from the protected asset to engage the aircraft before it has an opportunity to attack the protected asset.

There were deployment issues with the other Stinger sections as well as the second Stinger section. The first week out on field maneuvers was lessons learned for the entire platoon. Our platoon was so close to the DMZ that we couldn't afford to make any mistakes if faced with having to go to war. I would always tell the platoon that we must "make it happen" the first time because where we are located, we may not get a second time to redo a mistake. We don't get "do overs" in war; you get the aftermath of a very bad situation. I would often tell the platoon that "the threat is real," and we will always train as if we were fighting the real enemy across the border. "If we are not training to protect ourselves or our protected assets, then we have lost the meaning of training." During our training meetings back in garrison, we addressed our deficiencies in the field, and we worked on them during training sessions on a weekly basis until they were acceptable.

Saddam Hussein Invades Kuwait

I had been in South Korea about a little over a month when Captain Trip huddled the company leadership team together in his office and told us that Saddam Hussein, the president of the Republic of Iraq, had invaded the Emirate of Kuwait. He said that we must train to standard because we don't know what will happen with the Gulf situation. It could get worse before it gets better. Captain Trip said, "We face a threat right here in Korea, and we must be ready to go to war always." After a series of updates on upcoming events, we were released. In October 1990, the urgency of the situation in Kuwait had finally happened.

All United States Army personnel assigned to the Republic of South Korea were hereby under "stop-loss," which means that we couldn't be reassigned back to the States until the United States Army lifted the "stop-loss" freeze on personnel. We had stopped getting a regular influx of soldiers replacing departing soldiers. Any soldier scheduled to depart the country after October 1990 was automatically extended in the country.

In late October 1990, everyone's permanent change of service (PCS) dates changed to 1997. Everyone was just astonished at that new PCS date. This led one to assume that the Pentagon couldn't afford to lose the number of troops in South Korea because of the North's unpredictable leader in Kim Il Sung. We had about 37,000 troops throughout South Korea. The fact that we were building up our war machine in another hemisphere and this dictator to the North was a loose cannon made those of us in South Korea feel a little uneasy to say the least. It made us in Korea train harder and harder because we knew if something happened over here, we had no backup. The United States Armed Forces and the ROK Army would be it as far as defending South Korea.

My oldest son, Danny, graduated from his AIT at Fort Bliss, Texas, and was on orders to go to Germany. I got a call from him, and he said that his orders were being revoked and he was being reassigned to Fort Bliss in the First Air Defense Brigade. I already knew why; the First Air Defense Brigade was a rapid deployment unit and was probably building up its forces in preparation to deploy to Kuwait if necessary.

After receiving that message from my son, it made me pay more attention to what was going on in Kuwait and listening to the news more. I was hoping that Saddam's forces would withdraw before we invaded Iraq. Saddam not only didn't withdraw his forces from Kuwait, but he annexed Kuwait and made it his nineteenth province. Iraq owed Kuwait over $14 billion in loans for financing the Iraqi–Iran War. Saddam asked the Kuwait government to forgive the loans, but they didn't. Saddam also accused them of slant drilling of oil. Instead of drill on a vertical angle, he accused them of drilling on an angle to siphon the Iraqi oil. The reason that almost everyone on the planet believes is that Iraq invaded Kuwait to take the oil fields bearing hundreds of oil wells.

After Iraq invaded Kuwait, Saddam installed Ala'a Hussein Ali as the prime minister and Ali Hassan al-Majid as the governor of Kuwait. Saddam sent the Emir of Kuwait (Jaber al-Ahmad al-Sabah) into exile.

The United Nations Security Council (UNSC), North Atlantic Treaty Organization (NATO), and all major world powers condemned the invasion. It was now mid- to late November, and it was getting very cold at night. I turned on the Armed Forces Korea Network (AFKN) news station, and most of the talk was about President Bush sending the troops into Kuwait to liberate them from Saddam Hussein's army. The Iraqi government was criticized by every country in existence to include our nemesis, the Soviet Union and China. The coalition was building up, and it was a done deal; we were going to liberate Kuwait from the Iraqi Army. Saddam Hussein had no intention of leaving Kuwait under any terms. He was bent on having Kuwait confirmed as the nineteenth province of Iraq as well as its oil fields. By now, the possibility that my son, Danny, may be sent off to war was becoming increasingly a reality as the troop build-up continued. Within weeks, he was on his way to the battlefield.

With the build-up of soldiers and equipment in Kuwait, many of us thought that Saddam would withdraw his soldiers from Kuwait. He didn't think that we would assist in removing his soldiers out of Kuwait. A week prior to his invading Kuwait, Ambassador April Glaspie had a conversation with Saddam, and she failed to make it clear to him that if he attacks Kuwait, we would intervene. Instead, she told him that America would not interfere with Iraq and its Arab neighbor's disputes. Many believed that Ambassador Glaspie's meeting with Saddam confirmed in his mind that the United States was not going to react militarily to his invading Kuwait.

The United States gave Saddam an ultimatum: be out of Kuwait by January 15, 1991, or face war.

On January 16, 1991, allied aircraft targeted Iraqi aircraft and destroyed them. In late February 1991, Kuwait was officially liberated, and the emir and his family returned to Kuwait. Operation Desert Shield became the code name for the build-up of coalition force to thwart Saddam and his forces. Operation Desert Storm was the codename for the actual Gulf War (January 17, 1991–February 28, 1991) against Iraq. Over 1,000 Kuwaiti civilians were killed, and over 300,000 civilians fled the country during the Iraqi occupation. I did receive a phone call from my son during the build-up just prior to the invasion. He was fine and was tired of waiting.

Once the invasion started, I lost contact with him until the ground war was over. George H. W. Bush was the president of the United States, Dick Cheney was the secretary of defense, Colin Powell was the secretary of the army, and Norman Schwarzkopf Jr. was the commander of all military forces in Iraq.

Our next field maneuvers were in early February, and it was still under 20 degrees. We trained in the field more during the wintertime because the rice paddies were still frozen and this gave us more land to train on. During the summer months, the rice paddies were flooded with water to grow the nation's chief product (rice).

I decided to check on our first Stinger section, which was attached to an infantry unit out of Camp Casey. Team 3 from the first section was Alfa Company, and we had to cross a river to gain access to their position. We arrived at the river too late to the high tide coming in. We had to camp out at the river until morning. I decided to sleep on the hood of my Humvee. I got my sleeping bag out and rolled it out on top of the vehicle's hood, and I took my boots off and slid into my sleeping bag while zipping it over my head because it was so cold outside. The next morning, I woke up under a foot of snow. My driver slept very well inside the vehicle, and he had the heater going and I could thaw out. The tide had gone down low enough that we could leave for the Stinger team.

We found the Stinger team so that I could inspect their position. By the time we arrived, they had already eaten breakfast and set up their position. Their position looked great. The training the platoon received during the past several months certainly paid off. I praised them for during a great job even under adverse weather conditions.

Fourth Platoon

Two weeks after I came to RC-4, PVT Washkill arrived, and he was a 16S (Stinger gunner). I assigned him to Sergeant Barnes's team. PVT Waskill was a hardworking soldier and a very quick learner. He would always be a step ahead of his peers when it came to just about everything. You ask for a volunteer, the first hand that went up was always PVT Waskill's. He reminded me of myself when I was a PVT. I had about twelve privates in my platoon. Three months after Waskill arrived in my platoon, I was allocated two slots for PFC in my platoon. Out of the twelve PVTs, Waskill outranked two of the soldiers, but he outworked all twelve of them. I promoted Waskill to PFC. I explained to my soldiers that they must meet the "whole soldier concept." Meaning that you must give me 110 percent effort in everything you do as a soldier, you must perform your military duties as a team, you must never be late for platoon or company formation, and be at work every day that you are a soldier.

About eight months later, I received a slot for Specialist 4th class E-4 rank (Spec-4). I had about ten soldiers at this point eligible for promotion to Spec-4. I had soldiers that had almost twenty-four months of service to their credit. Unitizing my philosophy for promotion (the whole soldier concept) made it less difficult for me to choose the person for the promotion. I had one soldier that thought that by him having a Stateside tour completed prior to coming to South Korea automatically put him ahead of everyone else. That is not an automatic path to promotion. My reasoning is that just by being in the military is part of the eligibility process, but what puts a soldier in the limelight is performance. This soldier did not perform to standards in the categories that mattered.

I observe training in a field environment, the motor pool, the barracks, individual equipment, personal appearance, conduct both on and off duty, loyalty to the unit, one's attendance at work every day, works well with his peers, and if a soldier excels in all those categories, then that soldier is looked at very closely for promotion to the next rank.

Out of the ten soldiers in my platoon, I had four soldiers that were following that philosophy of soldiering; however, PFC Waskill was still "head and shoulders" above his peers when it came to assessing all those qualities. He was my selection for Spec-4. It was an easy choice, and I am sure the other soldiers understood that his selection was fair and impartial.

My leaving this platoon behind was not easy. The soldiers in my platoon knew that I led them by example. When we had training, I was there with them; every physical training session and three- to six-mile run, I led them all the way. On the firing range, they saw me as a fire expert; I would always max my APFT. When my soldiers were in the field, I was in the field with them. If they had personal problems, I assisted them in solving it. If they needed something that would improve themselves or the platoon, then I got it for them. Above all else, their problems were my problem.

My son, Danny, did return to Fort Bliss safely to continue soldiering in the air defense corps. The summer of 1991 was a year after my flight into Kimpo International Airport, and I was still in South Korea. A vacancy opened in the Security and Intelligence office at the battalion level, and I applied for the job at battalion headquarters (Camp Stanton). I was interviewed by Captain Laterza (the S-2 officer).

The next day, Captain Laterza called me back into his office, and he told me, "You have the job, SFC Kinsey, provided you pass the security clearance checks." He said, "Wait a minute, you are the Stinger platoon sergeant, right?"

I said, "Yes, sir."

He said, "You already have a secret clearance. You start work as soon as the RC-4 company commander releases you."

I said, "Thank you, sir!"

Captain Trip was okay with the transfer. I went back over to Camp Stanton because I was told by one of the sergeants at Camp Stanton that the gate guard, Mr. Choi, had an apartment for rent just outside the gate at Camp Stanton. I talked to Mr. Choi, and he did have an apartment, and he said that he would rent it to me for 200,000 won or $250.00. I said I will take it.

Prior to moving to Camp Stanton, I went to visit the Stinger section that was at Warrior Base Camp in the DMZ. We patrolled along the border and observed the North Korean soldiers on the other side of the

DMZ though a periscope. We tuned into the guard post directly across from our guard post, and there were two North Korean guards sitting on the outside of their guard shack looking in our direction. We just stared at each other. Prior to me leaving for RC-4, I briefed my soldiers on my transfer to a battalion staff job, and I praised them for such a fine job during my tenure as their platoon sergeant. They thanked me for demanding that they give a 110 percent effort every day to their unit. One of the soldiers looked at me and said that it made them better men and better soldiers. I told them that I cared about each one of them, and I wanted them to make it home safe to their families.

After our visit, I was off to RC-4 to begin moving to my new assignment. My driver and several soldiers from my platoon assisted us in moving over to Camp Stanton. Notifying my soldiers in garrison and on the DMZ that I was leaving was very hard.

My New Platoon

Meanwhile, over at battalion headquarters, our 1SG decided to make me the headquarters platoon sergeant, which placed me in charge of our administrative staff, our cooks, our maintenance soldiers, our communication soldiers, and the rest of the battalion staff. Our 1SG knew that I had experience when it came to equipment inspections, uniform inspections, motor pool inspections, and barracks inspections. When we had our annual Inspector General's inspection, SFC Kinsey was always the go-to guy for advice.

My job in the S-2 shop was a challenge as well. We were the experienced staff for the North Korean threat in the country. Each day, Captain Laterza and I would receive classified information to analyze and pass on to the battalion commander. We would often receive North Korean propaganda flyers and leaflets that were passed off to the villages by North Korean sympathizers, and we would have them translated so that we would know what the latest tricks the North would try to use to gain support for their political cause. We briefed all officers entering the country on the North Korean air threat. Although it is probably still to this day classified in part, we knew where the North Korean air threat would be coming from and what corridors specific aircraft would enter South Korean airspace. We knew where the North Korean aircraft were based at in the north, the type of aircraft, their fighting capabilities, fuel range (this played a big role in their attack strategy), wheels-up times, and even the amount of their annual budget that is spent on their military. We knew where the air threat was coming from based on the layout of the land coming from the north; we had to plan a defense against that air threat. We were very much prepared for such a threat; our air defense units were very proficient and reliable. Our command and control of our deployed units was very well-organized, and our gunners were very accurate and detailed in target engagement. Our soldiers were prepared very well for the impending air threat from the north.

Leisure Time in South Korea

There were times that Marlee and I would go into Camp Casey to pick up some items to send home for Christmas and other occasions. We caught the bus to Camp Casey, and as we were getting off the bus, I noticed a soldier that I thought I had seen before. I went up to the soldier and asked him if his name was McCrary, and he said yes. I said, "Man, do you remember me back at Fort Sill, Oklahoma?"

He said, "Are you Moose Kinsey?"

I said, "Yes." I asked him what happened to him after the accident on the Howitzer (tank) at Fort Sill. He said that after the accident, he was taken to the hospital, and they treated him for his hand. McCrary said that he was a holdover in one of the units until his hand was functioning well enough to go to another unit and complete his training. He said that after the completion of his job skill training, he went from there to Germany. I told him that I thought that he was discharged and went back to Albany, Georgia.

He said, "No, I really wanted to be a soldier, and besides there was nothing for me back in Albany." He missed his bus back to Camp Hovey, and we talked for several hours just catching up on how our careers went through the years.

I was glad that SFC McCrary could stay in the army after such a horrific accident. SFC McCrary finally left to go back to his post, and we went on into town to shop for the holidays. We picked up several items to send back home, and we were off to the bus stop so that we could make it home before dark. We made it back to Camp Stanton before dark.

Lessons Learned

The next event on our headquarters company calendar was the annual Inspector General's (IG) visit. This visit was to ensure that each soldier and his equipment and living areas was up to the army's standards. Many of the soldiers and their sergeants had not gone through such an important inspection. I had a platoon meeting with all my section sergeants to brief them on the inspection layout and what the IG team was looking for during the inspection. I explained to them that the IG would be looking to see if they have all issued field equipment (TA-50), the serviceability of the equipment (is it usable), and the cleanliness of that equipment. In the barracks, the IG will be looking at each room to see if humans live there, and not animals (general room appearance to indicate room organization between roommates). They will also look for room cleanliness overall and no safety hazards in the room, such as too many wires running all over the room. The final check is to ensure that the room is not being used as a storage bend (laundry not piled up or a room full of boxes).

I told them that the IG inspection was only two weeks away, and I wanted them to pick a room in the barrack of one of their soldiers. I wanted it set up and have one of the soldier display his TA-50 on the floor of that same room in two nights. I would come over and inspect it myself. Everyone else in the platoon could come and see the standards for inspection. I also informed the section sergeants to put together a detail to clean common areas within and outside of the barracks area as well.

The sections came to my office at 7:00 PM to inspect the rooms that they had designated as pre-inspection rooms. I went to the barracks and entered the first room and stood in the doorway. I looked at the ceiling and it looked good; the walls had spider webs in the upper corners and along the crevices around the room; the windows still had dirt in crevices; under the bed had dust and spider webs, which indicated that the floor had not been washed, waxed, and buffed; the bed had dust on the headboard. I turned to the section sergeant and asked him, "Where were you when they were preparing this room for inspection?"

He said, "I was in and out of the room, checking on the other soldiers in the section."

I said to him, "It does you no good to check on others when you can't get the first one right." I told the section sergeant, "I wanted that room up to standards before anyone goes to bed tonight!" I turned to the other section sergeants and said, "I am sure your rooms are not ready either, so I will be back for inspection at 11:00 PM tonight." I walked out of the room and began to observe the hallway, and it was in unsatisfactory condition. I had the four section sergeants accompany me as I walked around the outside of the barracks, and the grass had not been cut, and I saw a cigarette butt lying on the ground. I turned to all four of them and said, "If this isn't done tomorrow, guess what we will be doing this weekend?"

One of the section sergeants said, "We will, Platoon Sergeant."

I said, "You are learning."

I walked over to the barracks about 9:30 PM to check the progress in each section, and I was quite pleased; the section sergeants were in each of the four rooms assisting their soldiers in cleaning and organizing their rooms. I went around and asked all my section sergeants to come with me to my office. When we reached my office, I told them, "The point I wanted to make with you guys is that your sections are not going to perform the way you want them to unless you are there with them. You give them instructions and walk away. How are going to make corrections when they are doing what you told them to do? You must stay with them to not only keep them on task but to ensure that the standards are being met. You cannot lead from the rear; you must lead from the front (set the example and hold them to that example or standard). When you give them instructions and walk away, you are communicating that the task that you gave them is not that important to you. If you stay with them and supervise the task, then it tells them that the task is not only important, but you want it done correctly."

The section sergeants said that they understood and went back to the barracks to supervise their soldiers. When I went back over to the barracks at 11:00 PM, all four section sergeants were standing by the designated rooms for inspection and waiting for me to inspect. After inspecting all four rooms, I pointed out the minor issues that needed to be addressed in each room. I then let the soldiers know that they all did a great job and that we did so well that we will not have another pre-inspection until the day before the IG Inspection. I also complimented the section sergeants in front of their soldiers for doing a fine job with assisting them and preparing for my pre-inspection. Before I left, I turned to them all and said, "It's not so bad sometimes to burn a little midnight oil."

Over the next two weeks, my section sergeants took the initiative to do a pre-TA-50 inspection prior to me calling for one. They reported that they needed several items of TA-50 replaced because it was either unserviceable or the soldiers had lost the items. I arranged for them to go to our CIF to pick up the items. I sensed that the section sergeants finally figured out I wasn't going to accept shortcuts and that if they stayed a step ahead of me, then I would be very easy to get along with.

The day of truth was finally here, the IG Inspection. My platoon passed with excellence. The soldiers and my section sergeants were very excited after being pointed out by the inspection team that they had never seen a platoon do so well in all areas on the IG visit. The IG team went on to say that they excelled in every area above every unit that they had inspected so far. The soldiers begin to chant, "Midnight oil, midnight oil, midnight oil." I think the IG team got the message. I would always tell them, "It's about doing the right thing."

A few weeks later, my driver and I were on our way to another camp in the area to pick up classified materials when we passed by a Humvee parked on the side of the road facing our route of travel. We passed by the vehicle, and about a quarter mile down the road, we noticed a vehicle behind us. The vehicle got closer to us as we continued to move toward our destination. Finally, I told my driver to pull over and stop the vehicle to see what they wanted.

The vehicle did pull in behind us, and a soldier exited the vehicle from the passenger side and began to walk toward us. As he approached my side of our Humvee, the image of the soldier became very clear; he was a friend of mine from back home in Norman Park. He started to yell my name, "Mose, it's me, Al." He opened the door of the Humvee and grabbed my hand and we shook hands and greeted each other. He said that he was out on maneuvers with his unit and was waiting back there to link up with them.

Al and I were in school together in Norman Park. He was a grade ahead of me, but we all hung out together during lunch. I had not seen Al since high school. In fact, I had lost track of most of my friends from high school during the years that I was in the military. I saw very few friends of mine when I came home on vacation because I was only at home about one of two weeks and never went anywhere but home. Al had been in the military about the same number of years that I was in. We continued to talk about the good ol' days until his unit reached him. After Al departed, my driver and I continued our journey to complete our mission and returned to Camp Stanton, South Korea. Once we were back at Camp Stanton, I took the information to Captain Laterza.

In late fall of 1991, some soldiers began to receive transfer orders back to the States. The war had ended in the summer, and the army was trying to get back to its normal process of rotating soldiers throughout the world. I thought, "Great, my orders should be coming soon."

January 1992 came and still no orders reassigning me back to the States. I began to think that just maybe my branch had forgotten that I was rapidly approaching two years in this one-year assignment. So I decided to call the air defense branch to see if they overlooked me in the process. I called and talked to our branch manager back at the Pentagon to see if I could get my choice of assignment. He asked me if I wanted to teach the Reserve Officer Training Corps in college. I asked him what was available, and he said Brookings Institute, San Jose State, and Fresno State. I said that I needed to talk with my wife to see which one would be best for us.

I went home from my office and talked to Marlee, and she said that it was too cold at Brookings and that San Jose State was up around Silicon Valley, but Fresno was in a farming community and it's only several hours from Los Angeles.

The next night, I called the air defense branch again, and I asked my branch manager if I could go to Fresno State, and he said yes. He said that I should be receiving orders in about three to four weeks. I did receive my orders weeks later, and I was due to leave the country on April 22, 1992. My orders had me going to Fort Monroe, Virginia, for a two-week orientation for college ROTC. I was just glad to be placed on orders so we could go back to the States.

Meanwhile, I was in my office and in came Captain Laterza and said, "Hey, SFC Kinsey. Captain Price has a soldier fresh from the States in his battery, and he says that he knows you."

I said to him, "What's his name?"

Captain Laterza looked at me and said, "He is a 16S and his name is Danny."

I said, "My son is here?"

He said, "Your son is here?"

I got up and walked down to Bravo Battery's orderly room and talked the Captain Price's 1SG. As I was approaching 1SG's office, he yelled out, "Hey, SFC Kinsey, are you here to see your son?"

I said, "Yes, 1SG. Is he here?"

He said that he should be over at the barracks putting away his gear. I said, "Thanks 1SG, I will run over there."

He yelled, "No problem."

As I approached the barracks, he must have spotted me, and he came out and we hugged. I told him that I didn't know that he was coming to Korea. I know his intentions were to surprise me. He caught me up on what was going on back in the world and back home. I was sad that I only had a few weeks left in the country when he arrived. We did manage to spend some time together prior to me leaving for Fresno. He had gone through a lot in his short time in the military. As soon as he finished his basic and advanced individual training, his orders for Germany were revoked, and he was reassigned to Fort Bliss, and within a few months he was headed to Kuwait under the implicit name of Desert Shield. He was there for over eight months, returned to the States for only six months, and was on the plane to South Korea, which is a hardship tour for the remainder of his time in the military (eighteen months). I think he would have stayed in the military if he had not had almost all overseas assignments his first three years in the army.

ROTC at Fresno State University

The next few weeks in the country were spent making plans for my departure back to the States as well as out-processing the unit. Marlee left a week ahead of me to go visit her parents in Arizona. Upon completing my out-processing at Camp Corner, I flew to Arizona, and from there we departed for Fort Monroe, Virginia, to attend the ROTC Transition Course. We stopped by Houston, Texas, to visit my daughter, Cassandra, and her family. Norman Park, Georgia, was the next stop to visit my parents and family. While we were there, we decided to go to Bear Creek subdivision to look at some chow puppies and to get one as a pet. They were about six weeks old and full of energy. We got one of the males and named him Bear Creek. His riding space in the car was above the rear seat under the rear windshield. He loved crawling around under the windshield. On the way to Fort Monroe, as we stopped at rest areas to let him use the pet room, he would use it and jump back into the car and jump up under the rear windshield. He looked like a stuffed dog lying on the rear dash until he moved.

While in Virginia, we visited some friends of Marlee from Los Angeles, California. Karen and Linnie lived out in the suburbs, and Linnie worked for the federal government and was transferred from Los Angeles several years earlier. They all grew up in Grace Church under the direction of Reverend John McArthur. Unfortunately, Linnie was on the plane heading back into Washington, DC, that was commandeered by Bin Laden's hijackers on 911 and perished the same day the Twin Towers went down.

The ROTC course went by very quickly, and before we knew it, we were on our way back to California for my new assignment. We were traveling between Houston and San Antonio, Texas, when we stopped at a rest area and Bear Creek went to use the pet room outside, and he began to scoot his bottom on the ground. We knew why; he had developed stomach worms. We were about 100 miles from San Antonio, and we decided to go to Fort Sam Houston military installation and stop by the veterinarian's (vet) office to have him treated for the worms. After the vet's visit, we were on our way to Fresno.

We were now back in LA and on our way to Edwards Air Force Base where my kids, mom, and stepdad lived. We were going to pick them up to live with us. We got there, and the kids were all packed up and ready to go. Falisha, Dwayne, and Orenthal came with me to Naval Air Station Lemoore (NAS Lemoore), and Dedric was about to graduate and enter the air force, so he stayed with his mom.

We did move on to NAS Lemoore, and I worked at Fresno State University. The drive was forty-eight miles one way from my front yard to the university parking lot. It was good down time for me, as I could come up with ideas on how to improve different things that I felt needed a change.

Fresno State had over 20,000 students, and an army and an Air Force ROTC program. We had about seventy-five students. Some of the students had prior military service. but the majority did not. The ROTC program is designed to prepare college students to become commissioned officers in the United States Army and Army Reserve Forces. It's a four-year program where the cadets learn basic military skills, including military customs, courtesy and traditions, the wear of the military uniform, awards and decorations, map reading, first aid, ethics, infantry tactics, and much more.

When I arrived, Captain Willfong was the military science III (MS) instructor, and Major Gonzalez was the commandant of the program but was leaving at the end of the summer. Sergeant Major Dement was there but also would be leaving the following year for retirement. Mr. Harvey took care of our supply room. Vonda Epperson was our secretary, and Mrs. Davis was our administrative clerk.

We had several prior service cadets that worked on our work-study program. The work-study program would pay several students to come in after class to assist us with paperwork or assist Mr. Harvey in the supply room. I was handed the responsibility for getting the MS I (first-year cadets) and MS II (second-year cadets) trained. I was further assigned to ensure that first-year cadets were in-processed into the program, received all uniforms and equipment, and completed all administrative issues prior to the start of the semester.

Each semester, we took the cadets on a field training exercise, which lasted a weekend. There, we would put all their classroom training into practical application, and monitor their performance and critique them individually after their performance. The senior cadets (MS IV) ran the program under the supervision of the commandant (professor of military science). One of the main goals of the field training exercise was to prepare the MS IIIs for their Advanced Camp at Fort Lewis, Washington. The MS IVs and cadre monitored the MS III cadets' performance, from preparing the cadets to depart the university to Camp Roberts and return. The cadre is constantly making notes of the leadership decisions by both the MS IIIs and the MS IVs. The MS IVs are tasked with moving the student battalion from garrison to the field and conduct maneuvers utilizing the MS IIIs and safely returning the battalion back to garrison.

Kids in School

One of the first things we had to do when we moved out of the guesthouse into our house on base was to enroll the kids in school.

I had already talked to the kids about their schedules, that I would be the one that decides on what classes that they'll take. I told them that they would all take Algebra 1, Geometry, Algebra 2, and College Prep classes. They could choose one elective class.

The boys had no problem with the challenges that was put in front of them. When Falisha started taking Algebra 1, we would get calls from the teacher saying she is failing algebra. I called the teacher and told her the Falisha doesn't have an option; she must stay in and pass her algebra class. Her teacher recommended that Falisha drop down to Algebra B class for six weeks and then move back up to Algebra A once she gets the hang of it. I agreed to let her drop down to Algebra B and back up again once she gets the formulas down.

Dwayne had no problem with the math or any other subjects until his junior year. I would get phone calls from his teachers saying, "Dwayne is not turning in his assignments; he is not doing well in class at all." I talked to him and he said, "Okay, Dad, I will be fine."

The next week, it started all over again. So, I told Dwayne that when he comes home every evening, he should put the books of all his classes on the kitchen table. I normally arrive at home about 6:15 PM each day from work. I would come in from work and ask, "Where is Dwayne?"

He would always come out of his room and say, "I am here, Dad."

I would always say, "It's time to hit the books." We would go over every subject and make sure it was done right. Sometimes, it would be around midnight when we finished, but we finished all readings and assignment. After the second night, he turned to me and asked me, "Dad, can I just get my GED?"

I looked him in the eyes with a very angry look and said to him, "No GEDs will come in this house, buddy." I told him that he would get those grades up or the both of us will die trying. Every evening, we worked and worked and worked and finally, after about two-and-a-half months, he said, "Dad, don't worry about it, I got it from here on."

The next evening when I got home, he had already finished his homework. I gave it a week, then I called one of his teachers and she did confirm that he was doing great not only in her class but in all his classes. From talking to Dwayne's homeroom teacher, I learned that he sat next to a girl during her class period, and he doesn't sit by her anymore, and that may be why his grades took a turn for the worst. She also said that since he joined the cross-country team, he's doing a lot better. I said, "Yes, his brother, OJ, talked to him about joining the team."

OJ, on the other hand, loved school and especially math. He took every math class the school had to offer. He took accounting, chemistry, and anything to do with numbers. I remember going to their open house, and we went to OJ's chemistry class, and his teacher said he uses OJ as a peer instructor during class. When OJ took his SAT, he almost maxed the math portion of the test.

My kids were all either on the track team or ran cross-country or both. Falisha was on the track team during her eighth grade year. She and three other girls set a track record in the 4X100 for eighth grade girls' team at Lemoore Union High School. I sat down to watch them run for the first time, and they all ran past their competition. The girls were superfast on the track. I think that team could have beaten the varsity team very easily.

Ranger Challenge Team

I was also the Ranger Challenge Team coach. The cadets volunteered to participate on the Ranger Challenge Team. The team competed with other universities throughout California and Nevada.

The events were as follows:
- APFT – Two minutes of sit-ups, two minutes of push-ups, and two-mile run
- M16 Rifle – Reassemble an M16 rifle within two minutes.
- M60 machine gun – Reassemble an M60 machine gun, cock it, load it, and attempt to fire within two minutes
- BRM – Score marksman, sharpshooter, or expert on the firing range
- One-Rope Bridge – Construct, cross, and tear down a one-rope bridge within two minutes. The participants simulate crossing a 30-foot stream with their rope and tie the rope off on the pole on the far side of the stream. The Anker team member ties the rope off on the near pole, thus constructing a one-rope bridge. Five team members then mount the rope and cross the open stream to reach the other side. Once the fifth person is off the rope on the other side, the final team member secures his rope and brings it across the simulated stream to stop the time.
- 10K Rucksack Run – Each team must start with ten team members. They must wear regular battle dress uniform, boots, M16 Rifle, web gear with two full canteens of water, and a rucksack with thirty pounds. The team must start and finish together. The fastest team wins the event.

We would practice three days a week, and I would work out with the team. On Mondays, we would work on push-ups, sit-ups, and the two-mile run. On Wednesdays, we would work on the one-rope bridge. On Fridays, we would take our rucksacks to university vineyards and run six miles with our rucks. This was my favorite event because I would run it with the cadets. The incoming freshman would start out fast and wind up drifting way behind the pack. Before we start, I would always tell them, "If the old man falls out, don't stop. Keep going and once you finish, call 911." I would always finish ahead of the cadets, and I would run back along the way, encouraging them to keep moving. When all the cadets make it in, they would ask me how I do it. I tell them to start off at a regular airborne shuffle and don't let up, just keep that same pace throughout the run.

Lesson Learned for the Cadets

We were training young men and women to become commissioned officers in the United States Army, and we (cadre) must set the brightest example for them to take into the military service with them.

I remember the Reno, Nevada, Ranger Challenge meet. We had competed in the APFT and BRM the first day, and we went back to our barracks prior to going to dinner. We were trying to decide on what we wanted to eat for dinner. It was about half and half split that some of our cadets wanted pizza and the other half wanted a restaurant meal. I dropped off half of the group at the pizza shop, and the rest of us went to a restaurant to eat. We finished at the restaurant, and I paid the bill, and then we left to go pick up the other group. We reached the pizza shop, and we all went inside and started talking to the group there, and time passed and someone said, "It's time to go; we have that 10K waiting on us tomorrow."

We all got up and just walked out of the pizza shop, and then we went back to the barracks. We were in bed when I realized that I didn't pay the pizza shop for the team's meal. I got up from my bunk and asked the team members near me if they saw me pay for the meal at the pizza shop. No one could tell me that I paid the bill.

By this time, all the male cadets had made their way over to my bunk. I said, "I am going back to pay the bill."

One of the cadets said, "We are here now, they can't find us."

Another said, "Let's keep the money for something else."

Yet another said, "They wouldn't give it back to you, MSG Kinsey."

I said, "Guys, it's not right for me to keep their hard-earned money. They have bills like we do, and I can't take the money. Now, who wants to ride back into town with me to return it?"

Several cadets rode back into town with me to deliver the unpaid debt. We reached the restaurant, and we approached the locked door. One of the men in the store didn't want to open the door until I said that we came back to pay our bill. The man nearest the door opened it and asked us what we wanted. I told him that I had not paid for the pizzas the cadets had eaten. He walked over to the cash register, picked up a receipt, and brought it to me, and it was the unpaid bill. The bill was over $270.00.

On the way back, one of the cadets said, "You know, MSG Kinsey, they really didn't know who that bill belonged to."

I said to him, "But I know whose bill it is."

When we made it back and entered the barracks, a cadet asked, "Did we pay the bill or keep the money?" One of the cadets that rode with me to take the money back said, "We did the right thing."

The next day, we finished the competition in second place overall to San Jose State who came in first. We were proud of what we accomplished with such a young team. The trip back home was a good one because we didn't know where we stood as a team until this meet. We now knew what areas that required more practice and the team members that needed additional practice.

Good Friends Are Hard to Find

Our friends Craig and Kathy Carroll drove up from LA to visit us the following weekend. We hadn't seen them since we left for South Korea. Craig was an owner and operator of a printing company called "Tiger Printing." Craig's dad was a retired lawyer, and his mom was a retired schoolteacher. Craig's dad was a die-hard Dodger fan. Craig was an ice hockey fan of the LA Kings and of any team that Wayne Gretzky played on. He was a good hockey player himself. Craig was also a die-hard Republican, and he would always let me know it.

When he arrived, he would always make a comment about politics. He did not like President Clinton. The first thirty or forty minutes after him and Kathy arrived, he would talk about how bad Clinton was and how he should be sent back to Arkansas. I didn't have time to keep up with politics at that time and couldn't defend the president. After he had his say on how bad Clinton was, he was then ready to have a civil conversation about everything else that was going on in the world. He would talk in a kidding way so that he didn't offend me in any way. He was and still is a great friend.

Los Angeles Earthquake

We were visiting them in the LA when the earthquake of 1994 hit. I woke up to the house rocking back and forth. I awakened Marlee and I said, "The house is moving," and she started screaming, "It's an earthquake."

After about forty-five or fifty seconds, it stopped, and Craig knocked on the door and said, "We just had an earthquake." We went downstairs and some of Craig's mom's figurines had fallen over and a long crack was in one of the walls. We walked outside to see if there were any damage to the house. Craig's mom's house was okay, but the neighbor's chimney was leaning toward Craig's mom's house. This particular neighbor that lived to their left was one of the special effects men for the *Star Wars* movies that was released in the 1970s.

We went back in the house, and I got a phone call from my oldest son, Danny. Danny had gotten out of the service and was attending college and living with us in Fresno. He looked after his brother and sister while we were visiting Craig and Kathy.

He called and said, "Hey, Dad, have you seen downtown LA?"

I said, "No, we haven't had a chance to turn on the TV." He said the 14 Freeway collapsed, houses fell and are burning. Some roads in and out of LA are shut down. He asked, "How are you and Mrs. Marlee going to get out of LA?"

I said, "We will probably take side roads to get out."

Craig and I went to check on Kathy's mom over in Simi Valley. She was doing fine but had no water or power at that time. We went back to Craig's, and we planned a route through LA that could take us to Interstate 5, which would take us back to Fresno. The route through Simi Valley to the Interstate did get us out of LA and on our way to Fresno. We made it back to Fresno where we could watch TV and see all the damage down in LA. It caused a tremendous amount of damage throughout the LA area.

Where Did Some Parents Go Wrong?

Meanwhile, back in my office at the university, our office clerk (Vonda) asked me if I would consider being a guest speaker in her daughter's middle school class down in Fresno. I accepted the invitation and agreed to speak. It was an intercity middle school with some issues, which are common to most schools. I arrived at the school, and I was still wearing my military uniform from work. As I was walking into the classroom, I observed students attentively listening to the teacher, but at the same time I focused on some kids in the back talking to each other as Ms. Epperson was giving instruction to all students. I noticed girls looking in their purses and some were not paying attention.

Ms. Epperson introduced me, and I immediately started talking to the students. All of the students' eyes begin to focus on me as I approached the front of the classroom. I asked the students what they thought about school. Most said that it was okay, some said that they needed an education to get a good job, and others said that they must graduate high school so they could go to college. I asked the students their thoughts on the advantage of graduating from high school versus not graduating from high school. Some said more money, others said better job, yet others said better opportunities, and one kid said nothing will change.

I turned to him and asked him why wouldn't anything change, and he said, "My brother doesn't have a job."

I asked him if his brother has been looking for a job. He said, "He had one but he lost it."

I said, "Why did he lose it?"

He said, "I don't know."

I said there are many reasons people lose their job. They don't show up for work on time or don't show up at all; they don't give a 100 percent effort while on the job; they are not good neighbors; they violate company rules; or they just don't want to work. As I was talking, I noticed a male student carrying on a conversation the same time I was talking, and I stopped and looked at him. The student he was talking to noticed me looking at them, and he stopped listening to him and raised his head and looked at me. The other kid turned around and looked at me as well. I asked that kid if he planned to finish high school. He responded with, "When I turn sixteen, I am dropping out of school."

I said, "Why?"

He said, "I am tired of school."

I said to him, "What are you going to do when you drop out of school?"

He said, "I will get on welfare."

I was in total shock when he said that to me, and the class could probably see it in my reaction to his answer. My facial expression did not help the situation. I immediately came back with, "What if welfare goes away?"

He responded without hesitation, "I'll just rob somebody."

I asked him, "How you would take care of your family while you are in prison for robbing someone?"

He said, "Welfare will take care of them too."

I then turned to the class and said, "Most men I know work hard every day to take care of their families and their children." I shared with them that I started working when I was thirteen years old. This enabled my mom to buy me clothes from the dime store instead of Goodwill. I told them, "I knew at an early age that if I was going to have a family, I couldn't take care of them working in the cotton and tobacco fields." I continued talking to the class about my struggles when I was their age. I wanted to instill hope and inspiration that they can do better than just go on welfare. I wanted to plant a seed so that they would think of getting out of their environment and breaking the cycle of families on welfare. I talked to them about the military being an option for them as it was for me. Even getting a trade at their local community college so that they would have some form of income to start earning a living. Many of them were very receptive to the idea of earning a living and not being dependent upon someone else such as their parents, family members, or in even welfare. Some of them had goals that were very achievable, and some didn't know what direction they were going to take even after turning the age of sixteen. It was very evident that some parents had not talked to their children about life after high school. I left the class with education being the key to many successes in life.

I said to Ms. Epperson prior to leaving her class that she deserves the Nobel Peace Prize for patience, understanding, and dedication. Teachers are truly the unsung heroes of our time. I returned from the university, went to my office, marched straight to Vonda's desk, and told her what happened, and she was not surprised. She said that she talked to her daughter every night about situations in the classroom. Vonda said that she was not keen on the idea of Staci teaching in the inner city, but her daughter insisted that this was God's calling for her to teach in the inner-city school system.

Promoted to the Second Highest Enlisted Rank in the Army

I received orders from the Department of the Army congratulating me on my promotion to master sergeant. I was very excited to become a master sergeant (E-8). All my hard work over the years was finally being noticed. Air defense is a small branch within the army, and this rank was very hard to achieve. Major Masters was the new commandant over the program at Fresno State now, and he had a ceremony with all cadets and staff to pin the Master Sergeant stripes on me. The promotion ceremony was short-lived in that we had shifted to high gear in preparation for the cadet's Advanced Camp.

Minicamp

We were leaving the weekend for our minicamp at Camp Roberts near San Luis Obispo, California, to train our MS IIIs for Advanced Camp at Fort Lewis, Washington. The MS III cadet company commander was supposed to give the cadre a load plan for personnel and equipment prior to our departure. We received it an hour prior to pulling out the parking lot. I drove a 44-passenger bus, which I had borrowed from one of the local army reserve units in Fresno. We departed for minicamp on Friday morning, and we arrived early evening at Camp Roberts. The MS IIIs took control of the cadet training exercise, and the MS-IV cadets and cadre were evaluators for the exercise. The cadet commanding officer (CO) and executive officer (XO) took control as soon as we hit the ground at minicamp. The XO got all the cadets situated in the barracks and bedded down for the night. The next day, the CO and XO moved the cadets out to training and assigned cadets in key positions during all phases of training during the day.

Captain White (a new assistant professor of military science in our program) was evaluating one group of cadets, and one of them approached him and told him that they had landed on poison ivy during one of the missions. The cadet had already begun to blister with sores. We rushed the cadet to the hospital. By the time we reached the hospital, the cadet's face was unrecognizable (the cadet remained in the hospital for a week before being allowed to leave for home). At end of the day, we conducted an after-action review (AAR) with the cadet leadership team. The CO, XO, and other cadets in key leadership positions performed well but could have performed much better, and the AAR pointed those shortcomings out. We all stopped for the day and lights out was at 10:00 PM.

At 10:30 PM, I received a phone call from home. It was my wife reporting that Dwayne had been dropped off at the house by the military police for violating the base curfew for teenagers. Teenagers must be off any sidewalk on the base by 10:00 PM each night. I told her to tell him that he couldn't leave the house and that I would talk to him when I return from training. The cadets were up early Sunday morning preparing for our trip back to Fresno. Major Masters and some of the cadre went to the hospital to check on our cadet's condition, and the rest of the group traveled back to the university.

Once we arrived back at the university, the cadet CO and OX took control of the cadet group and ensured that all sensitive items and equipment were secured and stored and all cadets were accounted for. We conducted the AAR on Monday to let the cadet leadership know how they performed overall.

Curfew Violation

I arrived home late Sunday afternoon and Dwayne was my only thought when I walked in the house. I summoned him to the kitchen table and asked him to explain why he was out past curfew. He said that he and his friends didn't realize what time it was when they left the Youth Center (a place for teenagers on the base). I said, "Why didn't one of you have the responsibility of monitoring the time so that you wouldn't be walking home late?" I said to him, "We live only three blocks from the Youth Center, and you could have made it home within ten minutes." He insisted that they lost track of time. I told him, "The lost track of time is going to get him grounded for the next month." His punishment was no phone time; leave the house for school only; no friends over to the house; no sports at school; and all of this will last for one month.

The effects of his punishment were immediate; his cross-country coach called and asked if the sport ban could be lifted because of an upcoming track meet. I said, "Coach, with all due respect, I must teach my son lessons that will last him beyond high school." I said to him, "If my son would be going to jail for this crime, would you make this phone call?" I told him, "I don't want my children to think that if they get into trouble, Dad can get them out of it." This punishment is meant to change his behavior. If I alter any of it, then it defeats the purpose of trying to change him. I told the coach that I know how important cross-country is to Dwayne, and that's why it's in his punishment.

I went on to say to the coach that Dwayne had the privilege of going to the Youth Center while I was gone, and his only responsibility was to report back home on time and not break the curfew. He knew I wasn't home, and his intentions were to set a new set of standards, and that was to come home later than what he was told. I finished by telling him that I would not allow my children to set new standards in my house. The coach said, "I understand, Mr. Kinsey." The coach left me with, "Mr. Kinsey, I will have a conversation with Dwayne also on how he has cost the team by not living up to his responsibilities."

I said, "Thanks, Coach." The coach and I hung up the phone, and I turned around and looked at my wife, and she looked at me as if she had seen a ghost. I said to her, "I am sorry, but that's how I feel about what he's done."

She said, "I didn't mean to get him into this much trouble."

I said "You didn't do anything; he did." I said to her, "If you hadn't called me, he would go through life thinking that everyone should give him a break. He must be accountable for everything that he does good, bad, or indifferent."

After several weeks of being on restrictions, seeing his brother Orenthal leave and visit his friends, and his friends not coming over, he came to me and asked if he could go to the gym to play basketball. I turned to him and said, "No, you have two more weeks to go on your restrictions." He turned and walked back to his room.

At the end of the third week of his restriction, I was sitting on the couch and he came in walking very slowly, and he sat down on the couch and said, "It's a great day outside."

I turned to him and said, "You have one more week." He got up and went back to his room.

The next week, he was off restriction, and finally he was eligible to leave the house. He asked if he could go to the gym, and he asked me if I would go with him, Orenthal, and their friends to play basketball, and I said, "Yes."

Orenthal Was Not Mistake-Free

Our good friends, the Franklins, were a navy family and lived several blocks from us on the base. They had a son and a daughter that would often visit our house with their parents when they would come over. Their son (Ivan) were very good friends with Dwayne and Orenthal. What none of us knew was that their daughter Brenda had a crush on Orenthal.

One Sunday evening, the Franklins came over unexpectedly. We invited them in, then Randy said, "Hey, Marlee and Mose, we have a problem. Brenda has been slipping out the window and meeting a boy on the playground near where we live. The boy is Orenthal."

After being in shock for a few seconds, we summoned Orenthal from his room to understand why this was happening. He came in the living room, and as he looked around the room and saw everybody seated, he knew that he was in trouble. I asked him what was going on with him and Brenda, and why were they slipping out the window late at night? He said that they were just talking.

I said, "What reason would you have to slip out the window to talk? Is it that private that you must wait until everyone is asleep and leave your homes to go talk?"

They said, "No, just everyday stuff."

I said, "As of today, it will not happen again."

Randy and his wife agreed that slipping out the window was over. If they wanted to talk, they could talk on the phone. We talked to them about getting through school and getting prepared for their future. Orenthal apologized to Randy and his wife and said it wouldn't happen again. Meanwhile, Dedric had decided on the United States Air Force as a career and headed off to basic training.

Surprise! You Are Pregnant!

After completion of the ROTC Advanced Camp at Fort Lewis, Washington, Marlee flew there, and we went to Victoria Island, British Columbia, Canada. We had to drive the car on a ferry boat to go to Lake Victoria from Bremerton, Washington. We camped out a week at Lake Victoria. Wade and Jo (Marlee's parents) met us there. We fished and relaxed for a week, and the four of us had a great time. On the way back home, we stopped in the city to shop for souvenirs. We returned to Fresno just prior to the start of the new school year. Marlee and I had talked about adopting a child when we were in South Korea, and for some reason, that conversation came up again.

She was over thirty years old and thought that maybe we couldn't have kids. We decided to give it one more year, and then we would proceed in trying to adopt. About six weeks after that conversation, she called me at work to let me know that she was so sick on her stomach and that she had to go to see the doctor.

When I returned home from work, she said, "Surprise! I am pregnant." We both were in shock after talking about adopting. We elected not to find out the sex of the baby.

It was an extremely tough pregnancy because Marlee was sick seven of the nine months. On May 26, 1994, I left for work, and when I walked into my office at the university, the clerk said, "You need to go back to Lemoore. Your daughter (Roanea Bluecloud Kinsey) was born a few minutes ago."

I turned around and went back to NAS Lemoore's hospital. The nurse said that Roanea had to be sent to the Children's Hospital in Fresno. I went in and talked to Marlee prior to leaving for the Children's Hospital in Fresno. I arrived at the Children's Hospital in Fresno and went to the Intensive Care Unit. There, Roanea was in a bed with tubes running out of her throat. They were getting the excess fluids to run out of her lungs.

The doctor said that at Lemoore, the doctors had lost her heartbeat and had to do an emergency C-section operation. The fluids that would have been squeezed out of her lungs during natural childbirth did not occur, and those fluids are still in her lungs. The doctor said that they had to allow those fluids to exit her lungs. The child next to her was the smallest baby I had ever seen. It must have weighed only a pound. She remained in the hospital for four days. After four days, she could drink at least 2 oz. of milk, and the doctors would allow her to leave. I took her home, and everyone was excited to see her. I didn't have to go to Advanced Camp that summer due to the anticipated birth of Roanea.

The Kids Were Making Career Decisions at an Early Age

Danny decided that he would travel back to Georgia. We followed him back to Moultrie, and he would live temporarily with his Grandma Flossie. He eventually started working for the Lowndes County Sheriff's department. We returned to Fresno, and within a week, Dedric came home to visit from the United States Air Force. We were very excited to see him. The group got caught up on things that were going on with each other. He was glad to see his little sister, Roanea. They all spent a lot of time playing and loving her. Dedric asked me if he could take his brother to see a movie in the car. I said yes, that was fine. We were all happy to have him back home.

Three or four hours later, a vehicle brought the boys home with one of their friends as well. They entered the house and Dedric said, "Dad, I had an accident." The friend that rode with them was roughed up some, I could tell by looking at him. I asked him if he was okay, and he said, "Yes, sir." I told them not to worry about the car. They were fine, and that's all that matters. Dedric said that he was going under a bridge that had sand under it, and he just lost control of the car, and it ran off the road and flipped into the ditch. I knew the bridge that he rode under, and it always has sand under it and along the road side because of farmland in that area.

We all had a great visit prior to Dedric heading back to his assignment. Orenthal graduated from high school, got a job at McDonald's on the base, and enrolled at the local junior college in Lemoore.

The kids have all had a clear understanding that when they graduate from high school, they could stay at home for free, get a job, and go to college or stay at home for free, work one year, save their money, and get their own apartment. They were often told that when they graduate, I would be standing on the other side of the graduation stage with their favorite dinner plate and a hammer. When they receive their diploma, the plate would be broken. It never happened, but it was fun saying it to them over the years.

In the fall of 1994, Dwayne decided to enlist into the army while still in high school. He came to me and asked if he could enlist into the army. I asked him if he was sure that this was what he wanted to do, and he said, "Yes, sir." I asked him why didn't he want to go to college, and he said, "I don't want to right now." He said he wanted to do something different. I asked when did he want to go talk to the recruiter, and said, "I have already talked to the recruiter." I said when, and he said, "At school." He said if it's okay, he will take me to take the ASVAB at MEPS in San Bernadino, California, on Sunday evening. He said that he would take his physical on Monday and enter the delayed entry program. Dwayne asked me if I would come to MEPS on Monday help in getting him a job. I asked him what career field he wanted to go in. He said finance. I said, "Okay, I will certainly have to go with you if you wanted to go into that field."

I knew the first jobs the counselors would offer him would be combat arms such as infantry, armor, or field artillery. I went to MEPS around noon and waited on Dwayne to complete his physical. After he completed his physical, he came to the counselor area to select a job. The recruiters had already notified the counselors that I was there with Dwayne. The counselor working with Dwayne asked me what Dwayne wanted to do in the army, and I told him that Dwayne wanted something in finance. He immediately turned to me and said, "Master Sergeant, it will probably be at the end of the day before I will be able to get that job for him because I have to sell the combat arms jobs first."

I said that I was a recruiter before, I understand, and we can wait or return another time when it's available. He said, "Master Sergeant, we will get it for him."

The counselor came back in an hour and said to Dwayne and I, "I have finance and accounting, is this okay for you?"

Dwayne said, "Yes, sir?"

On August 20, 1995, Dwayne departed for basic training at Fort Jackson, South Carolina. In October 1995, Marlee, Roanea, Orenthal, and I drove from California to South Carolina for Dwayne's graduation from basic training. The trip to South Carolina was not a good one. There was a hurricane coming through Mississippi and Alabama, and we ran into it. Orenthal was sick with a stomach virus and had to ride in the back of the truck under the camper top. We had to take an alternate route through Mississippi. The winds were so high, we had to pull off the road and behind a store to ride out the storm. We stayed in the truck overnight. The next day, we started back on our way, and there were trees down for a good part of our trip through Mississippi. We did make it to South Carolina in time for Dwayne's graduation. Dwayne was able to spend the day with us prior to him signing into his new unit at Fort Jackson. We met many of his platoon buddies. Fort Jackson had not changed over the last twenty-two years since I was there.

After our visit with Dwayne, we headed to Georgia. Prior to us leaving Georgia, we looked at a double-wide mobile home sitting on eight acres of land. The house and land was located on Indian Lake Drive in Norman Park, Georgia. We talked to Helen Whitney of Landmark Realty Company. The property required making the owners an offer, and we did. Once we returned to California, the owners and I started negotiating a price that together we could live with. It was rather peculiar, because of all the last names the owners could have had, theirs was the same as mine (Kinsey), and we were not related. I was really amazed that our paths crossed in little Norman Park. During the negotiations, we never saw each other. We got a good deal on the place, but I have always thought it was because of our last name. Helen sealed the deal with a $10,000 check that I sent her to start the buying process. A month or so later, we closed the deal on the house.

Just a few weeks after the visit with Dwayne, Orenthal drove in the driveway from work and walked up to me with a worried look. Before he said anything, I asked him "When do you want to go in the army."

He said, "How did you know?"

I said, "I know that you have been talking to Dwayne."

He said, "I want to go in now."

I said, "Call Dwayne's recruiter and let him know that you want to go in the army." I asked him what job did he want to go in, and he said, "The medical field."

The recruiter stopped by the house, and he and I talked. He said that he would get Orenthal something in the medical field. I asked the recruiter if I needed to go to MEPS, and he said, "No, Master Sergeant. They know you are serious."

Orenthal came home from MEPS and he was going to be a dental assistant. Orenthal departed for the army on January 6, 1996.

Back to College

I had gotten my associate's degree in liberal arts from El Paso Community College while stationed at Fort Bliss, Texas. It was now time to fulfill my promise to myself that I would get my college degree. I could have gone to Fresno State and received two classes free per semester because of my position there at the school. However, I decided to go to Fresno Pacific College. They had a program where I could go to school at night and I could earn my bachelor's degree within sixteen months. I had to pay full tuition and books with no financial aid.

I enrolled into the Management Program. Our primary instructor was Mrs. Consuela Maux. We met for four-hour sessions, two nights a week. The class required an extensive amount of research, writing, and reporting. It was mandatory for graduation that each student to complete a thesis project, present it to at least two faculty members, and receive a pass or fail on it. If you pass, you graduate, and if you fail, you don't. The course was very challenging, and it kept the entire class busy. When we went to minicamp, I would take my homework with me. I would be up sometimes until 2:00 AM, studying.

One of my classmates worked at Cochran State Prison at Cochran, California. Cochran prison is where Charles Manson was serving his time. Charles Manson was responsible for killing actress Sharon Tate and her unborn child. My classmate said that Charles Manson has been in solitary confinement ever since he has been at Cochran Prison. He comes out for exercise after everyone else is gone back to their cell.

All of us were students with daytime jobs and other responsibilities. Some were secretaries or teachers; there was a prison guard, and some were housewives. I was the only military, and the college itself was Mennonite based. Our class started at 5:00 PM, so all daytime students were gone home or at their dorm by the time I hit the campus in uniform. It was mandatory that at least six semester hours of curriculum had to be biblical classes. It was fine with me because I love the teachings in the Bible.

One of our class requirements was that we had to perform community service and report on what we did. I decided to volunteer to work and serve meals at a soup kitchen in Fresno. I report to the kitchen about 1:00 PM, and they put me to work immediately. I was assigned to the vegetable-cutting team. I was escorted to the potato-cutting side of the kitchen and given a knife and other equipment to help me perform the task. Each team was preparing their portion of the meal by 3:00 PM, and it was passed on to the teams that we assigned to cook the meal. We were set to start serving the meal at 5:00 PM. Some of the volunteers were performing community service as part of their court-ordered sentence for law violations.

After we turned over our team's food for cooking, we just sat around talking until it was time to serve the patrons. We also served the food when the people came in to eat. What I didn't know or notice before is that there are a lot of people that are homeless or living in poverty today. The biggest surprise for me that day was not the number of people that came through the line, but it was how young many of them there were; women with children; families; and former white-collar workers that came through the line. It was an explicit reminder to me how many people are still living in poverty not only in Fresno but in our country.

In the meantime, my thesis project was almost done, and I was preparing for the presentation to the group. The countless hours of pulling it together was a major sacrifice. I had put the computer in the bedroom so that Roanea wouldn't be distracted when she was playing in the living room. However, she knew that I was in the bedroom, and she would come to the door and knock on it and she would say "Dah-Dah," and I would always open the door and play with her until she was ready to see what Ma-Ma was doing.

Once the thesis project was completed, I took the twelve floppy disks to Kinko's in Fresno for binding. The presentation went very well. I received an A on the project. All the late nights coming home from class, countless hours of research, community service time, classroom assignments, and weekends at the library finally paid off when I received my degree.

South Korea, a Third Tour: Why?

I had been at Fresno State for almost four years. I was in a leadership position, but it was not like running my own company as the 1SG. I looked back on my career in the military, and as a sergeant, my goal was always to be in a command position.

I talked to Marlee about the possibility of going back to South Korea. She now was pregnant with my fifth son, Lincoln Meadows Kinsey.

This was not what she expected me to come home and talk to her about, with her being pregnant. I explained to her that since I was not on orders, I would have to write to the Department of the Army and ask to be placed on orders. I think the reason she agreed is that she didn't really think the army would grant me the request. She said that she would be all right and that she would get Mom Jo to come several weeks prior to Lincoln being born.

I sat down in my office and typed the letter requesting to return to South Korea so that I could perform the duties as company 1SG. About four weeks after the letter was sent to the Department of the Army, a response came in, orders reassigning me from Fresno State to South Korea. Marlee was in shock. She really didn't think they would send me for a third tour in South Korea. I talked to Major Masters and CPT White about me returning to South Korea. I am sure they had mixed emotions. I am sure they were happy that I was going to command troops again, but not wanting me to leave the cadre at Fresno State. I had trained SSG Collins very well and he knew my job well enough to take care of the cadets. Master Sergeant Anderson would assist SSG Collins if needed. SSG Collins had come on board a year earlier. He came to us from Hawaii. SGG Collins was from Thailand, and while stationed in Hawaii, SSG Collins was on special duty assignment to translate and assist in recovering the bodies of American soldiers from Vietnam and Cambodia. His team did recover several bodies from Vietnam. The cadets were well covered with regard to the instructors.

Prior to leaving to South Korea, something got into my head about going back home to Georgia. So I decided to fly home to visit my parents. When I arrived, I had a long talk with my sister, Leatis, and brother, Leroy. They told me that Dad was in the advanced stages of Alzheimer's. Leatis told me that they were going to have to move the locks on the doors up over the top of the doors so that he couldn't reach them. They told me that on several occasions, they had gotten calls from the neighbors at 1:00 or 2:00 AM, and that Dad was walking down the road in his pajamas. They had started dressing him with adult pull-ups because he didn't know when it was time for a bowel movement. When I talked to him, he would call out one of our names but didn't know who he was talking too. I didn't go anywhere or visit any friends. I just stayed with them for the entire week. I could tell that Mom was losing her memory as well. She was not as far along as Dad. It was tough for me to see my dad in this state of mental and physical shape because I had always seen him in a different way. At this point, I had been in the military for over twenty-two years. When I left home, I was a scrawny nineteen-year-old, and my dad could get around just as good as me. To see him now was very painful to me. I felt very guilty that I had gone into the military and not settle down near home so I could have spent more time with him and Mom during the later years in life. This was something that I would wrestle with in my mind for the next eight months. With three of the boys still in the military, it would give me a lot to think about outside of my other responsibilities as a soldier and a husband.

I flew back to Fresno to prepare for my third tour of duty in South Korea. I was able to get everything in order at home prior to leaving for my new assignment. I arrived in South Korea on June 23, 1996. While in-processing in country at Camp Corner, my battalion command sergeant major (CSM) came down the Camp Corner and welcomed me into the battalion as its newest 1SG. He said that I would be taking over Delta Battery Fifth Battalion Fifth Regiment Second Infantry Division located at Camp Stanley, South Korea. He followed that statement with, "The 1SG in Delta Battery quit last week and the job is yours."

I said, "Thank you, CSM, for allowing me this opportunity." I was thinking, why did the previous 1SG quit? He, his driver, and I gathered all my gear and we headed back to Camp Stanley. We went straight to battalion headquarters and into LTC Wrenn's office, and he stated, "Sir,

I am here with 1SG Kinsey." LTC Wrenn reached in his desk drawer and pulled out a set of 1SG stripes, and he and the CSM pinned them on me to make it official.

LTC Wrenn said, "Congratulations, 1SG. We look forward to working with you."

I said, "Thank you, sir."

LTC Wrenn and I discussed my previous assignment and other things of importance. After our discussion, CSM and I went on to my new orderly room to meet CPT Choi, my battery commander. I knew CPT Choi from my previous tour here in 1990. CPT Choi was a second lieutenant platoon leader at that time. CPT Choi and I had served as evaluators for the Stinger certification in 1990. He was a soldier's officer who believed in allowing the NCOs to do their job without interference from the officers. He simultaneously demanded that the standards are met. CPT Choi called in all the platoon leaders and platoon sergeants to introduce them to me. We talked about what the company needed to become successful in the future, things that I saw as PL and PSG responsibilities. CPT Choi asked me to introduce myself to the battery as a whole and let the soldiers know my goals for the company going forward, at the evening formation. I told them that I looked forward to meeting them.

My driver picked me up at the orderly room and took me to the supply room so that I could sign for my quarters, linen, and settle in prior the evening formation. We returned to my quarters, and while unpacking, I discovered that I had not put my checkbook in my suitcase. I had about $47.00 on me until my wife mails me the checks. Calling back to the States was a bit complicated. You either go into town to where they were set up for an international operator or get a control number from battalion headquarters to make an overseas phone call. When it's night here, its day back in certain states back home. I had to call at midnight to talk to someone during the day. It is now about time for the evening formation, and I walked to the motor pool.

New Battery 1SG

When I arrived in the motor pool, the battery was assembling, and once assembled, CPT Choi called the battery to attention and back at ease and began to introduce me as the their new Battery 1SG. He then called the battery back to attention and called out "1SG." I walked around and turned in front of CPT Choi and rendered him a hand salute, and he returned it and walked around behind the formation and waited on me to address our soldiers.

I about-faced and instructed the soldiers to stand at ease. I introduced myself and told them that this was my third tour in South Korea. The following are some excerpts for that address as I remember them: I said, "I wanted to cover a few responsibilities and goals for all of us as a battery. We are now an average battery of average accomplishments. My goal is to move from where we are now to a battery of great accomplishments. We must start with ourselves. We must take pride in our unit. Assist our fellow soldiers in their shortcomings and work as a team. When someone is down, you lift them up. If your buddy has a problem, then you have a problem, because problems affects everyone in each platoon. I understand that we have good leaders in this battery. Good leaders must take care of their soldiers. Soldiers make good leaders and good leaders take care of those that make them great. Some of the things that will make us successful are:

Training:

I emphasized to them that we must train our soldiers with the thought that we could be attacked by North Korea tomorrow. Training that is critical to our mission as air defenders is map reading, air craft recognition, and target engagement. This training will appear on our training schedule every week until we are proficient in that training. I said that we must train with a sense of urgency and take no shortcuts. I warned them, "A shortcut we take today could mean a loss of life tomorrow." More than anything else, we must train to standards.

Health and welfare:

Soldier's care will be a top priority in this unit. Individuals that give a 110 percent day in and day out will be rewarded. The expectation for success by everyone in our unit should remain high. I explained that our soldier's barracks will be maintained in very high state of cleanliness. We need our soldiers healthy to accomplish our mission.

Equipment:

Our personal equipment such as uniforms and field gear should be worn correctly, clean, and serviceable at all times. Our vehicles should be operational, and no deadlined vehicles in our motor pool. I explained that our sensitive items such as weapons, radios, and night vision devices should be operational always.

Conduct:

I said to them that our conduct on and off Camp Stanley will always remain professional. I reminded the soldiers that we were visitors in South Korea, and we must honor their customs, traditions, and laws the same as we would expect them to do in America. I said, "Don't be the soldier that beats his girlfriend (*yobo*) in the village and winds up in a Korean prison."

Safety:

I explained to everyone that this was not my first tour in South Korea. I told them that I have seen soldiers get into a lot of trouble over the years that I was in the country. Soldiers that lost their careers, their ranks, and some that wind up in Korean jail. There will be a safety briefing every Friday afternoon on safety. "CPT Choi and I want you to leave this country in the same condition in which you arrived."

Upcoming events:

I explained to the battery that we had several major events on our agenda that we must train for very quickly. Our annual Inspector General's inspection, our Avenger certification, our annual Team Spirit exercise. "Finally, I wanted to let everyone know that I have an open-door policy, and if anyone would like to talk to me about anything, I will be available to talk with them." I thanked them for their loyalty to our unit, and that I would see them at the morning formation for physical training. After the battery formation in the motor pool, I came back to the orderly room and put together the Charge of Quarters (CQ) roster for the NCOs. The CQ is a sergeant that is on duty from 5:00 PM to 5:00 AM. His job is to watch over the company after hours. He records emergency phone calls and notifies the individual and the battery leadership team (1SG and CO), and he checks the barracks to ensure that it's safe and secure throughout his shift.

CPT Choi arrived a few minutes later and we planned a strategy on motivating our soldiers. I told him to give me a week or to get out and talk with the soldiers and try and find out what's going on within the battery. Soldiers are not shy; they will tell you if you ask. The only thing is that if you don't do anything about the problem, they want talk to you about it again. They will assume that you don't care about their problem. Several weeks passed and after many conversations with our soldiers, I was ready to talk with CPT Choi about how to motivate our soldiers. I explained to him that the soldiers are under a lot pressure to perform and some of them don't feel that they are valued. They are 10,000 miles away from home; they're in a foreign country and they can't speak the language; many have personal issues involving back home; McDonald's is no longer down the street; they seldom are authorized a three- or four-day pass to leave the installation; and the possibility of North Korean soldiers crossing the border just five kilometers away is wearing on them.

I told CPT Choi that the first thing I was going to do was to have a cook-out for the battery. The second thing I was going to do was to increase the percentage of soldiers allowed to leave the post for time away from the battery. They can go down to Seoul to relax. I also told him that I was going to encourage the platoon sergeants to compliment their soldiers more often when they do a good job or when they complete a certain mission.

There were other rules put in place to help improve the morale in our unit. A couple of days after the battery party, SFC Calvin Bolden, one of my platoon sergeants, came up to me while I was inspecting the battery motor pool and said, "1SG, the soldiers and all the NCOs are very glad that you are our battery 1SG." He said, "1SG, if you ask these soldiers to leave right now and drive across the border to fight, they will ask, 'When does the 1SG want me to go?'"

I told SFC Bolden, "I could implement changes all day long, but if you and the other six platoon sergeants would not support those changes, then they would not have worked." I told him, "You and your peers are the ones that are instrumental in reviving this battery to what it should be." I also told SFC Bolden to continue encouraging his fellow platoon sergeants to maintain a positive attitude because if they are happy, their soldiers will display a positive attitude as well.

Within a few weeks after we began to relax the rules a bit, CPT Choi said to me, "Hey, Top (1SG), the soldiers seemed happier to be here. You have really made a difference here."

I said, "The entire leadership team is making a difference here, sir."

He replied, "You are right, Top. I have seen a big difference in the platoon sergeant's motivation as well. When they come in to see you and talk to you, you listen to them and make notes as they are talking."

I said to him, "Sir, I need their buy-in that this is the best unit in South Korea. I receive input from them as what and how we want change certain things, and I simply ask questions to steer them into the direction that I want them to take, but they get the credit because it's their idea."

He said, "Top, I like that."

I said, "Sir, I am leaving for the evening formation down in the motor pool. Are you going to attend?"

He said, "No, Top."

At the evening formation, I praised the battery for being disciplined enough to not get into trouble down in the village. We ended the formation with a safety briefing aimed at keeping them out trouble over the weekend.

It has now been almost a month and my checks had not arrived in country, and I am down to about $9.00. I just happened to walk to the post exchange (PX) to pick up me some soap and I ran into Lieutenant Frances Moss. Lieutenant Moss was a former cadet at Fresno State University. I essentially put him through the program. I was there for his entire cadet career at Fresno State. He knew Marlee and the kids. Francis, his wife, and several of the cadets would come to Naval Air Station Lemoore to watch the annual air show, and they would stop by the house before they headed back to Fresno. We had a long chat about our assignments. He was a signal officer and was doing a great job at it. LT Moss was just a few months from being reassigned back to the

States. LT Moss wind up loaning me $50.00, and Marlee would repay him once he returned to the States. His wife and family were in Fresno. Marlee was to pay him back for me. LT Moss did stop by my battery several times prior to him departing for his stateside assignment.

Several months had passed and when I called home, Marlee told me that LT Moss and his wife stopped by to check on her, and she said that she paid him for me. The army needed more Frances Mosses in the officer's ranks simply because he was very clean-cut, dedicated to his job, and very compassionate and caring about his fellow soldiers.

All-New Delta Battery

The first big test for us was our bi-annual Avenger Team certification. Soldiers had put in a lot of hard work preparing the certification. Going through aircraft recognition, map reading, target engagement, fire commands, upload and download sequence, and other areas that composed the certification.

All teams certified, which was very pleasing to our leadership team. CPT Choi and I congratulated the platoon sergeants, platoon leaders, and their soldiers for during such a great job. CPT Choi told them that it took a lot of hard work, late-night studying, and many man hours of training to achieve the goal of every team being certified. He said that he wanted to thank the entire battery for a job well done. I echoed those sentiments also during my speech to the battery. Our soldiers were not afraid to say that they were a part of Delta Battery 5/5 ADA.

Although we were now doing what the army asked us to do as soldiers, some of us will have setbacks. One of the Second Platoon's soldiers had a little too much to drink one night, and I was called by the military police to come pick him up. The soldier's conduct downtown warranted disciplinary actions at the battery level. I explained to CPT Choi what happened and that I would work with the soldier rather than tarnish his military career permanently for a one-time mistake that young soldiers make yet minor enough to overcome. I talked with the soldier's platoon leader and platoon sergeant, and I explained to them what my punishment would be for the soldier and they were totally surprised, but in agreement that it was appropriate for this situation.

About 7:00 PM that evening, the soldier's section sergeant, platoon sergeant, and platoon leader were all present in my office when we asked him to report to me for his disciplinary hearing. The soldier entered the room and stopped in front of my desk. He rendered a hand salute and stated, "Specialist Gray reports as requested, 1SG."

I returned the salute and instructed him to stand at ease. I then read the charges against him and asked him how would he plead. He says, "Guilty, 1SG."

I told him, "On each end of my desk is a red can, and under each can is a list punishment." I asked him to lift the first red can and he did so. I asked him, "What's under that can?"

He said a Battery grade Article 15; range from reduction in rank, loss of pay, and confinement to post, which will be administered by the battery commander. I said, "Put it back and lift the other one."

He lifted the other one and his eyes opened wide. I said, "Read it," and he said, "Two Sundays in church with 1SG Kinsey."

I asked him, "What punishment would you prefer?"

He said, "Two weeks in church, 1SG."

His leadership team all scratched their heads in disbelief. I dismissed the soldiers and explained to them why I elected to give this soldier a break. I went on to discipline a couple more of our soldiers under those methods, and I received a phone call from our battalion CSM. He said, "1SG, I know you are doing a great thing in your battery and you are looking out for your young soldiers, but you know you can't discipline that way." He said, "You know, if the IG finds out, we will be in a little trouble."

I said, "10-4 (understand), CSM, I will change my tactics."

The next formation I did tell all the soldiers that the red cans were going away, and that they must keep out of trouble because if they incur an Article 15, it will harm them later in their career if they elect to stay in the military.

College Professor: 1SG Kinsey

Several of my platoon sergeants knew that I had a college degree, and they felt that I would support a request by their soldiers in allowing them to enroll in college classes at Camp Stanley.

We talked the about field training exercises and other training requirements in our battery. The platoon sergeants explained that our soldiers would often fall behind in the studies, and in some cases, drop out of class because of us having to go to the field. I told them that I would go over to the education center and talk to the office manager and the registrar.

I went over and to the education center, and the administrator and I sat down to come up with a strategy to make this work for our soldiers. As we were talking, she knew that I was very concerned and wanted this to go forward for my soldiers. She said to me, "Do you have your degree, 1SG?"

I said, "Yes, I do."

She asked, "In what?"

I said, "In management."

She said, "Guess what?"

I said, "What?"

She said, "We don't have an instructor for management classes."

I said, "You want me to be the instructor?"

She said, "Yes, and then if your unit goes to the field, you have the option of working with the students on making up their work once they return from the field." She said, "The only catch is that I must open the class up to all the soldiers on the installation." She said that I needed to send for my transcripts and degree certificate to start the classes. She also said that I would be a paid faculty member of Central Texas College.

I was very ecstatic of what I had learned from the learning center. After the evening formation, I held back all the platoon sergeants back so that I could pass that good news on to them. I asked them to talk to their platoons and explain to them that this was an opportunity for them to earn some college credits while in South Korea. Once my credentials arrived, I took them to the administrator, and within two weeks, the education center was advertising that management classes were available at Camp Stanley.

My first class had about twenty-two students signed up, and eight were soldiers from my unit. Several weeks after our classes began, I was attending our weekly training briefing with the CSM and the other 1SGs in the battalion. The CSM turned to me and said, "1SG Kinsey, I see where you briefed that you have eight soldiers out of your battery attending college classes."

I said, "Yes, CSM."

He said, "I heard something else."

I said, "What did you hear, CSM?"

He said, "I heard that you are their professor!"

I said, "It's true, CSM."

He said, "You know, 1SG Kinsey, I think that is just great that you are looking out for your soldiers in that way!"

I said that they had complained to their platoon sergeants that they couldn't go to school because of being in the field all the time. It was a means of taking excuses away from the soldiers that really wanted to attend school versus the ones that were just complaining. I said, "We do have soldiers in our unit that have set high goals and expectations for themselves, and I am just happy to help in some small way."

CSM finally said to me, "Keep doing what you are doing, 1SG!"

I thanked him and left. By the time, I reached the orderly room, I received a call from the States, and my son, Lincoln Meadows Kinsey, was born on October 29, 1996. He weighed in well over nine pounds and was over twenty-four inches long. He was huge, to say the least.

The rice paddies had been harvested, and we could now conduct field training exercises. The entire battery went out for a train-up exercise, and it went very well. The Avenger fire units and crew performed well. We returned to Camp Stanley from our field training exercise and began equipment clean-up.

As our unit was coming into the motor pool to unload their field equipment, I noticed Third Platoon was off-loading their equipment, and their platoon sergeant was not present. I went over to their platoon area and asked one of the section sergeants where their platoon sergeant was, and they said that, "As we were coming into the post, they pulled out of the convoy."

I said "Okay, I will see you later." I began to walk from one platoon to the next ensuring that everyone's sensitive items (weapons, radios, night vision devices, and protective masks) were all accounted for and turned in. I was in the motor pool for over two hours. I went back over to Third Platoon sergeant's location in the motor pool, and he still had not showed up in the motor pool to check to see if his platoon's sensitive items were turned in. I told one of his section sergeants to report to me in the orderly room once his platoon's sensitive items were all accounted for and turned in.

About an hour later, the section sergeant came by and said that all of their sensitive items were accounted for and turned in. I thanked him and asked him what happened to his platoon sergeant. He said that he talked to the platoon sergeant's driver, and he said that he dropped him off to take a shower at his quarters. I told him to give his platoon sergeant a message to see me at 8:00 am in the orderly room. All the other platoon sergeants came by my office and reported that their platoon sensitive items were all accounted for and turned in.

The Third Platoon sergeant came to the orderly room the next morning at 8:00 am and reported to me. I asked him why wasn't he in the motor pool with his platoon when we arrived from the field. He said he had his driver dropped him off at his quarters to take a shower and clean his gear and that he had briefed his section sergeants on what to do in the motor pool. I asked him, "What would you have done if one of your soldiers were missing a night vision device?"

"My section sergeant would have notified me, and I would notify you."

I said to him, "It doesn't work that way. Platoon sergeants are not to leave the motor pool or the company area until all sensitive items are turned in. You never showed up in the motor pool to find out whether your soldiers were missing any items at all, not to mention sensitive items. The idea of having all platoon sergeants in the motor pool with their people is one of motivation as well. Platoon sergeants are with their soldier to let them know that you are concerned about them returning back in garrison safely and with all of their equipment. They are dirty prior to finishing up for the day, and you should be there with them, dirty as well."

I told the platoon sergeant that he may not have a job in my battery after his lack of concern for his soldiers and their equipment. I told him that I was going to talk with the CSM about status in my battery. I told him that he was dismissed. I called the battalion CSM and explained to him my reasoning for firing the platoon sergeant. He said that he understood but needed to talk with LTC Wrenn, battalion commander.

Five minutes later, I received a phone call from CSM, and he said to have the platoon sergeant report to him on Monday morning for a new assignment within the battalion. Soldiers will resent following someone that they don't think is capable of leading them. The platoon sergeant clearly showed no interest in motivating his soldiers or leading them by example. He is one of those sergeants that I refer to as leading from the rear.

While his soldiers are conducting physical training, he goes back to his quarters or during platoon training; he is never around to ensure that training is effective. I appointed a very sharp and dedicated SSG to that position. The next day, I announced that the Third Platoon's platoon sergeant had resigned and would be working within the battalion in another job; his former platoon erupted with cheers. I then announced his replacement and more cheers came from Third Platoon. The cheers were the soldiers' way of venting frustration and relief. Frustration because of being led by someone that only cared about himself. Relief because now they have a leader that will put the platoon and its soldiers first.

Meanwhile, with a fifth son (Lincoln) being born and three of his brothers still serving in the military, it made me a little concerned that they were all doing well. Danny was now out of the military and was now a deputy sheriff in Valdosta (Lowndes County), Georgia; Dedric was serving a tour of duty in Guantanamo Bay, Cuba; Dwayne was serving a tour of duty in Germany; Orenthal was serving a tour of duty at Fort Meyer, Virginia. My oldest, Cassandra, was married and living in Houston, Texas. The middle daughter, Falisha, was about to graduate from high school, and little Roanea was assisting her mom in caring for Lincoln. I really felt good about my immediate family; it was my mother and father that I often thought about while I was gone this time. I knew that Dad was not doing well and hoped that he would be okay until I returned to the States. Dad was now eighty-eight years old, and Mom was seventy-eight. Their ages had me concerned that something might happen prior to me coming back home.

The next time I called home, I asked Marlee to call and check on them for me. She was told that they were doing fine according to my sister, Leatis. That made me feel better, and I was looking forward to taking some vacation time there with them again upon my return to the States.

The battery was functioning excellent, and morale was very high among the soldiers. Our soldiers took pride in our unit and performed at the highest level. The Christmas holidays were rapidly approaching, and our next major event for the battery was a monthlong training up on the border (DMZ). We were scheduled to operate out of Warrior Base Camp in the DMZ on the month of February 1997. With the holidays near, we arranged it so that our soldiers could take turns going "down range" (go to the village) to buy Christmas presents for loved ones back home and mail them out. It reminds me when I was in this country in 1991. Danny had made a special request to send him something with the Los Angeles Lakers on it. I found a pair of tennis shoes that were gold and purple with Los Angeles Lakers on them. I sent them to him and he loved those sneakers. He confessed a few years ago that there were bidding wars going on in his platoon for the sneakers. He told me that there was an offer that he just couldn't refuse. He sold them for $200.00.

I said, "Wow, I paid $29.95 for them, and you made a huge profit." He just smiled. I told him I would have done the same for that kind of money.

The other special request came in 1996 from Dwayne while he was still in Germany. He wanted a Green Bay Packers full-length parka coat. The local village (Song Do) at RC-4 (Alfa Battery 5/5 ADA) didn't have one.

I traveled to Camp Humphreys (Pyongtec, Korea) to find such a coat. It took me several hours of going from shop to shop until I found the coat. I tried not to get excited or I knew I would pay more than I was prepared to pay for the coat. If the item is something that adishi (Korean salesman) knows that you can't live without, then he will budge on the market price. The Green Bay Packers short-length coats were plentiful, but the full-length ones were harder to find. To try and throw him off of my real interest, I began looking at the short-length or regular-length coats first. I asked him how much for the regular-length coat, and he said, "$59.00."

I said, "How about $39.00?"

He came back with, "$55.00, okay you take that."

I then walked over to the full-length coats and turned to him and said, "Adishi, how much?"

He said, "$110.00."

I said, "How about $75.00?"

He looked at me and said, "$99.00."

I looked back at him and said, "$80.00."

The expression on his face displayed some frustration with me at this point in our intense negotiations, and he said, "Okay, GI, $89.00."

I said to him, "Okay, Adishi, I will take it." I mailed the coat to Germany, and several weeks later, Dwayne responded to receiving the coat by saying that he loved the coat. He also said that all of his buddies wanted to know how he got it. I said, "Tell them that it was the last one in South Korea." He just cracked up laughing.

The holidays were over and we were preparing for our departure to the DMZ. We would train during the day and move into Warrior Base Camp for the night. Warrior Base Camp had temporary living quarters for our soldiers. My orderly room was set up in an administration building, and my clerks and I had cots set up to sleep in while the radios were being monitored.

On February 7, 1997, I received a phone call at about 4:00 AM. One of my clerks picked up the landline and answered the phone, and he said, "Hold on, ma'am, he is right here." He walked over and said, "1SG Kinsey, it's your wife on the line."

I got the phone and said hello. Marlee said, "Mose, I just got a phone call from your sister, Leatis. She said that your dad passed away." I took a long pause, and she asked if I was still there. I said, "Yes I am here." I told her that I would call her back later.

I hung the phone up and told my clerks that I was going for a walk and would be back in a few minutes. I walked about a half mile just thinking about how much he meant to me, and I was gone during this time in his life. I shed a lot of tears on that walk.

I returned to the orderly room and CPT Choi had gotten up and he said, "1SG, I have assembled the battery to let them know that your father has passed and that you will be leaving for his funeral back in the States."

CPT Choi talked first and then turned the battery over to me. I simply told them that I enjoyed working with each and every one of them, and to continue on their path to success. I then turned the released the battery back to their platoon sergeants. CPT Choi and I talked for a few minutes.

My driver and I left for Camp Stanley. We arrived at Camp Stanley, and I packed my gear for traveling to the States. That night, the battalion commander and my driver picked me up and brought me to his on-post quarters. When we were driving up, there must have been twenty Humvees parked outside his residence. I walked inside and all of my platoon sergeants, LTC Wrenn, CPT Choi, CSM, and other key officers and sergeants were there.

LTC Wrenn thanked me for being such a dedicated soldier and turning Delta Battery around. So did the CSM. I told my platoon sergeants to continue taking the "hard right, instead of the easy left. Take the extra time to do it right instead of quick fixes. Above all else, continue being loyal to your unit." I thanked them all for their support and asked them to be excused so that I could go back to my quarters.

When I arrived at my quarters, I called Marlee and told her what time I would be arriving at Los Angeles International Airport (LAX). The next morning, my driver picked me up and drove me to Kimpo International Airport. I thanked my driver for his loyalty and dedication and gave him the keys to my quarters to give to SFC Bolden. SFC Bolden was going to periodically check on my quarters for me.

Return Home

When I arrived at LAX, Marlee, Roanea, and Lincoln were there at the gate to pick me up. We went from the airport to the Interstate 10 Freeway and headed to Georgia. It took us about two-and-a-half days to make it home. Leatis was at Mom and Dad's house when we arrived, and she explained that Dad just didn't wake up. I just couldn't believe that he was gone, although I knew that his time was near the end when I visited them prior to leaving for South Korea.

It was very difficult for me understand why God would ever take him away from us because he was such a good man. He always did what was right, no matter what. If something or someone frustrated him, he would not retaliate. He would go to God with it in prayer. He taught us how to live our lives right. If we did otherwise, it wasn't because he didn't teach us the right thing to do. It was because we chose a different path from what he wanted us to take. Above all else, he was an honorable man in the eyes of God. My dad wasn't armed with money, property, or an education. He was armed with character, humility, integrity, and a big heart. He was big on taking care of his family. He was the reason I never got into any trouble with the law or disrespected anyone. Men like him rarely exist anymore.

My sister said that Mom was in the early stages of Alzheimer's, according to her doctor. I asked Leatis, "Who's going to look after her?" She said that her daughter, Kim, was not working, and they would share the duties of caring for her. She said that if the brothers and sister would give her something for Kim, it would help her out as well.

Later that night, Marlee and I were talking and I told her that I was thinking of not going back to South Korea. She said that it was up to me, but she asked what I would do here. I said I only needed two classes added on my transcripts in order to teach social studies in school. I told her that I would call CPT Choi back in South Korea to let him know. She said okay.

The next day, I called CPT Choi, and I talked with him and told him to have SFC Bolden send my hold baggage to me at my home in

Georgia. He too thanked me for working with him. I then went to the local National Guard unit and explained to them that I was going to Fort Benning to put in for my retirement and that I would put them down as my unit of contact. I traveled to Fort Benning to the retirement point. I requested to be separated under the retirement code.

After giving them all of my information and last duty assignment, I was ready to head home. After Dad's funeral, I went to Brewton Parker College in Norman Park and signed up for the two classes that I needed in order to teach school. I went by the Colquitt County Sheriff's department because I had heard there may be an opening for a lieutenant jailer position. I talked to the sheriff, and he told me that the position had been filled. He also said that he wouldn't mind hiring as a jailer. I told him I wanted to think about it.

While redoing our house inside and out and going to school at night, I decided to go to the superintendent's office and talk to him about a possible job in this county as a schoolteacher. I talked to the assistant superintendent of schools here in Colquitt County. He said to me, "Since you are retired military, we have a disciplinary program in our school system that you might be interested in." He sent me to see CPT Stancil (the coordinator).

I went to CPT Stancil's office and talked to him. As soon as I said that I was retiring in August from the army, he said "Don't look anywhere else for a job, you have a job on August 18, 1997." I said, "Okay, I won't."

We continued talking about the program and how it was ran. He explained to me that it was a program designed to correct juvenile's behavior in our local school system and the juvenile justice system.

After the meeting with Captain Stancil, I called the sheriff back and told him that I was going with the Student Transition and Recovery program (S.T.A.R.) in the school system. He thanked me for considering them as an employer.

I was able to spend more time with Roanea and Lincoln as I renovated the house. I would have Lincoln in my arms as I drove the lawn mower while cutting grass in the yard. He would just sit there and watch the trees and the birds as they flew back and forth around the house. I had to be careful not to get him too dirty from being on the lawnmower. I would play with Roanea on her easy-bake oven and pretend to eat all the food she would prepare for me. She loved preparing food for her daddy.

My official retirement date was August 1, 1997. The next day was one of the saddest days of my life. After twenty-four years of wearing the military uniform, I was not required to put it on anymore. I began that day to reflect back on my military career, the many friends I had made, some of the soldiers that I had served with, assignments along the way, good times, bad times, and the security umbrella that the military provides for the soldier and their families, and now what the future holds for me. I would now have to reestablish myself in the civilian world. *A Hero's Journey 2* will cover that portion of my life.

What's a Hero?

Heroes come in all shapes, sizes, ages, male or female. They are everyday people in our communities and society. The label "hero" is given to someone for many different reasons. The first thing that comes to mind is acts of bravery on the battlefield; a police officer in the line of duty; a firefighter pulling someone from a burning car or building. The word "hero" is a very complex term and it has evolved over time. A hero can be someone who inspires others to do a common good for themselves and others in their community. One that sets high standards for himself or herself. Someone whose deeds and accomplishments are worthy of praise by others. One that overcame tremendous odds against them and inspired others to do the same. They are people who are not afraid to stand up for what they believe is right. Someone who helps when the benefit is knowingly going to someone else. Soldiers who chose to defend our country while knowing and understanding that they may not survive their journey of service to their country.

By Mose M. Kinsey

A Hero's Journey

SFC MOOSE M. KINSEY
4th Platoon Sgt.

Top Stinger

SFC Cadre

Top Stinger

Get that rebound, Big Mose . . .

With only one month preparation Tack team placed 4-th in Region and had two team members to go to Olympics I in Jefferson. Glen Hamm placed 5-th in the mile run while Mose Kinsey placed 3-rd in the 440 yard dash and 5-th in the 220 yard dash in State competition.

A HERO'S JOURNEY

- Grew up in poverty
- Earned a degree while in the military
- Military retiree
- All five sons served in the military

A Hero's Journey (2) the second book
- First black Chief Magistrate Court judge in Moultrie, Georgia
- Ran a strict juvenile program for wayward kids
- Human resources director for a major beef company

U.S. Army Ranks, Grades and Insignia

Commissioned Officers
Ranks Grades Insignia
General 0-10 Four silver stars
Lieutenant General 0-9 Three silver stars
Major General 0-8 Two silver stars
Brigadier General 0-7 One silver star
Colonel 0-6 Silver eagle
Lieutenant Colonel 0-5 Silver oak leaf
Major 0-4 Gold oak leaf
Captain 0-3 Two silver bars
First Lieutenant 0-2 One silver bar
Second Lieutenant 0-1 One gold bar

Warrant Officers
WO – 5 Grade 5 Silver bar with five enamel white squares
WO – 4 Grade 4 Silver bar with four enamel black squares
WO – 3 Grade 3 Silver bar with three enamel black squares
WO – 2 Grade 2 Silver bar with two enamel black squares
WO – 1 Grade 1 Silver bar with one enamel black square

Noncommissioned Officers
Sergeant Major of the Army E-9 Three chevrons above three arcs with two five-pointed stars
with a wreath around the stars between the chevrons and arcs

Command Sergeant Major E-9 Same as above but with one star
Sergeant Major E-9 Three chevrons above three arcs with a five-pointed star between the chevrons and arc
First Sergeant E-8 Three chevrons above three arcs with a diamond between the chevron and arcs
Master Sergeant E-8 Three chevrons above three arcs
Sergeant First Class E-7 Three chevrons above two arcs
Staff Sergeant E-6 Three chevrons above one arc
Sergeant E-5 Three chevrons
Corporal E-4 Two chevrons
Specialist Forth Class E-4 Eagle device
Private First Class E-3 One chevron above an arc
Private – 2 E-2 One chevron
Private – 1 E-1 None

ACRONYMS:
ADISHI - Adult Korean male
AFKN - Armed Forces Korea Network
AIT - Advanced Individual Training
ARB 15 Boat – Army Rubber Boat
ARTEP - Army Training and Evaluation Program
ARTICLE 15 - Non-judicial punishment
BNOC - Basic Noncommissioned Officer Course
BRM - Basic Rifle Marksmanship
CADRE - Staff at a training unit
CAMP CORNER – In-processing post in South Korea
CPL - Corporal (E-4)
CPT - Captain (0-3)
CO - Commanding Officer
COMMO - Communications
CONNEX - Metal storage building
DEADLINED - Inoperational vehicle
DMZ - Demilitarized Zone
DOWN RANGE - In the local village
ENTRENCHING TOOL - Small folding shovel
FA - Field Artillery
GARRISON - Main post
GUIDON BEARER – Soldier that carries the platoon or company flag

KATUSA - Koreans Augmented To the United States Army
LANDYARD - Pull-card for an artillery Howitzer
LATRINE - Rest room
LAX - Los Angeles International Airport
LT - Lieutenant (0-1)
LTC - Lieutenant Colonel (0-5)
MACHETE - Big knife
MAJ - Major (0-4)
MANPADS - Man Portable Air Defense System
MEDIC - Medical Personnel
MEPS - Military Entrance Processing Station
MOS - Military Occupation Specialty
MOTOR POOL - Area where military vehicles are kept
MOTOR STABLES -
MSA - Maximum Security Area
MSG - Master Sergeant (E-8)
NCO - Noncommissioned Officer
ORDERLY ROOM - Office
PCS - Permanent Change of Station
PFC - Private First Class (E-3)
PL - Platoon Leader
PMCS - Preventive Maintenance Checks and Services
PNOC - Primary Noncommissioned Officer's Course
POINT MAN - Leader soldier on a patrol
PVT - Private (1, 2)
PX - Post exchange
RANGER EYES - Illuminated tape cut in one-inch squares spaced one inch apart on the back of the Kevlar helmet
ROKA - Republic of Korea Army
RUCKSACK - Backpack
SERGEANT - Sergeant (E-5)
SFC - Sergeant First Class (E-7)
SGM - Sergeant Major (E-9)
SHELL - Ammunition
SHORAD - Short-Range Air Defense System
SOG - Sergeant of the Guard
SPECIALIST - (E-4)
SSG - Staff Sergeant (E-6)

SUPPLY ROOM - Maintain supplies for the battery
SWISS SEAT - A rope tied around the buttocks to form a seat
TA-50 - Field equipment
WON - Korean currency
YEN - Japanese currency
YOBO - Girlfriend
1LT - First Lieutenant (0-2)
#1 MAN - Main operator while on the Howitzer
1SG - First Sergeant (E-8)
16S - Stinger Missile Crewmember

Index

A

after-action review (AAR), 202–3
Alabama, 13, 17, 25, 98, 131, 210
Albany, 59, 79, 181
Alfa Battery, 78, 80, 85, 228
America, 27, 95–96, 123, 169, 175, 218
Armed Forces Korea Network (AFKN), 83, 175, 240
army physical readiness test (APFT), 161–64, 178, 192, 194
army training and evaluation program (ARTEP), 100, 240
Atlanta, xii, 5, 25, 33, 60, 63, 72, 79

B

Baez, Antonio, 136–38
basic noncommissioned officer course (BNOC), 124
Behrens, Stephanie, 166–67
Bevard (private), 98
Bin Laden, Osama, 187
Black (company commander), 71–72
Boatwright, Michael, 151, 156, 158, 161–65, 167
Bolden, Calvin, 219–20, 230–31
Bowers (staff sergeant), 134
Bridgewaters (staff sergeant), 74, 82
Bush, George H. W., 176

C

Camp Ames, 74, 78, 80–82, 84
Camp Casey, 74–75, 78, 80, 87, 172, 176, 181
Camp Corner, 74, 85, 168, 187, 215
Camp Hood, 86
Camp Red Cloud, 83–84
Camp Roberts, 189, 202
Camp Stanley, 215, 218, 224–25, 230
Camp Stanton, 178–79, 181, 185
Carroll, Craig, 196–97
Carroll, Kathy, 196
Chagres River, 107–9, 111
Chaparral, 94–95, 124
Chapin, Ken, 153–55, 158, 166
Charlton (staff sergeant), 90–91
Cheney, Dick, 176
China, 74, 76, 93, 175
Choi (gate guard), 178
Choi (second lieutenant platoon leader), 216–20, 222, 229–31
Collins (Leroy's boss), 54
Collins (staff sergeant), 214
Combat Support Company (CSC), 97, 112, 128
command sergeant major (CSM), 102, 143–44, 215–16, 223, 225, 227, 230
Corben (third-grade English teacher), 7
Coutemarsh (trainee under Kinsey, Mose), 145–46

Croft, Danny Lamar, xi, 78, 114–15, 139, 168, 174–75, 178, 186, 197, 209, 227–28
curfew, 75, 83–84, 202, 204

D

Davis, Robert, 58–61, 73, 83–84, 150, 152, 154, 156, 158, 161–62
Dawson (coach), 50
Dawson (private), 68
Deep South, 4, 25, 27
delayed entry program (DEP), 151–52, 155–56, 210
Demilitarized Zone (DMZ), 74, 168, 173, 178–79, 228–29
Dorothy (Mose's sister), 4–5, 13, 16
Dukes (captain), 92

E

education, 3, 13, 126, 198, 231
  civilian, 102, 126
  military, 102
El Paso, 123, 126, 133, 144
El Paso Community College, 126–27, 130, 212
Epperson (teacher), 198, 200

F

Fort Benjamin Harrison, 144, 150, 168
Fort Benning, 4, 129, 131, 133, 136, 141, 144, 146, 148, 150–51, 166, 232
Fort Benny, 5
Fort Bliss, 94–95, 122–27, 129, 131, 143–45, 168, 174, 178, 186, 212
Fort Clayton, 114

Fort Davis, 105, 110
Fort Hood, 86, 90–93, 127
Fort Jackson, 5, 63–64, 67–68, 71, 84, 210–11
Fort Kobbe, 97, 105, 110, 114–16, 118, 120, 128
Fort Lewis, 189, 202, 207
Fort Meyer, 227
Fort Monroe, 185, 187
Fort Sam Houston, 187
Fort Sill, 69, 71, 73, 181
Fresno, 5, 185–86, 188, 197–98, 202–3, 207, 209, 213, 215, 220–21
Fresno State University, 185, 187–88, 201, 212, 214, 220

G

Georgia, xi–xii, 1–2, 4–5, 7, 9, 15, 25, 27, 31–34, 46–47, 54, 72, 78–79, 81, 98, 102, 129, 131, 133–34, 141, 149, 166, 181, 187, 209, 211, 215, 227, 231–32
Georgia Christian School, 33, 42, 46
Germany, 86, 174, 181, 186, 227–29
Glaspie, April, 175
Grantham (coach), 47
Gulf War, 176
gunslingers, 151, 165
Guyana, 116–17

H

Hart High School, 151, 153, 155–56
honor platoon, 135, 145–46
Hooker (first-grade teacher), 7
Horne, Fleming, 2
Huizinga, Steve, 152, 156, 158

Hussein, Saddam, 174–76

I

Incheon, 78, 80, 83–84
Iraq, 174–76

J

Jackson (platoon sergeant), 80–81
James (drill sergeant), 68–69
Japan, 78–79, 242
Johnson (drill sergeant), 68–69
Jones, Jim, 116–17

K

Kasem, Casey, 84
Kinman (senior drill sergeant), 149
Kinsey, Dedric McLoyd, xi, 78, 114, 188, 206, 209, 227
Kinsey, Dwayne McLoyd, xii, 102, 139–40, 188, 190, 202, 204, 206, 210–11, 227–29
Kinsey, Falisha, xii, 121, 130, 139, 188, 190–91, 227
Kinsey, Lincoln Meadows, xii, 207, 214, 225, 227, 231–32
Kinsey, Lola Mae, xiii, 2–4, 6, 12, 16–23, 26, 28–29, 53, 74, 87, 123, 199, 227
Kinsey, Mose McLoyd, xiii, 13, 17–19, 29, 31–33, 35, 42, 44, 46–48, 57–60, 69, 71–72, 76, 82, 87–89, 92–93, 110, 120, 129, 132–33, 137–38, 145–46, 148, 154, 158, 161–62, 164, 171, 178, 180–81, 184–86, 194–95, 204, 206–7, 211, 216, 223–25, 229
Kinsey, Orenthal Juan, xi, 5, 93, 139–40, 188, 205–6, 209–11, 227
Kinsey, Roanea Bluecloud, xii, 5, 207–10, 213, 227, 231–32
Kinsey, Thomas Elbert, xiii, 1–4, 13, 19, 21, 23, 26–28, 35, 48–50, 52–55, 57, 71, 79, 119, 153, 157–58, 215
Kinsey, Thomas Elbert, Jr., 2, 4
Kinsey, Timothy, 6, 21
Koreans Augmented to the United States Army (KATUSA), 76, 241
Kuwait, 174–76, 186

L

Ladowski (private), 148–49
Laterza (captain), 178, 180, 185–86
Leatis (Mose's sister), 4–5, 29, 35, 215, 228–29, 231
Lemann (first sergeant), 86, 89
Leroy (Mose's brother), 11, 16, 20, 23, 54–55, 215
Los Angeles, 151–52, 158–60, 171, 185, 187

M

Macon, 33, 46, 72
malaria, 99
Manford (sergeant), 119–20
Manson, Charles, 212
Mary Nell (Mose's sister), 4, 6
Masada, Greg, 157–58
maximum security area (MSA), 75, 77, 80, 83
McCrary (private), 17–18, 72–73, 181

McCrary (teacher), 17–18
Meadows, Marlee, 5, 168, 181, 185, 187, 197, 206–7, 210, 214, 220–21, 228–31
Middison, Rachael, 156
Middlebrooks (Mose's summer boss), 40, 48–49
military entrance processing station (MEPS), 61, 63, 152–56, 161, 210–11, 241
Mississippi, 14, 17, 25, 210–11
Morrow (staff sergeant), 151, 158–59
Moss, Frances, 220–21
Moultrie, 4, 12, 15, 25–26, 38, 40–41, 58, 60, 73, 209
Munson, 168, 170
Murphy (coach), 50

N

Nobel Peace Prize, 131, 200
Noncommissioned Officer (NCO) Academy, 124, 127, 129
Norman College, 17, 31, 35, 54
Norman Park, xiii, 2, 9, 12–13, 15, 18, 24–25, 27, 35, 38, 47, 50, 72–73, 79, 81, 159, 184–85, 187, 211, 232
Norman Park High School, 13, 16, 33, 38, 47
North Korea, 74, 168, 217

O

Owens, Eddie, 31–32, 34, 56–57

P

Paceli (platoon leader), 80–81
Panama, 93–94, 97, 99, 104–5, 113, 116–17, 119, 122–23, 128
Patton, George S., 88
Powell (staff sergeant), 151, 156, 165
Powell, Colin, 176
Presley, Elvis, 86, 104, 123
Primary Noncommissioned Course (PNOC), 105, 113, 241
private first class (PFC), 77, 128, 177
Promotions, 82, 102–4, 125, 127, 144, 163–64, 177, 201

R

Reagan, Ronald, 112, 130–31
recruiters, 58–61, 145, 151, 158, 168, 210–11
Reserve Officer Training Corps (ROTC), 64, 66, 185, 187–88, 207
Revere (coach), 50
Roth (sergeant), 170–71
Ryan (congressman), 116

S

Sanchez, Robert, 152, 154, 156, 158, 161–62, 165
San Jose State, 185, 195
Schwarzkopf, Norman, Jr., 176
Smokey Joe, 37, 40
South Carolina, 5, 63, 68, 122, 210–11
South Korea, 73–74, 77–79, 82–83, 86, 92, 168, 170, 174, 177–78, 180–81, 185–86, 196, 207, 214–15, 217–18, 220, 224, 229, 231, 240

Spivey, Phyllis, 152, 154–55, 164–65, 168
Stallings, Betty, 42–44

T

Tomlinson (sergeant), 127
Torrijos, Omar, 97–98, 112
trainees, 68–69, 94, 129, 131–37, 141, 143, 145–49
training
  airborne, 142
  basic, 5, 67–71, 94, 147, 150, 206, 210
    Nuclear Biological Chemical (NBC), 144
  physical (PT), 69, 71, 98, 104, 134, 136, 141–42, 172, 178, 219, 227
  survival, 139
Trip (captain), 169, 195
Turner, Cassandra Irene, xi, 73, 187, 227

U

Underwood, Mary Lee, 54
United States, 74, 78–79, 86, 98–99, 112, 116, 123, 130, 159, 175
United States Army, xi–xii, 4, 86, 88, 98, 123–24, 144, 147, 174, 194, 239

V

vacation, 29, 74, 78, 86, 122–23, 134, 139, 166, 185, 228
Vietnam War, 100, 131, 142
Virginia, 13, 185, 187, 227

W

Warrior Base Camp, 178, 228–29
Washington, 150, 187, 189, 202, 207
Waskill (private), 177–78
Weaver (dairy farmer), 29, 46
welfare, 199, 218
Wise (fifth-grade teacher), 7
World War II, 68, 88, 131
Wrenn (lieutenant colonel), 215–16, 227, 230

Y

yellow fever, 99

Made in the USA
Monee, IL
05 October 2020